STATISTICS FOR
SIX SIGMA MADE EASY!

STATISTICS FOR
SIX SIGMA MADE EASY!

Warren Brussee

McGraw-Hill

New York   Chicago   San Francisco   Lisbon
London   Madrid   Mexico City   Milan   New Delhi
San Juan   Seoul   Singapore   Sydney   Toronto

The **McGraw-Hill** Companies

11 12 13 14 15 16 17 18 DOC/DOC 1 5 4 3 2 1 0

ISBN 0-07-143385-6

This publication is designed to provide accurate and authoritative information in regard to the subject matter covered. It is sold with the understanding that neither the author nor the publisher is engaged in rendering legal, accounting, or other professional service. If legal advice or other expert assistance is required, the services of a competent professional person should be sought.
— *From a Declaration of Principles jointly adopted by a Committee of the American Bar Association and a Committee of Publishers*

McGraw-Hill books are available at special quantity discounts to use as premiums and sales promotions, or for use in corporate training programs. For more information, please write to the Director of Special Sales, McGraw-Hill, 2 Penn Plaza, New York, NY 10121. Or contact your local bookstore.

CONTENTS

INTRODUCTION

WHO SHOULD USE THIS BOOK

Manufacturing Managers, Engineers, and Technicians: Implementing Six Sigma gives manufacturing and engineering teams a common language and approach to problem solving. No matter what skills people currently possess, the use of Six Sigma makes those skills more effective. *Statistics for Six Sigma Made Easy!* emphasizes using data to drive actions and get measurable results.

Sourcing: Six Sigma is equally valuable when applied to suppliers. The joint use of these tools makes your vendors an extension of your company. Suppliers are eager to participate, since they know that the Six Sigma process will both improve their product and strengthen the bond with their customer. These are almost always win-win situations.

Design Engineers: Production problems are best solved in the design stage. Six Sigma uses data and customer input to assist in designing products and production equipment that are more likely to be problem-free. Of special interest are the chapter on tolerances, which emphasizes reality-based tolerances, and the various customer input tools.

Marketing and Sales: Being able to demonstrate how your company uses Six Sigma tools to improve and control processes is a powerful marketing and sales tool. Many leading companies use Six Sigma and a degree of prestige and perceived technical prowess comes with incorporating it. In addition, the tools are an assist in spotting significant changes in demand or sales.

Accounting, Software Development, Insurance, etc.: Although most of the initial Six Sigma applications have been in manufacturing, there is a growing awareness that these techniques work equally well in reducing

costs or errors in other fields. These techniques can be used to compare people, processes, companies, events, etc. to spot significant differences or
trends. Use the various customer input tools to benefit from the knowledge
of everyone affected and to get maximum buy-in.

WHY *STATISTICS FOR SIX SIGMA MADE EASY!*

There are many books on Six Sigma. Most are just general overviews, with
little detail on actually *using* the Six Sigma tools. *Statistics for Six Sigma Made
Easy!* gently guides the user through the required statistics and enables someone to quickly apply Six Sigma tools to real-world problems.

Six Sigma is a structured methodology for solving problems with tools
that can be applied to the problem-solving process. Its use generates insights
that may not otherwise be obvious. Although initially designed to improve
quality, Six Sigma is now used by many companies to make cost-saving
improvements. Implementers of this methodology are often called "green
belts." This book simplifies the learning of Six Sigma and its application to
green-belt-level projects.

One company's green-belt training in Six Sigma includes seven books,
four software packages, and three weeks of class work. It is very intensive in
high-level statistics. Although this kind of course is excellent, not all companies or individuals want to commit to that level of instruction. *Statistics for Six
Sigma Made Easy!* includes only the tools used by most successful Six Sigma
practitioners. The only software package needed is Excel. Included is a brief
review of using Excel to analyze data. The 14 formulas and five tables included here enable you to do all the Six Sigma work described in this book.

All required statistics are completely and simply detailed. Using these
tools will enable a person to do much the same work as a green belt who
has completed more extensive training, such as described above!

It is not necessary to master all the tools to become effective at utilizing
Six Sigma. Even the application of a few of the tools can have a strong impact
on driving savings.

Many of the Six Sigma tools that are covered in this text are labeled as
"simplified." This simplification in no way reduces their effectiveness. It just
puts a degree of reality into the tools. In all cases I give reasons for the simplifications and give reference texts for those wishing to use the traditional,
non-simplified tools.

This book can be used as a stand-alone or as a supplement to other Six
Sigma texts.

TEACHING SIX SIGMA

Many of you who use this text will get involved in teaching Six Sigma. The people you will teach will have various educational backgrounds and various interest levels. I will share with you how I got involved in using, teaching, and finally writing this text on Six Sigma. Perhaps my experiences will be valuable to you as you begin to teach this methodology.

I had already been at GE for many years and was managing a very successful engineering team when Six Sigma was introduced. GE initially had a limited number of very bright people trained by outside consultants deemed experts in Six Sigma. This group of newly trained people then put together a set of modules to be used to train the next group of people, which mostly consisted of managers.

Since these original trainers had no experience in actually using Six Sigma and had various degrees of ability in statistics, both the modules and the training were rather haphazard. The training consisted of two one-week sessions, which included introduction to several software packages specific to Six Sigma.

In addition to these class sessions, GE brought in some outside consultants who covered additional Six Sigma tools and the corresponding software. Because of the software requirements, most people had to order new computers.

So, there was a dichotomy in the training. The homegrown training modules, written and taught by non-experts in Six Sigma who had no application experience, were often weak. The training done by the consultants was often overwhelming. It was problematic that there was no practical text for teaching the use of the Six Sigma tools.

Over a period of months, this training was given to most of the engineers and to various other groups, such as marketing and sales. After taking these classes, the people were to start using Six Sigma; the goal was that everyone, within one year, would complete two meaningful Six Sigma projects, document the savings, put in the necessary controls, and do a formal presentation. Those completing this would become "green belts." Everyone was also to take a test at the end of one year on his or her competence in Six Sigma.

After most of my engineering team had completed the classes, I asked them for feedback. At first I got the "they were OK" type of response. As I queried further, however, I found that the engineers had not truly learned or understood enough. The major weakness in the instruction was an assumption that the participants understood probability and statistics completely;

little effort had been made to walk them through practical applications.

Since I took great pride in my team being one of the best, I decided to start teaching a more practical version of Six Sigma to my team. I proceeded to schedule four-hour Six Sigma sessions with my team every other week, in which I would cover some specific area of Six Sigma. The first sessions were a general review of statistics, emphasizing only what was needed to actually do Six Sigma work. After several months, the general manager asked me to start the training over with another team, which I did.

Everyone attending the classes became a green belt by the one-year target and the teams taking these classes beat all other teams on the test that was given on Six Sigma at the end of the year.

In the classes I had to overcome the problem of a great diversity of skills and abilities. There were participants with two-year technical degrees, non-technical degrees, engineering degrees, and even several doctorates in physics. I explained to all of them that I was going to start with the basics and move slowly, with applied problems as examples. I asked those who already had a good understanding of statistics to assist those that didn't. I made no attempt to identify the people who were in each group. This approach seemed to work. Even those who felt they already had an understanding were surprised how much they learned from these classes.

How did I prepare for the classes? The weekend before, I would get every resource I could find on the subject I was going to cover, then do my best to glean the important points and attempt to present them in an understandable manner. Since the people I was teaching knew me well, feedback (positive and negative) was not an issue. This enabled me to fine-tune the course material. Hopefully this text will spare you this level of preparation.

After several months of this, you could sense the pride building in these teams as their comprehension grew. They were even bragging to other teams that they were going to blow them away on the year-end test (which they did).

Another issue I had to address in these classes was related to a few very skilled individuals who over the years had done well without using Six Sigma. It was a difficult sell to get them to put much effort into learning and applying this methodology. However, these people were bright enough that they were able to acquire some degree of competence just by attending the classes.

Another facet of teaching Six Sigma comes when you start to actually use the methodology. You have to provide some training to all the people you will be asking to contribute input or to help gather data. These people must get some feel for what the Six Sigma process does. An initial meeting of two to three hours is needed before involving them in the process. In the meeting, emphasize that Six Sigma needs input from knowledgeable people (them) and that data, which they will help gather, will drive the decisions. Explain that you will be doing some statistical tests on the data, that they don't need to understand all the details, but you will share the results. This means that you also need to have one or two additional meetings with them to keep them up to date.

There will be a few people within any group who will want to understand the Six Sigma process in far more detail. These people are extremely important to you, so you should have additional meetings for those wishing to understand more. They will be your best ambassadors!

There will be some fear that Six Sigma will be used to discipline employees in their jobs or even to reduce employees. Be very hesitant to do a Six Sigma project that has discipline or reduction of employees as a primary goal, since you will probably never get the people to work with you again on Six Sigma. Obviously no one can guarantee that a reduction may not occur because of business conditions, but the project should not have that as a direct goal.

After several years of using Six Sigma and having a team that generated an additional several millions of dollars of savings because of this methodology, I realized that I should go back and revisit the training method and material. This triggered the eventual writing of *Statistics for Six Sigma Made Easy!* The hope is that this book will fill the current void of a practical book on the use of the Six Sigma tools.

ACKNOWLEDGMENTS AND DEDICATION

Special thanks to Bonnie Burnick, a Six Sigma black belt, who encouraged me to write this book and who has been an invaluable assist throughout the process.

Others who have given valuable input are Donald Brussee, Sharon Curtright, Jean-Patrick Ducroux, Roy McDonald, Cheri Sims, Russ Sims, and Christopher Welker.

Of course, none of the above people are responsible for any errors or omissions, since the final decision on content was mine. Comments are encouraged by e-mailing Warren Brussee at wbsixsigma@aol.com.

This book is dedicated to my wife, Lois, who over the years has tolerated many of my idiosyncrasies, which include writing this book. Too bad it isn't a novel so she would actually read it!

STATISTICS FOR
SIX SIGMA MADE EASY!

PART I

**Overview of
the Six Sigma Process
and the DMAIC Roadmap**

CHAPTER 1

Six Sigma Methodology and Management's Role in Implementation

W hat you will learn in this chapter is the basic structure of the Six Sigma process and its purposes. You will also see how management's support of this methodology will ease its implementation and improve its likelihood of success.

Six Sigma Methodology

The Six Sigma methodology uses a specific problem-solving approach and Six Sigma tools to improve processes and products. This methodology is data-driven, with a goal of reducing unacceptable products or events.

The technical goal of the Six Sigma methodology is to reduce process variation such that the amount of unacceptable product is no more than 3 defects per million parts.

The real-world application of Six Sigma in most companies is to make a product that satisfies the customer and minimizes supplier losses to the point that it is not cost-effective to pursue tighter quality.

DEFINITION

I am going to get into some Six Sigma terminology, but before I do I want to explain what the Six Sigma methodology is about.

AVERAGE AND VARIATION

First, no one knows how to make anything "perfect." If you order 50 1.000" diameter ball bearings and then measure the bearings once you get them, you will find that they are not exactly 1.000" in diameter. They may be extremely close to 1.000", but if you measure them carefully, with a very good calibrated measuring device, you will find that the bearings are not exactly 1.000".

The bearings will vary from the 1.000" target in two ways. First, the *average* diameter of these 50 bearings will not be exactly 1.000". Whatever amount the average deviates from the target 1.000" is due to the bearing manufacturing process being off-center. Second, there will be a spread of measurements around the average bearing diameter. This spread of dimensions may be extremely small, but there will be a spread. This is due to the bearing process *variation*.

If the combination of the off-center bearing process and the bearing process variation is small compared with your needs, then you will be satisfied with the bearings. If, however, the combination of the off-center and variation is large compared with your needs, then you will not be happy. The Six Sigma methodology strives to make the total effect of an off-center process and process variation small compared with the need (tolerance). This is illustrated below in Figure 1-1.

Figure 1-1. Off-center and variation

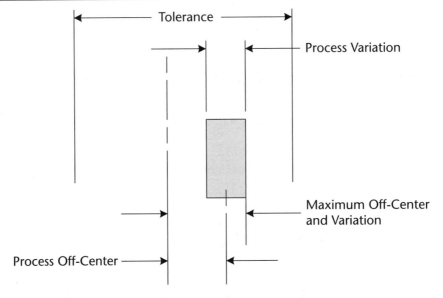

If you understand the general concepts I just discussed, what follows is just terminology and detail.

SIGMA

One of the ways to measure the variation of a product or a process is to use a mathematical term called *sigma*. We will learn more about sigma and how to calculate this value as we proceed, but for now it is enough to know that the lower the sigma value, the smaller the amount of process variation and the higher this sigma value, the greater the amount of the process's variation. Since the sigma calculation is normally done on a computer or calculator, it is more important that you gain a sense that sigma is a measure of the data spread (variation) than it is to be too involved with the detailed actual calculation of sigma.

Ideally, the sigma value is low in comparison with the allowable tolerance on a part or process. If so, the process variation will be small compared with the part or product tolerance a customer requires. When this is the case, the process is "tight" enough that, even if the process is somewhat off-center, the process produces product well within the customer's needs and specifications.

Most companies have processes with a relatively large variation compared with their customers' needs (a relatively high sigma value compared with the allowable tolerance). These companies run at an average ±3-sigma level (a 3-sigma process). This means that 6 sigma (±3 sigma) fit between the tolerance limits. The more sigma that fit between the tolerance limits, the better.

Figure 1-2. ±3 Sigma

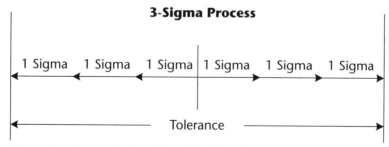

Sigma level is calculated by dividing the process's allowable tolerance (upper specification minus lower specification) by twice the process's sigma value, since the sigma level of a process is normally stated as a ± value.

Process Sigma Level

$$\text{Process Sigma Level} = \pm \frac{\text{Process Tolerance}}{2 * \text{Process Sigma Value}}$$

As an example, suppose a process machining shafts has the following measurements:

Sigma = 0.001"
Maximum allowable shaft diameter = 1.003"
Minimum allowable shaft diameter = 0.997"
So, the tolerance = 1.003" - 0.997" = 0.006"
We put these values into the above formula:

$$\text{Process Sigma Level} = \pm \frac{\text{Process Tolerance}}{2 \times \text{Process Sigma Value}}$$

$$\text{Process Sigma Level} = \pm \frac{0.006"}{2 \times 0.001"}$$

Process Sigma Level = ±3

So, this process is running at ± 3 sigma or, in the terms of Six Sigma, this is a 3-sigma process.

As you will see later in the book, a ±3-sigma process generates 99.73% good product, or 997,300 good parts out of every 1,000,000 parts produced. This means that there are 2700 defective parts out of every 1,000,000 parts produced (or 2700 input errors per 1,000,000 computer entries, etc.). These defects are very costly, causing scrap, rework, returns, and loss of customers. Eliminating this lost product has the potential to be a very profitable "hidden factory," because all the costs and efforts have been put into the defective product, but it's unusable.

Some companies, like aircraft manufacturers, attempt to run very critical parts at a 7-sigma level. This means that the variation is so low that ±7-sigma fit between the specification high/low limits. This targeted extremely low defect level (low process variation vs. the allowable tolerance) is sought due to the catastrophic potential of a defect (a part being outside tolerance).

A Six Sigma process runs with a variation such that ±6 sigma (including some process drift), or 12 sigma, fit within the tolerance limits. This will generate three defects per million parts produced. This was the original quality goal of this methodology and it's how the name "Six Sigma" became associated with this methodology. This extremely low defect incidence is not required in most real-world situations and the cost of getting to that quality level is usually not justified. However, getting the quality to the level where the customer is extremely happy and supplier losses are very low is generally a cost-effective goal.

Companies that embrace the Six Sigma philosophy train people to various skill and responsibility levels and assign the following titles.

Green Belt

A Six Sigma green belt is the primary implementer of the Six Sigma methodology. He or she earns this title by taking classes in Six Sigma, demonstrating a competence on Six Sigma tests, and implementing projects using the Six Sigma tools.

Black Belt

A Six Sigma black belt has Six Sigma skills sufficient to act as an instructor, mentor, and expert to green belts. A black belt is also competent in additional Six Sigma tool-specific software programs and statistics.

Master Black Belt

A Six Sigma master black belt generally has management responsibility for the Six Sigma organization. This could include setting up training, measuring its effectiveness, coordinating efforts with the rest of the organization, and managing the Six Sigma people (when Six Sigma is set up as a separate organization).

DEFINITION

Much of Six Sigma is not new. The Six Sigma methodology includes elements from SPC (statistical process control), the scientific method of problem solving, and procedures to incorporate expert knowledge. Practical application of statistics and probability is inherent in the Six Sigma process. However, the Six Sigma methodology brings all these elements together in a synergistic and disciplined fashion that has proven to be effective in driving process improvement. The use of Six Sigma doesn't change someone's job; it just makes him or her more effective in doing that job.

IMPLEMENTING SIX SIGMA

Commitment of Top Management

The easiest way to implement Six Sigma into an organization is to have complete commitment from top management. This commitment would include company-wide communications explaining the process and its goals, with some explanation of the reasons why the company was going to invest the time and energy into implementing the Six Sigma methodology. This buy-in demonstrates to the whole company that management believes in this methodology. This way the required investment in people and training will happen, along with everyone's active participation. When incorporating Six Sigma, many companies start with outside consultants/instructors and then transition to in-house people as trainers.

Six Sigma Separate

Some companies set up Six Sigma as a separate organization, which then services the rest of the company. As a separate organization, the Six Sigma people work in parallel with the various groups already in place, identifying and implementing Six Sigma projects in addition to whatever projects the groups have already defined.

The advantage of this approach is Six Sigma can be implemented with fewer people trained initially and the effect of the methodology can be more readily tracked. The downside of this approach is that the separate Six Sigma organization is often looked at as a group of prima donnas, with their own set of agendas. This causes some resentment among others in the organization and stifles cooperation. It also discourages the input of experts into Six Sigma projects, since many of these experts feel threatened. There can also be some feeling that current ideas are "stolen" and then labeled as Six Sigma.

Six Sigma Integrated

An alternate approach is to incorporate Six Sigma as part of the organization, not as a separate entity. Six Sigma then becomes an integral part of everyone's job, using a relatively few highly trained Six Sigma people as reference instructors. This is a somewhat more difficult way to implement Six Sigma, because of the large number of people to be trained, but a common Six Sigma language and philosophy will then permeate the organization. As the Six Sigma methodology unfolds in the coming chapters, it will be seen that Six Sigma is helpful to everyone in the organization and therefore it should become an integral part of everyone's job.

Six Sigma from the Bottom Up

Sometimes some high-level managers and/or people throughout the company feel that the company can't afford the training, software, computer upgrades, etc., to implement Six Sigma. Managers may also be dubious whether the skill level in the company will support the perceived high technical competence required. In these cases, complete management buy-in is unlikely. Although a complete commitment from management is the easiest way to implement Six Sigma, it is possible for individuals or teams to start this process from the bottom up.

Six Sigma Tools

Many of the Six Sigma tools will work independently. The tools can also be simplified and do not require the rather esoteric special software often associated with Six Sigma. Excel is sufficient for all calculations and graphs. Even the implementation of two or three Six Sigma tools can make a measurable difference in a company's performance! There is no need to try to implement the whole methodology at once.

Of course, the individual planning to use Six Sigma should first review his or her implementation plans with the manager, but usually a manager will not discourage this extra effort. Usually there will be a caveat from the manager not to incur any additional costs and not to delay any ongoing projects.

After someone has demonstrated the success of the Six Sigma method, others will often follow this lead. Then tool use and training can expand. Although this takes individual initiative on the part of the person initiating Six Sigma, it is a great way to get noticed and truly influence a company's success! Even when a company is supportive of Six Sigma, it generally takes a few dynamic individuals to lead.

WHAT WE HAVE LEARNED IN CHAPTER 1

1. The Six Sigma methodology uses a specific problem-solving approach and select Six Sigma tools to improve processes and products.
2. People with expertise in Six Sigma are called green belts, black belts, or master black belts.
3. The name Six Sigma came from the goal of reducing defects to 3 parts per million, which is ±6-sigma (including some process drift).
4. Most companies produce at an average ±3-sigma quality level (99.73% good product), which generates 2700 defects per million parts. For most real-world situations, this is a level of defects that is excessively high, but the optimum quality level is usually not as tight as ±6 sigma. A realistic goal is to make a product that satisfies the customer and minimizes supplier losses to the point that it is not cost-effective to pursue tighter quality.
5. Excessive defects are very costly, causing scrap, rework, returns, lost customers, etc. This lost product has the potential to be a profitable "hidden factory."

6. The easiest way to implement Six Sigma in an organization is with complete commitment from top management.

7. Although complete corporate commitment is desired, many of the Six Sigma tools can be used independently to make substantial improvements. This approach can cause bottom-up acceptance of Six Sigma. *It is not necessary to use all the tools to have a measurable effect on reducing defects.*

8. Some companies set up Six Sigma as a separate organization. This can cause some animosity. Another approach is to incorporate Six Sigma into the current organization, as an integral part of everyone's current job.

9. There are task-specific software programs for many of the Six Sigma tools, but these are not required to begin implementing Six Sigma.

10. The Six Sigma tools can be simplified to make them more practical without significantly reducing their value.

RELATED READING

Strategic Six Sigma: Best Practices from the Executive Suite, Dick Smith and Jerry Blakeslee (Hoboken, NJ: John Wiley, 2002).

The Six Sigma Way: How GE, Motorola, and Other Top Companies Are Honing Their Performance, Peter S. Pande, Robert P. Neuman, and Roland R. Cavanagh (New York: McGraw-Hill, 2000).

Six Sigma: The Breakthrough Management Strategy Revolutionizing the World's Top Corporations, Mikel J. Harry and Richard Schroeder (New York: Random House/Doubleday/Currency, 1999).

CHAPTER 2

DMAIC: The Basic Six Sigma Roadmap

What you will learn in this chapter is the DMAIC problem-solving approach used by green belts. This is the roadmap that is followed for all projects and process improvements. Which tools are used and what statistics are needed are dictated by each project. Appendix A has a Six Sigma Statistical Tool Finder Matrix to assist in picking the correct tool.

DMAIC Problem-Solving Method

DMAIC (Define, Measure, Analyze, Improve, Control) is the Six Sigma problem-solving approach used by green belts. This is the road map that is followed for all projects and process improvements, with the Six Sigma tools applied as needed.

D—Define This is the overall problem definition. This definition should be as specific as possible.

M—Measure Accurate and sufficient measurements/data are needed.

A—Analyze The measurements/data must be analyzed to see if they are consistent with the problem definition and to identify a root cause. A problem solution is then identified. Sometimes, based on the analysis, it is necessary to go back and restate the problem definition and start the process over.

I—Improve Once a solution is identified, it must be implemented. After the solution has been implemented, the results must be verified with independent data.

DEFINITION

C—**Control** A verification of control must be implemented. A robust solution (like a part change) will be easier to keep in control than a qualitative solution.

As we learn to use each tool in the following chapters, I will refer back to its use in the DMAIC process.

D—Definition

A problem is often initially identified very qualitatively:

- "The customer is complaining that the quality of the bearing races has deteriorated."
- "The new inventory tracking software program keeps crashing."
- "The losses on line #3 seem higher."

Before one can even think about possible solutions, the problem must be defined more specifically. Only then can meaningful measurements or data be collected. The above examples after some additional definition:

- "The inside diameter of the MQ18 bearing race became more varied starting week #14."
- "When the number of inventory items exceeds 1000, the inventory-tracking software crashes several times per day."
- "The number of line #3 product being scrapped for loose wiring has doubled in the last week."

If there were quantitative values available, like the specific measurements related to the bearing diameter, they would be included in the problem definition. The more specific the initial problem definition, the better.

To get a good definition of the problem may be as simple as talking to the customer. In this text are several excellent tools for quantifying customer input. Often, however, the improved definition will require much more effort. Some preliminary measurements may have to be taken to be sure that there even *is* a problem. It may be necessary to verify measurements and calculate sample sizes to ensure that we have valid and sufficient data. Sometimes the resultant measurements and analysis will show that the initial problem definition was erroneous and you then have to back up and formulate another definition.

M—Measure

Once the problem is defined, we must decide what additional measurements must be taken to quantify the problem. We will discuss several tools that will help identify the key process input variables to be considered and/or measured.

Samples must be sufficient in number, random, and representative of the process we wish to measure.

A—Analyze

Now we have to see what the data are telling us. We have to plot the data to understand the process character. We must decide if the problem as defined is "real" or just a random event without an assignable cause. These data will also be the base against which we will measure any implemented improvement. We may also have to measure appropriate key process input variables.

I—Improve

Once we understand the root cause of the problem and have quantitative data, we identify solution alternatives. Tests may be required to understand any interaction between or among the input variables. Tolerances have to be examined. We analyze the error contributed by each component to see if one component is causing most of the error.

We then implement the solution and verify the predicted results.

C—Control

Quality control data samples and measurement verification can be scheduled. Control charts can be implemented to help the operator keep the process in control. Updated tolerances should reflect any change.

USING DMAIC

It is strongly recommended to follow all the DMAIC steps when problem solving. Especially don't make major process changes without doing all the DMAIC steps. Remember: trying to fix something without working through all the applicable steps may cause you to spend more time responding to the resultant problems than if you had taken the time to do it right!

The DMAIC roadmap is not only useful for problem troubleshooting; it also works well as a checklist when doing a project. In addition to any program management tool that is used to run a project, it is often useful to make a list of Six Sigma tools that are planned for each stage of the DMAIC process as the project progresses. This Six Sigma tool check-off list should be regularly reviewed and updated as the project progresses.

There is an example of a Six Sigma tool check-off list in Appendix B that relates to the case study below. By the time you get to Appendix B, you will be familiar with the specific Six Sigma tools that are shown in the check-off list example.

CASE STUDY: USING THE DMAIC PROCESS FOR PROJECT CONTROL AND REVIEW

Six Sigma was implemented into a company and the engineering team began to follow the DMAIC process religiously. Not only did the team's project performance improve, but also the customer plants now felt that they were a part of the process. This is because many of the Six Sigma tools required input from the customers. Even when there were temporary issues, everyone felt they were part of the problem and therefore felt like they should be part of the solution.

Here's a comment from one of the program managers, who is currently managing 17 diverse programs in several plants, with a total project value of over $2,000,000:

> I can't imagine ever going back to managing programs without the DMAIC Six Sigma process. Not only are more of my programs meeting the goals, but also it is easier now that the plants, and my manager, can track the steps in each project. Every project is reviewed per the DMAIC format. At the start of every project a list of Six Sigma tools is identified that is specific to that program. At every program review this Six Sigma tool check-off list is reviewed to make sure that every element is being followed. There are no surprises. The DMAIC process minimizes the 'panic' and catch-up that often accompanied projects before Six Sigma.

> The advantage of doing the Six Sigma tool check-off list at the start of the project is that it is less likely that a tool will not be used. In the middle of a project, when all sorts of things are happening, including the pressure of other projects, it is easy to skip a tool. That is less likely to happen when you know that the tool is already on a review list against which you will be measured.

> As an example, on a project that was completed a year ago, we were in the last steps of verifying that a new inspection gauge was working as designed. It had already passed the tests with sample products, and it was then to be tested on actual production parts, with its performance measured against historical data.

The project was running a few days late, and the production manager wanted to skip the last test with production products, since he was sure the test with the sample products was sufficient. The project would then be on time. I insisted we do the test as planned, even though that meant the project would be perhaps a week late.

The inspection device failed the test with production products. The device was rejecting a statistically significant lower number of production products for rim diameters than historical (population) rejects on the old gauge. After a week of testing production product on the new and old devices, it was discovered that there was a type of rim diameter that had a small amount of distortion, and the new inspection gauge was not able to measure the diameter correctly because of this distortion. No one was aware of this particular distortion because the old dial indicator gauge was not sensitive to it. After a very minor modification on the new gauge, however, rim diameters having this distortion were readable. Products with the distorted rims were added to the sample products, the tests were redone, and the new gauge then passed with flying colors.

The inspection device was two weeks late because of the time needed to identify and fix the problem, and to redo the tests. However, if the test with production product had *not* been run, the problem would not have been found until the customer started finding more rim diameter defects in the products. Then we would have had a very angry customer, would had much product to re-inspect, and would have lost faith in the Six Sigma process! As it was, the two-week delay was forgiven when everyone realized how the Six Sigma tool check-off list had saved us *all* a lot of grief!

WHAT WE HAVE LEARNED IN CHAPTER 2

1. The DMAIC process (Define, Measure, Analyze, Improve, and Control) is the process roadmap Six Sigma green belts use to solve problems.
2. The Six Sigma tools are used in different steps in the DMAIC process. The project or problem dictates which tools are used and where in the DMAIC process.
3. The DMAIC process not only is useful as a problem-solving guide, but also can be used as a standardized format for project reviews. A Six Sigma tool check-off list is an effective way to make sure applicable tools

are identified and used. An example of a Six Sigma tool check-off list is shown in Appendix B.

4. The use of Six Sigma—both the DMAIC process and the Six Sigma tools—gets involvement and buy-in from both customers and management.

5. There is less "panic" and more control when this methodology is followed. Effectiveness improves measurably, as does job satisfaction and reward.

RELATED READING

Rath & Strong's Six Sigma Pocket Guide, Rath & Strong Management Consultants (Lexington, MA: Rath & Strong/Aon Consulting Worldwide, 2000).

The Six Sigma Handbook, Revised and Expanded: A Complete Guide for Green Belts, Black Belts, and Managers at All Levels, Thomas Pyzdek (New York: McGraw-Hill, 2003).

PART II

Qualitative
Six Sigma Tools

CHAPTER 3

Simplified QFD

What you will learn in this chapter is that what a customer really needs is often not truly understood during the design or change of a product, process, or service. A simplified QFD, if done carefully, will minimize issues arising from this lack of understanding.

QFD originally stood for *quality function deployment*. Year ago, when quality departments were generally much larger than now, quality engineers were 'deployed' to the customers to rigorously probe the customer's needs and then create a series of forms that transitioned those customer needs into a set of actions for the supplier to take. The simplified QFD attempts to accomplish the same task in a condensed manner.

What is presented here is a simplified version of the QFDs likely to be described in many Six Sigma classes. Some descriptions of these traditional QFDs and the rationale for the simplification will be given later in this chapter. The simplified QFD is usually used in the Define or Improve steps of the DMAIC process.

A simplified QFD is a Six Sigma tool that does not require any statistics. But it is usually necessary to do a simplified QFD to understand what actions are needed to address a problem or implement a project. The specific actions that are identified in the QFD, or in any of the other qualitative tools, are often what trigger the application of the statistically based Six Sigma tools.

Many product, process, and service issues are caused by not incorporat-

Simplified QFD

The simplified QFD converts customer needs into prioritized actions. Here are some examples of how a QFD is used.

Manufacturing Use the simplified QFD to get input from customers on their needs at the start of every new design or before any change in process or equipment.

Sales and Marketing Before any new sales initiative, do a simplified QFD, inviting potential customers, salespeople, advertisement suppliers, etc., to give input.

Accounting and Software Development Before implementing a new program language or software package, do a simplified QFD. A customer's input is essential for a seamless introduction.

Receivables Do a simplified QFD on whether your approach to collecting receivables is optimized. Besides those directly involved in collections, invite customers who are overdue on receivables to participate. (You may have to give them some debt relief to get their cooperation.)

Insurance, etc. Do a simplified QFD with customers to see what they look for to pick an insurance company or what it would take to make them switch.

ing inputs from customers and/or suppliers of components and raw materials early in a design or process change. Often the manufacturer decision makers just assume that they and the people from whom they source already know what the customers want.

The customers in this case include everyone who will touch the product while or after it is made. This would include employees in production, packaging, shipping, and sales and the end users. They are all influenced by any design or process change. The people who operate equipment, who do service work, or who implement can be both customers and suppliers.

The most difficult (and important) step of doing any QFD is getting the suppliers, operators, and customers together to do the required QFD form(s). Every group affected by the project should be represented. The desires of one group will sometimes cause limitations on others and simultaneous discussions among the factions will often identify options not previously considered, to arrive at the best possible overall solution. As you read the following details, refer to the simplified QFD form (Figure 3-1) to see the application.

SIMPLIFIED QFD INSTRUCTIONS

The simplified QFD form is a way of quantifying design options, always measuring these options against customer needs. The first step in doing the simplified QFD form is to make a list of the customer needs. Then, put a value of from "1" to "5" on each need:

- "5" is a critical or a safety need, a need that must be satisfied.
- "4" is very important.
- "3" is highly desirable.
- "2" is a "nice to have."
- "1" is "wanted if easy to do."

You can do a more elaborate rating system, but you will find you spend too much time assigning numbers! The customer needs and ratings are listed down the left side of the simplified QFD form.

Across the top of the simplified QFD form are potential actions to address the customer needs. Note that the customer needs are often expressed qualitatively (easy to use, won't rust, long life, etc.), whereas the design action items listed will be more specific (tabulated input screen, stainless steel, sealed roller bearings, etc.). Under each design action item and opposite each customer need, you will determine a value ("1" to "5") to rate how strongly that design item addresses the customer need:

- "5" means it addresses the customer need completely.
- "4" means it addresses the customer need well.
- "3" means it addresses the customer need somewhat.
- "2" means it addresses the customer need a little.
- "1" means it addresses the customer need very little.
- "0" or blank means it does not affect customer need.
- A negative number means it is detrimental to that customer need. (A negative number is not that unusual, since a solution to one need sometimes hurts another need!)

Put the rating in the upper half of the block beneath the design item and opposite the need. Then, you multiply the design rating times the value assigned to the corresponding customer need value. Enter this result into the lower half of the square under the design action item rating. These values will have a possible high of 25.

Once all the design items are rated against every customer need, add up the values in the lower half of the boxes under each design item and enter the sums into the "Totals" row at the bottom of the sheet. The solutions with the highest values are usually the preferred design solutions to address the customer needs.

Once these totals are reviewed, someone may feel that something is awry and want to go back and review some ratings or design solutions. This second (or third) review is extremely valuable. Also, the customer "5" ratings should be discussed one at a time to make sure that they are being addressed sufficiently.

Figure 3-1 is an example of a simplified QFD. The simplified QFD form can be done by hand or in Excel. In any case, the building and rating should be done "live" in the meeting to get maximum interaction and participation.

In the simplified QFD form, near the bottom, design action items are grouped when only one of the options can be done. The priorities within a group are only among the items in that group.

In this case, the priorities showed that the supplier should cast a plastic license plate cover with built-in plastic lens. This precludes the need for a separate lens, which is why the NA (not applicable) is shown in that priority. The unit should be mounted using plastic screws, with holes for all plates cast in. Gold or silver plating is an option that can be applied to the rim of the plastic.

Note that some of the luxury items (like steel casting) weren't picked because other factors were deemed more important. Having the customers there for these discussions is very critical, so they don't feel the supplier is giving them other than what they really want. Often customers will start out with a wish list of items that is then trimmed down to the critical few.

The form can be tweaked to make it more applicable to the product/process/service it is addressing. The importance is in getting involvement from as many affected parties as possible and using the simplified QFD form to drive design direction.

The simplified QFD form should be completed for all new designs or for process modifications. The time and cost involved in having the required meetings will be more than offset by making the correct decisions up front, rather than having to make multiple changes later.

CASE STUDY: A SIMPLIFIED QFD ON A TEST CUTTING MACHINE

A simplified QFD was being done to determine what adjustments were to be incorporated on a test in-line cutting machine for extruded tubing. The intent of this project was to instrument a cutting machine sufficient to test all reasonable combinations of settings to identify an optimum cutting process. The cutting machines currently would leave a rough end on the tubing as they cut it. This caused excessive material losses.

Figure 3-1. Simplified QFD example and form

License Plate Holder Option for Luxury Automobiles Ratings: 5 = Highest 1 = Lowest (or negative number)	Design Items	Metal Cast Rim	Plastic Cast Complete	Stamped Steel Rim	All Holes Already In	Optional Punched Holes	Gold/Silver Plating	Hex/Slotted Plastic Screws	Hex/Slotted Plated Steel Screws	Plastic Lens, Separate	Tempered Glass Lens, Separate
Customer Needs	**Ratings**										
Embossed Name	5	5	5	3	0	0	0	0	0	0	0
		25	25	15	0	0	0	0	0	0	0
Place for Dealer Name	5	5	5	5	0	0	0	0	0	0	0
		25	25	25	0	0	0	0	0	0	0
Must Hold All State Plates	5	5	5	5	5	5	0	0	0	0	0
		25	25	25	25	25	0	0	0	0	0
Solid Feel	3	5	3	2	0	0	0	1	4	2	5
		15	9	6	0	0	0	3	12	6	15
Gold/Silver Option	2	5	5	3	0	0	5	5	5	0	0
		10	10	6	0	0	10	10	10	0	0
Easy to Install	4	3	5	3	5	3	0	5	3	3	2
		12	20	12	20	12	0	20	12	12	8
Corrosion Resistance	4	3	5	2	0	0	3	5	3	4	5
		12	20	8	0	0	12	20	12	16	20
Light Weight (for MPG)	1	1	4	5	0	0	0	5	2	5	1
		1	4	5	0	0	0	5	2	5	1
Luxury Look	4	5	2	1	2	4	5	1	5	2	5
		20	8	4	8	16	20	4	20	8	20
No Sharp Corners	5	4	5	2	4	2	0	5	3	5	2
		20	25	10	20	10	0	25	15	25	10
Transparent Lens	4	0	3	0	0	0	0	0	0	3	5
		0	12	0	0	0	0	0	0	12	20
Last 10 Years	5	4	4	3	0	0	3	5	4	3	5
		20	20	15	0	0	15	25	20	15	25
Low Cost	2	1	5	4	5	2	1	5	3	4	2
		2	10	8	10	4	2	10	6	8	4
Keep Appearance 10 Years	4	4	3	2	0	0	2	5	3	3	5
		16	12	8	0	0	8	20	12	12	20
Groupings Totals Priorities		203 1	225	147	83 3	67	67 4	142 2	121	119 NA	143 NA

Future production machines would be designed with features dictated by the results found using the test cutting machine. The simplified QFD was to identify what items were to be tested on this test in-line cutter. Then, equipment design engineers would have to design that test capability into the test machine.

In attendance at this simplified QFD meeting were several Ph.D.s who had studied the process, equipment design and process engineers, customers who emphasized what issues had to be addressed, and some operators and maintenance people knowledgeable of the current cutting equipment.

The machine operators were quiet until the end of the meeting, when they became insistent that an additional support spring be added. None of the "experts" felt that this additional support spring was needed and opposed adding it because the operators could not logically explain the rationale for the spring. The operators' experience, however, made them adamant that the support spring was needed. Since the operators were so insistent and the worst thing that would happen is that the added spring would prove to be not needed, it was decided to include the additional support spring against the advice of the "experts."

When the test was run to find the optimum settings, it was found that this additional support spring was critical. The cutting process was very unstable without this support spring being optimized. Without the simplified QFD, this spring would not have been incorporated and the process optimization would not have been as successful.

The knowledge gained from this piece of test equipment was incorporated into the design of 12 in-line extruded tubing cutters, saving $1,500,000 per year.

TRADITIONAL QFDS

A traditional QFD, taught in most classes on Six Sigma, is likely to be one of the following.

The first is a QFD consisting of four forms. The first form is the "House of Quality." This form covers product planning and competitor benchmarking. The second form is Part Deployment, which shows key part characteristics. The third form shows Critical-to-Customer Process Operations. The fourth is Production Planning.

Two other QFDs are the "Matrix of Matrices" QFD, consisting of 30 matrices, and the "Designer's Dozen," consisting of 12 QFD matrices.

Needless to say, these other QFDs take much more time and effort than the simplified QFD. Meetings to complete the traditional QFDs generally take at least four times as long as the meetings required for the simplified QFD on an equivalent project.

Are the traditional QFDs worth the extra effort versus the simplified QFD? Perhaps so on very large and very complex programs. However, the benefit of being able to use the simplified QFD on *every* project or change, which is not realistic with the more complex QFDs, gives it a decided advantage. The customers' inputs are needed on *all* levels of projects!

The major benefit of any QFD comes from getting the input of everyone affected. If the form is too complex or the meeting to do the form is too long, people lose focus, their eyes begin to blur, and the quality of the input diminishes. The simplified QFD is designed to get needed input with the minimum of hassle! Simplified QFD meetings are often only two or three hours long.

WHAT WE HAVE LEARNED IN CHAPTER 3

1. The simplified QFD is usually used in the Define or Improve step of the DMAIC process.
2. Many product, process, and service issues are caused by not incorporating inputs from customers and/or suppliers of components and raw materials early in a design. Often the manufacturer just assumes that what the customers really want is already known.
3. The use of a simplified QFD can minimize a lot of issues before a design or modification is implemented.
4. Everyone affected by the project—such as operators, suppliers, users, engineers, maintenance staff, and customers—must participate in generating the simplified QFD form.
5. The simplified QFD should be done as early in a project as possible.
6. Revisit the simplified QFD's priority results several times to make sure they truly reflect the group's intent.
7. The cost of doing a simplified QFD will be more than offset by the benefits of a superior design with fewer modifications required.
8. The simplified QFD should be used on *every* new product or product/process change.
9. There are more complex and detailed QFDs that may be worth considering for very large and complex programs. However, the effort and people required for these QFDs usually preclude their being used on *all* designs and changes. The simplified QFD is extremely practical, since it *can* be used be used on *all* designs and changes.

RELATED READING

QFD: The Customer-Driven Approach to Quality Planning and Deployment, Shigeru Mizuno and Yoji Akao, editors (Tokyo: Asian Productivity Organization, 1994).

Quality Function Deployment: How to Make QFD Work for You, Lou Cohen (Upper Saddle River, NJ: Prentice Hall PTR, 1995).

Basic Statistics: Tools for Continuous Improvement, Mark J. Kiemele, Stephen R. Schmidt, and Ronald J. Berdine, 4th edition (Colorado Springs, CO: Air Academy Press, 1997).

CHAPTER 4

Simplified FMEA

W hat we will learn in this chapter is that on any project there can be collateral damage to areas outside the project. A simplified FMEA (failure modes and effects analysis) will reduce this likelihood. A simplified FMEA will generate savings largely through cost avoidance and it is usually used in the Define or Improve steps of the DMAIC process.

As was true for simplified QFDs, as presented in the prior chapter, the simplified FMEA will be less complex than the FMEA taught in most Six Sigma classes. A brief discussion of the traditional FMEA and the reason for the simplification comes later in the chapter.

Note that the simplified FMEA format is very similar to that used for the simplified QFD. This is intentional, since the goal is to use *both* on *every* new product or change. Since many of the same people will be involved in both the QFD and the FMEA, the commonality of both forms simplifies the task.

Simplified FMEA

Manufacturing Before implementing any new design, process, or change, do a simplified FMEA. An FMEA converts qualitative concerns into specific actions. You need input on what possible negative effects could occur.
Sales and Marketing A change in a sales or marketing strategy can affect other products or cause aggressive response by a competitor. A simplified FMEA is one way to make sure that all the possible ramifications are understood and addressed.

APPLICATIONS

Accounting and Software Development The introduction of a new software package or a different accounting procedure sometimes causes unexpected problems for those affected. A simplified FMEA will reduce unforeseen problems and trauma.

Receivables How receivables are handled can affect future sales. A simplified FMEA will help to understand concerns of both customers and internal salespeople and identify approaches that minimize future sales risks while reducing overdue receivables.

Insurance The balance between profits and servicing customers on insurance claims is dynamic. A simplified FMEA helps keep people attuned to risks associated with any actions under consideration.

A simplified FMEA is a method to review things that can go wrong even if a proposed project, task, or modification is completed as expected. Often a project generates so much support and enthusiasm that it lacks a healthy amount of skeptics, especially in regard to any effects that the project may have on things not directly related to the project. Everyone is working on the details of getting the project going and little effort is spent on looking at ramifications beyond the specific task!

The simplified FMEA form is a way of giving a project a critical look before it is implemented; it often saves a lot of cost and embarrassment. In doing a simplified FMEA, it is assumed that all inherent components of the direct project will be done correctly. (They should have been covered in regular project reviews.) The emphasis in a simplified FMEA is to identify affected components or issues downstream or tangentially related processes in which issues may arise because of the project.

Just as in the simplified QFD, the critical step is getting everyone together who has anything to do with the project, especially those having to deal with the effects of the project. These people could be machine operators, customers, or even suppliers. The proper group of participants will vary per project.

SIMPLIFIED FMEA INSTRUCTIONS

The left side of the simplified FMEA form (see Figure 4-1) is a list of things that could possibly go wrong, assuming that the project is completed as planned. The first task of the meeting is to generate this list of concerns. On this list could be unforeseen issues on other parts of the process, safety issues, environmental concerns, negative effects on existing similar products, or even employee problems. These will be rated in importance:

- "5" is a safety or critical concern.
- "4" is a very important concern.
- "3" is a medium concern.
- "2" is a minor concern.
- "1" is a matter for discussion to see if it is an issue.

Across the top of the simplified FMEA is a list of solutions already in place to address the concerns or additional solutions that have been identified in the meeting. Below each solution and opposite the concern, each response item is to be rated on how well it addresses the concern:

- "5" means it addresses the concern completely.
- "4" means it addresses the concern well.
- "3" means it addresses the concern satisfactorily.
- "2" means it addresses the concern somewhat.
- "1" means it addresses the concern very little.
- "0" or a blank means it does not affect the concern.
- A negative number means the solution actually makes the concern worse.

Enter this value in the upper half of the block, beneath the solution item and opposite the concern. After these ratings are complete, multiply each rating times the concern value on the left. Enter this product in the lower half of each box. Add all the values in the lower half of the boxes in each column and enter the sum in the Totals row indicated near the bottom of the form. These are then prioritized, with the highest value being the #1 consideration for implementation.

As in the simplified QFD, these summations are only a point of reference. It is appropriate to reexamine the concerns and ratings.

CASE STUDY: A POTENTIALLY LIFE-SAVING SIMPLIFIED FMEA

A high-speed production machine was experiencing wear. This wear caused the tooling to have too much play, which allowed it to rub against the product at one specific location on the machine, causing quality issues. The cost of rebuilding the machine was very high, so the manufacturing plant wanted other options of solving this problem.

An engineer came up with what seemed like an ingenious solution. Powerful magnets would be mounted just outboard of the machine at the problem area, near the tooling. These magnets would hold open the tooling as it went by, eliminating the chance of the tooling rubbing against the product. This solution was especially attractive because it would be inexpensive and easy to do, and it would solve the problem completely! The initial engineering study found no "show-stoppers" in regard to installing the magnets. Bench tests with actual magnets and tooling indicated that it would work extremely well.

Everyone was anxious to implement this project, since all the parts were readily available and would be easy to install on the machine for a test. But a requirement of the Six Sigma process was to first do a simplified FMEA to see if this could cause other issues. So, a group of production engineers, foremen, operators, maintenance people, and quality technicians were invited to a meeting to do the simplified FMEA.

Below is the simplified FMEA as derived in the meeting.

Figure 4-1. Simplified FMEA example and form

FMEA: Magnets Holding Tooling Open Ratings: 5 = Highest 1 = Lowest (or negative number)		Mount a degausser after magnets	Mount ProxSwitch and use breakaway mounts	Use electric magnets; adjust current and turn off to clean	Check with pacemaker mfg; shield if required
Concerns	**Ratings**				
The tooling will become magnetized	4	4	0	0	0
		16	0	0	0
Caught product will hit magnets, wreck machine	5	0	3	0	0
		0	15	0	0
Magnets will get covered with metal filings	2	2	0	3	0
		4	0	6	0
One operator has a heart pacemaker	5	?	0	0	?
		?	0	0	?
Magnets will cause violent tooling movement	2	0	0	3	0
		0	0	6	0
Totals **Priorities**		?	15	12	?

Most of the concerns that surfaced had doable and effective solutions. However, the concern that one operator had a heart pacemaker was a complete surprise; no one had any idea of how the magnets would affect the pacemaker.

On following up with the pacemaker manufacturer, it was discovered that even representatives of the manufacturer were not sure how the powerful magnets would affect the device. They did say, however, that they had serious reservations. They didn't want to commit to what level of shielding would suffice to protect the operator and were afraid of any resultant liability.

Other options were discussed, like reassigning the operator to another machine, but all of those options raised issues (such as union issues on the reassignment). The machine operator had to be free to access all areas of the machine, so a barrier physically isolating the area around the magnets was not an option.

At that point, the option of using magnets was abandoned, because there seemed to be no way to eliminate the possible risk to the operator with the pacemaker! No other low-cost solution was identified. The machine had to be rebuilt despite the high cost.

Without the simplified FMEA, the project would have been implemented, with some real risk that the operator could have been hurt or even lost his life.

Although this example is more dramatic than most, seldom is a simplified FMEA done without uncovering some issue that was previously unknown. Most of these issues can be resolved and it's easier to resolve them up front than afterwards! In this case study, the machine was rebuilt. This would probably have been the outcome in any case; the simplified FMEA prevented the risk, cost, and embarrassment of installing the magnets, dealing with the effects, and removing the magnets.

TRADITIONAL FMEAs

As mentioned earlier, the simplified FMEA is less complex than the traditional FMEA normally taught in Six Sigma. A traditional FMEA requires the people doing the form to identify each potential failure event and then the failure mode, the consequences, the potential cause, the severity, current design controls, the likelihood of detection, the frequency, the impact, risk priority, the recommended action, and likelihood of the action succeeding. This traditional FMEA requires multiple forms, much time, and many people. Is the extra time and effort worth it?

As with the traditional QFD, perhaps it is worthwhile on very complex and large programs. However, since the simplified FMEA takes far less time, it can be used on *every* project or change, which is unlikely to happen with a traditional FMEA. This gives the simplified FMEA a real advantage, because collateral damage can occur on *all* levels of project or change.

Both the traditional and simplified FMEAs trigger consideration of collateral damage, so one of the two should be used. Obviously the author prefers the simplified FMEA.

WHAT WE HAVE LEARNED IN CHAPTER 4

1. A simplified FMEA is usually used in the Define or Improve steps of DMAIC.
2. Much effort goes into making sure the specific details of a project, process, or service are correct. However, areas not inherently tied to the project are often ignored.
3. A simplified FMEA emphasizes identifying concerns in other affected areas and prioritizing potential solutions to these concerns.
4. Everyone affected by the proposed project, process, or service should participate in the simplified FMEA.
5. Revisit the results of the simplified FMEA several times to make sure that they truly reflect the group's intent.
6. The cost of doing a simplified FMEA will be more than offset by the costs avoided on the project's potential negative effects on other areas.
7. Traditional FMEAs are more complex, but may be justified on extremely large and complex programs. However, they are unlikely to be used on *every* program or change, which is the value of the simplified FMEA.

RELATED READING AND SOFTWARE

Failure Mode and Effect Analysis: FMEA from Theory to Execution, D.H. Stamatis, 2nd edition (Milwaukee, WI: American Society for Quality, 2003).

The Basics of FMEA, Robin E. McDermott, Raymond J. Mikulak, and Michael R. Beauregard (New York: Quality Resources, 1996).

Basic Statistics: Tools for Continuous Improvement, Mark J. Kiemele, Stephen R. Schmidt, and Ronald J. Berdine, 4th edition (Colorado Springs, CO: Air Academy Press, 1997).

Relex FMES/FMECA, Relex Software Corporation, Greensburg, PA, www.relexsoftware.com.

CHAPTER 5

Cause-and-Effect
Fishbone Diagram

What we will learn in this chapter is that it's critical to identify and examine all of the possible causes for a problem. This chapter explains how a cause-and-effect diagram is used.

The fishbone diagram is used primarily in the Define, Analyze, and Improve steps of the DMAIC process. It helps identify which input variables should be studied further and gives focus to the analysis.

The purpose of a fishbone diagram is to identify all the input variables that could be causing the problem of interest. Once we have a complete input variables list we identify the critical few key process input variables (KPIVs) to measure and further investigate.

Fishbone Diagram

Manufacturing Do a fishbone diagram to list all the important input variables related to a problem. Highlight the KPIVs for further study. This focus minimizes sample collection and data analysis.

Sales and Marketing For periods of unusually low sales, use a fishbone diagram to identify possible causes of the low sales. The KPIVs enable identification of probable causes and often lead to possible solutions.

Accounting and Software Development Use a fishbone diagram to identify the possible causes of unusual accounting or computer issues. The people in these areas respond well to this type of analysis.

APPLICATIONS

Receivables Identify periods of higher than normal delinquent receivables. Then, use a fishbone diagram to try to understand the underlying causes.

Insurance Look for periods of unusual claim frequency. Then, do a fishbone to understand underlying causes. This kind of issue usually has a large number of potential causes; the fishbone diagram enables screening to the critical few.

FISHBONE DIAGRAM INSTRUCTIONS

The specific problem of interest is normally the "head" of a fishbone diagram. There are six "bones" on the fish; on these "bones" we list input variables that affect the problem "head."

Each "bone" has a category of input variables that should be listed. Separating the input variables into six categories, each with its own characteristics, helps us make sure that no input variable is missed. The six categories are Measurements, Materials, Men, Methods, Machines, and Environment. (Some people remember these as the five M's and one E.) The six categories are what make the fishbone diagram more effective than just simply listing the input variables.

Ideally, the input variables on a fishbone should come from a group of "experts" working together in one room. This enables a high degree of interaction among the experts. However, if this is not feasible, it *is* possible to do this process on the telephone, using a computer to regularly send updated versions of the fishbone diagram to all the people contributing. It is important for all contributors to be able to see the fishbone diagram as it evolves. This will cause everyone to constantly be triggered by the six categories. Below is an abbreviated example of a fishbone diagram (Figure 5-1) done on the problem "Shaft Diameter Error."

After listing all the input variables, the same team of experts should pick the two or three KPIVs they feel are most likely to be the culprits. Those are highlighted in boldface and capital letters on the fishbone diagram.

There are software packages that enable users to fill in the blanks of standardized forms for the fishbone diagram. There are also free downloads from the Internet that have forms that tie in with Excel. However, other than for the sake of neatness, doing them by hand works just as well.

As you will see later, in Chapter 8, the fishbone diagram is the recommended tool to identify what should be sampled in a process and to know what variables need to be kept in control during the sampling process. Without the kind of cause-and-effect analysis the fishbone diagram sup-

Figure 5-1. Fishbone diagram example (input variables affecting shaft diameter error)

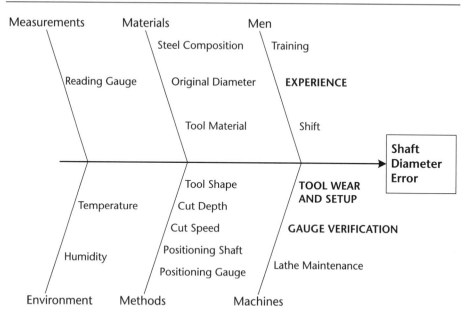

ports, the sampling will be less focused and more likely to be fraught with error. This is because the effort and control needed for good sampling and data collection is not trivial, so the amount of sampling must be minimized to allow everyone to get it right!

Sometimes just the process of doing the fishbone diagram leads to the solution, because you are getting the "experts" together to discuss the problem, which doesn't happen without a scheduled purpose.

WHAT WE HAVE LEARNED IN CHAPTER 5

1. The fishbone diagram is used primarily in the Define, Analyze, and Improve steps of the DMAIC process.
2. Look for possible cause-and-effect relationships using a fishbone diagram. The purpose of a fishbone diagram is to have experts identify all the input variables that could be causing the problem of interest. Once we have a complete input variables list, we must attempt to identify the critical few key process input variables (KPIVs) to measure and further investigate.
3. The fishbone diagram is the preferred Six Sigma tool for identifying what should be sampled in a process and which variables need to be

kept in control during the sampling process. Without the kind of cause-and-effect analysis the fishbone diagram supports, the sampling would be less focused.

4. Sometimes just the process of doing the fishbone diagram leads to the solution, because you are getting the experts together to discuss the problem with a specific focus.

5. Use of the fishbone diagram is not limited to manufacturing. Virtually any problem can be tackled using this powerful tool.

RELATED READING AND SOFTWARE

Rath & Strong's Six Sigma Pocket Guide, Rath & Strong Management Consultants (Lexington, MA: Rath & Strong/Aon Consulting Worldwide, 2000).

Basic Statistics: Tools for Continuous Improvement, Mark J. Kiemele, Stephen R. Schmidt, and Ronald J. Berdine, 4th edition (Colorado Springs, CO: Air Academy Press, 1997).

MINITAB 13, Minitab Inc., State College, PA, www.minitab.com.

CHAPTER 6

Simplified Process Flow Diagram

What you will learn in this chapter, as in the previous chapter, is that it's critical to identify and examine all of the possible causes for a problem. In addition to the fishbone diagram discussed in the previous chapter, you can use the simplified process flow diagram to help identify key process input variables (KPIVs) in a process. But there's a difference between these two tools.

It is important to know where and when input variables affect a process so you can see if that makes sense with where the problem is being seen. Of special interest are positions in the process where inspection or quality sorting takes place or where process data is collected. By looking at data from these positions, you may see evidence of a change or a problem. By noting where different operations take place, you can also see where issues can arise. Simplified process flow diagrams are used primarily in the Define, Analyze, and Improve steps of the DMAIC process

Simplified Process Flow Diagrams

Manufacturing The simplified process flow diagram will focus an investigation by identifying where and when in the process KPIVs could have affected the problem. Of special interest is where data is collected in the process.

Sales and Marketing A simplified process flow diagram will assist in identifying if the cause of low sales is region, personnel, etc. This allows the team to focus on the likely area.

APPLICATIONS

Accounting and Software Development A simplified process flow diagram will help pinpoint the specific problem areas in a system or program. This simplifies the debug process. Software developers are very familiar with this process.

Receivables Identify periods when delinquent receivables are higher than normal. A simplified process flow diagram may help in designing procedures, like discounts for early payment, to minimize the problem.

Insurance Look for periods of unusual frequency of claims. A simplified process flow diagram may help identify them.

A simplified process flow diagram works well when used in conjunction with a fishbone diagram. It can further screen the KPIVs that were identified with the fishbone, minimizing where you will have to take additional samples or data.

There are software packages that enable users to fill in the blanks of standardized forms for the fishbone diagram and the process flow diagram. There are also free downloads from the Internet that have forms that tie in with Excel. However, other than for the sake of neatness, doing them by hand works just as well.

SIMPLIFIED PROCESS FLOW DIAGRAM INSTRUCTIONS

A process flow diagram shows the relationships among the steps in a process, or the components in a system, with arrows connecting all of the pieces and showing the sequence of activities. Some texts and software for traditional process flow diagrams use additional geometrical shapes—circles and inverted triangles and so on—to differentiate among types of functions in the process. I choose to keep it simple. Figure 6-1 shows a simplified process flow diagram.

Just as with the fishbone diagram, the simplified process flow diagram is not limited to uses related to solving problems in a manufacturing process. Also, a simplified process flow diagram is not limited to a physical flow map. The flow could be related to time or to process steps, not just place.

Finally, process flow diagrams are not just for solving problems. They can also be used to configure a proposed new process.

Figure 6-1. Simplified process flow diagram, shaft machining

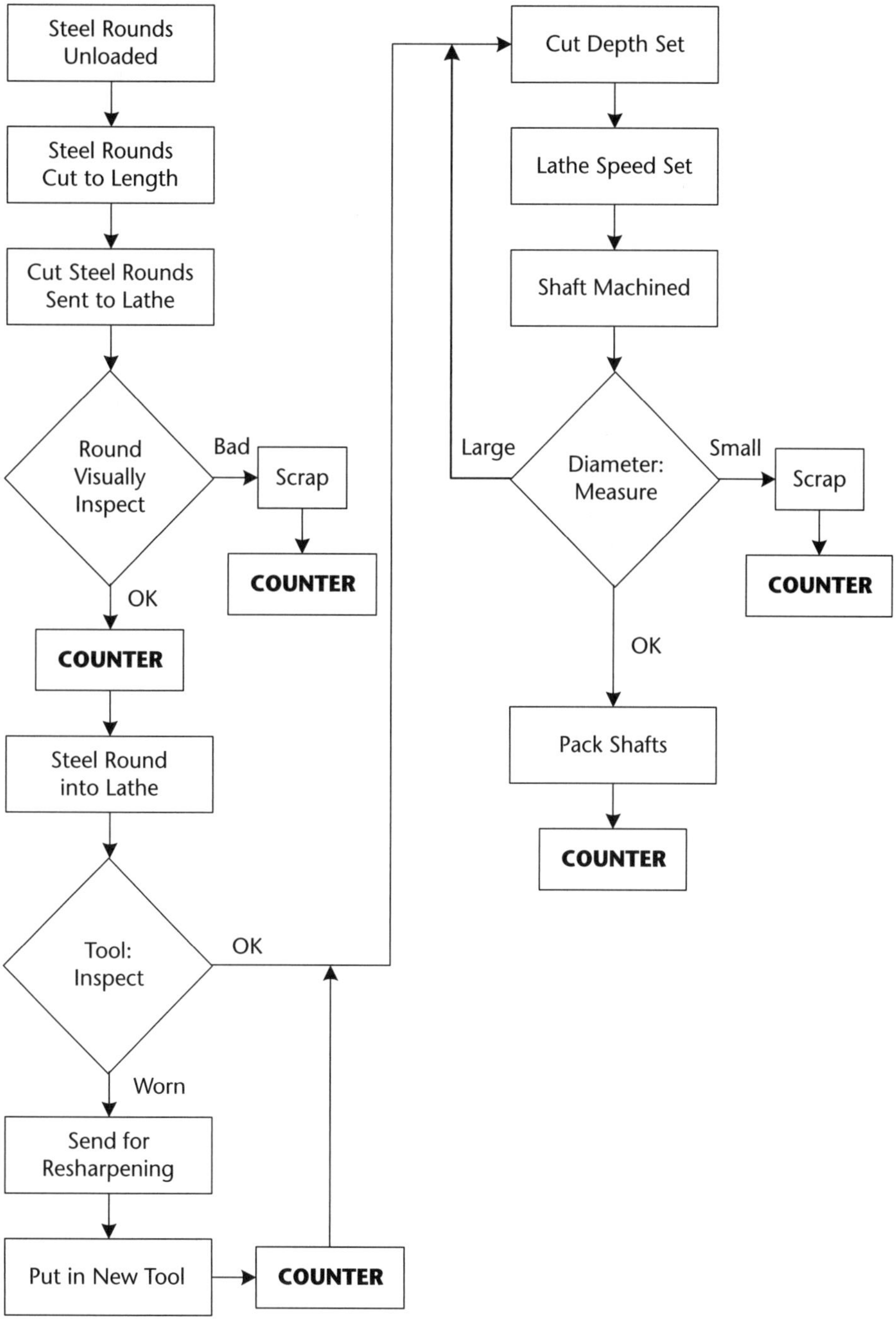

WHAT WE HAVE LEARNED IN CHAPTER 6

1. Simplified process flow diagrams are used primarily in the Define, Analyze, and Improve steps of the DMAIC process.
2. A simplified process flow diagram will help further pinpoint the area in which efforts should be concentrated. Of special interest in a process is where data are collected, since this will often help focus the study to a defined process area.
3. Simplified process flow diagrams work well in conjunction with a fishbone diagram. By using the two, the areas to further investigate and sample are minimized.
4. A simplified process flow diagram is not limited to a physical flow map. The flow could also be related to time or to process steps.
5. Besides being used for problem solving, process flow diagrams can be used to configure a proposed new process.

RELATED READING AND SOFTWARE

Rath & Strong's Six Sigma Pocket Guide, Rath & Strong Management Consultants (Lexington, MA: Rath & Strong/Aon Consulting Worldwide, 2000).

Basic Statistics: Tools for Continuous Improvement, Mark J. Kiemele, Stephen R. Schmidt, and Ronald J. Berdine, 4th edition (Colorado Springs, CO: Air Academy Press, 1997).

MINITAB 13, Minitab Inc., State College, PA, www.minitab.com.

CHAPTER 7

Correlation Tests

What you will learn in this chapter is how to discover the key process input variables (KPIVs) that may have caused a change in a process or product. For that, we will be doing correlation tests.

In some Six Sigma classes, regression analysis is used to find correlations. A mathematical curve is fit to a set of data and techniques are used to measure how well the data fit these curves. The curves are then used to test for correlations.

These methods require a high degree of skill and generally are not friendly to those who are not doing this kind of analysis almost daily. Thankfully, most Six Sigma work can be done using the tools already covered, as long as we are willing to do some visual examination of data and their related graphs. Correlation tests are used primarily in the Define, Analyze, and Improve steps of the DMAIC process.

Something changed in a process or product and we would like to discover the KPIV(s) that caused it. Time and position are the critical factors in doing the analysis.

Correlation Tests

Manufacturing Do a time plot showing when a problem first appeared or when it comes and goes. Do similar time plots of the KPIVs to see if a change in any of these variables coincides with the timing of the problem change. If so, do a controlled test to establish the cause-and-effect relationship for that KPIV.

APPLICATIONS

41

Sales and Marketing For periods of unusually low sales activity, do a time plot showing when the low sales periods started and stopped. Do similar time plots of the KPIVs to see if a change in any these variables coincides with the low sales period. If so, do a controlled test to establish the cause-and-effect relationship for that KPIV.

Accounting and Software Development Do a time plot of unusual accounting or computer issues. Do similar time plots of the KPIVs to see if a change in any these variables coincides with the issues. If so, do a controlled test to establish the cause-and-effect relationship for that KPIV. The people in these areas respond well to this type of analysis.

Receivables, Insurance, etc. Identify periods when delinquent receivables are higher than normal or the frequency of claims is unusual. Then do a time plot of the problem and the related KPIVs. For any variable that shows coincident change, check for cause-and-effect relationships with controlled tests.

CORRELATION TEST INSTRUCTIONS

We first isolate when and where the problem change took place. We do this by doing a time plot or a position plot of every measurement of the process or product we have that is indicative of the change. From these plots we can often define the time and/or the position of the change to a very narrow range. If the change indicated by the plot is large compared with other data changes before and after the incidence and the timing corresponds to the observed problem recognition, it is generally worthwhile to check for correlations.

The next thing to do is to look for correlations with input variables, often using graphs of historical data. If we don't know the KPIVs, we must do a fishbone diagram or a process flow diagram to identify them. We do time plots or position plots of every KPIV, centering on the previously defined time period or position. Any input variable that changed at nearly the same time or position as the problem is suspect.

When we find multiple time/position agreement of change between the problem and an input variable, then we must do controlled tests where we control everything but the suspicious variable. In this way we can establish cause-and-effect relationships.

If more than one KPIV changed, there could be an interaction between these variables, but usually one KPIV will stand out. Looking at extended time periods will often rule out input variables that do not correlate consistently.

Later in the text we will learn numerical methods to test for statistically significant change. These tests can be used to test for significant change on the data from immediately before and immediately after the problem begins. These tests can be used on both the problem data and the KPIV data. However, if there is multiple time agreement on change between the problem and the KPIV, these extra tests are often not needed. In any case, we will have to run controlled tests to prove cause-and-effect relationships.

Below are simplified plots (Figure 7-1) of a problem and the process KPIVs (A, B, and C). You can see how this visual check is very easy, and often obvious, once plots of the problem and the KPIVs are compared with each other.

Figure 7-1. Correlation illustration plot

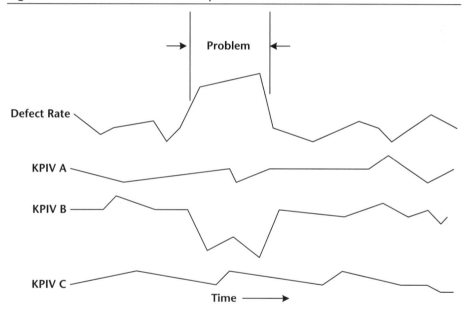

KPIV B certainly looks suspicious, given that it had a change in the same time interval as the problem, matching both the beginning and end of the time period. As a first test, I would expand the time of the data for both the process defect rate and the KPIV B to see if this change agreement is truly as unique and correlated as it appears in this limited data. Remember, however, that this test will never be definitive. It will only hint at the cause. A controlled test involving controlling all possible variables (except for KPIV B in Figure 7-1) will be required. We would intentionally change KPIV B per the above plot and see if the problem responds similarly. Only then have we established a cause-and-effect relationship.

When time plots of variables are compared with the change we are studying, it is important that any inherent time shift be incorporated. For example, if a raw material is put into a storage bin with the inventory from three days previous, this three-day delay must be incorporated when looking for a correlation of that raw material to the process.

Showing Cause-and-Effect

TIP

Correlation doesn't prove cause-and-effect. It just shows that two or more things happened to change at the same time or at the same position. There have been infamous correlations (e.g., stork sightings versus birth rates) that are just coincidental or have other explanations.

To show cause-and-effect, you must run controlled tests where only the key test input variable is changed and its effect is measured. Normally, historical data can't be used to prove cause-and-effect because the data are too "noisy" and the other variables are not being controlled.

Case Study: Incorrect Cause

A glass container was heated to very high temperatures in an indexing device and it was critical that the glass softened at the same position on this indexing heating machine. This was critical because several processes on this machine relied on the glass having a certain viscosity at different stations on the machine. The people running this indexing heating device had historically complained that the glass container softened at various positions on the machine, causing issues with the processes that occurred at the different machine stations and therefore hurting the quality of the final product.

It was believed that the cause of this problem was large variation (high sigma) within the glass wall of each container. This was not a new problem and over the years the tolerances had been tightened on the container wall variation. These tolerances were so tight that large losses were occurring in the container plant trying to meet these tight specifications. Because the complaints continued, however, a major project was started to further reduce the wall variation within each container.

To find out how critical variation in wall thickness was, the project team ran a large group of containers with great variation in wall thickness on the indexing heating machine and compared the results against the results of running a group of containers with little variation in wall thickness. Using the statistical tests that will be covered later, the project team found *no* statistically significant difference between the two groups.

The historical belief that the wall thickness sigma within each container was causing the container to soften at different positions was wrong!

A search was started to find the KPIVs that influenced the position at which the glass softened. Looking at periods of time when the complaints were highest versus times when the complaints were reduced, one of the KPIVs found to correlate was the *average* wall thickness of each container—not the wall *variation* within each container. When a test was run with containers grouped with others having similar average wall thickness, each container softened consistently with others in the group, at different positions on the machine. Again, the variation (sigma) within each individual wall had no effect. The test was repeated, in different plants on similar machines with the other variables in control, and the results supported the cause-and-effect.

This subtle finding that the average wall thickness was the KPIV and that variation within each container wall did not correlate changed the way the container was manufactured. This saved the container manufacturer $400,000 per year, because it had been scrapping containers with large variations within the wall. It also saved the plants running the heating machines $700,000 per year through better yields.

The tool that triggered the realization that container wall *variation* was not the culprit was visually checking for correlations on plotted data on wall variation versus softening position on the indexing machine. No visual correlation was seen. However, there *was* a visual correlation between *average* wall thickness change and softening position.

These initial observations were followed up with quantitative statistical tests that checked for significant change, but the correlation tests done on visual plots were the breakthrough trigger. And, of course, controlled tests were needed to prove cause-and-effect.

WHAT WE HAVE LEARNED IN CHAPTER 7

1. Correlation tests are used primarily in the Define, Analyze, and Improve steps of the DMAIC process.
2. In some Six Sigma classes, regression analysis is used to find correlations. These methods require a high degree of skill and generally are not friendly to those who are not doing this kind of analysis almost daily.
3. Something changed in a process or product and we would like to discover the key process input variables (KPIVs) that caused it. Time and position are the critical factors in doing the analysis. Using data plots, we first isolate when and where the problem change took place.

4. Look for a matching time period or position change on data plots of all input variables. Identify all KPIVs that have a change that correlates with the problem.

5. Test for a cause-and-effect relationship by running controlled tests with only the suspect KPIV being changed.

6. Statistical tests for significance, which will be covered later in the text, can also assist in checking for correlations. But often the visual correlation using data plots is sufficient, especially when you see multiple correlations of timing between the problem and a KPIV.

RELATED READING AND SOFTWARE

Rath & Strong's Six Sigma Pocket Guide, Rath & Strong Management Consultants (Lexington, MA: Rath & Strong/Aon Consulting Worldwide, 2000).

Basic Statistics: Tools for Continuous Improvement, Mark J. Kiemele, Stephen R. Schmidt, and Ronald J. Berdine, 4th edition (Colorado Springs, CO: Air Academy Press, 1997).

MINITAB 13, Minitab Inc., State College, PA, www.minitab.com.

PART III

Foundations for Using
Statistical Six Sigma Tools

CHAPTER 8

Getting Good Samples and Data

What you will learn in this chapter is how to take good samples and get good data. Otherwise, the best thinking won't matter much because you won't be able to put it to the test properly. In later chapters you will see how to calculate minimum sample size and how to verify that a gauge used to measure a product is giving data that are sufficient for your needs. Just as important, however, is making sure that your sample and data truly represent the population of the process you wish to measure. The whole intent of sampling is to be able to analyze a process or a population and get valid results without measuring every part or component, so sampling details are extremely important.

Issues in Getting Good Data

Manufacturing Samples and the resultant data have to represent the total population, yet processes controlling the population are often changing dramatically, due to people, shift, environment, equipment, etc.

Sales Sales forecasts often use sampling techniques in their predictions. Yet the total market may have many diverse groups to sample. These groups may be affected by many external drivers, like the economy.

Marketing What data should be used to judge a marketing campaign's effectiveness, since so many other factors are changing at the same time?

APPLICATIONS

Software Development What are the main causes of software crashes and how would you get data to measure the "crash-resistance" of competing software?

Receivables How would you get good data on the effectiveness of a program intended to reduce overdue receivables, when factors like the economy exert a strong influence and change frequently?

Insurance How can data measuring the satisfaction with different insurance programs be compared when people covered by the programs are not identical?

We have all seen the problems pollsters have had in predicting election outcomes based on sampling. In general, the problem has *not* been in the statistical analysis or in the sample size. The problem has been picking a group of people to sample who truly represent the electorate!

The problem of sampling and getting good data has several key components. First, the people and the methods used for taking the samples and data affect the randomness and accuracy of both. Second, the product population is diverse and often changing, sometimes quite radically. These changes occur over time and can be affected by location. To truly reflect a population, anyone sampling and using data must be aware of all these variables and somehow get valid data despite them.

I will share some of the difficulties or challenges my teams have experienced in getting representative samples and data. I will then discuss some approaches to get useful and valid data despite these issues. Most of the examples pertain to manufacturing, but I will explain later how the approach recommended for getting good data applies to many other applications.

HAWTHORNE EFFECT

As soon as anyone goes out to measure a process, things change. Everyone pays more attention. The process operators are more likely to closely monitor their process and quality inspectors are likely to be more effective in segregating defects. The resultant product you are sampling is not likely to represent that of a normal process. This is even true when people are polled on an issue, in that the answer may be the result of far more careful thought than the impulses or knee-jerk reactions that might guide those people in their daily actions.

There have been many studies done on how people react to having someone pay attention to them. Perhaps the most famous is the Hawthorne

Study, which was done at a large Bell Western manufacturing facility—the Hawthorne Works—in Cicero, Illinois, from 1927 to 1932. This study showed that any gain realized during a controlled test often came from the positive interaction between the people doing the test and the participants and also the interaction among the participants. The people may begin to work together as a team to get positive results. The actual variable change being tested was often not the driver of any improvement.

One of the tests at the Hawthorne facility involved increasing the light level to study the influence of the increased light on productivity. Productivity did indeed increase where the light level was increased. But, in a control group, where the light level was *not* changed, productivity also improved by the same amount. It was apparently the attention given to both groups that was the positive influence, not the light level. In fact, when the lighting was restored to its previous level, the improvement in productivity continued for some period of time. This effect of attention has become known as the Hawthorne Effect.

Any data you take that show an improvement that you think is the result of a change you have implemented must be suspect due to the Hawthorne Effect. Your best protection against making an incorrect assumption about improvement is to take data simultaneously from a parallel line with an identical process (control group), but without the change. However, the people in both groups should have had the same attention, attended the same meetings, etc. An alternative method is to collect line samples just before the change is implemented, but after all the meetings, interaction, etc. These "before" samples would be compared with the "after" samples, with the assumption that any Hawthorne Effect is included in both.

There was a different result, however, in another study in the same Hawthorne facility. In this case, the participants of the study were afraid that the test results were going to negatively affect their jobs and, as a group, they had agreed that their productivity would *not* improve, no matter what changes were implemented, so of course it didn't. Doing a test in this environment would make it very difficult to ascertain whether a change was good or bad, since the experiment could be undermined. In this kind of environment, the only way to get good data is to do a surreptitious change, unless the change is so basic to the process that its results can't be denied.

If you ask an inspector to pick up and inspect a product at random, there is a good chance the sample will be biased toward any product with a visible defect. This is because inspectors are accustomed to looking for defects and because they believe you are there because of problems with defects, so they want to be helpful.

I once ran a test where product was being inspected on-line, being paced by the conveyor speed. I collected the rejected product and isolated the packed "good" product from this same time period. Without telling the inspectors, I then mixed the defective product back with the "good" packed product. Without telling the inspectors that they had already inspected the product, I had the same inspectors inspect this remixed product off-line, where the inspectors weren't machine-paced. The defect rate almost doubled. (Interestingly, the customer had not been complaining about the product coming through the on-line inspection.)

When the product was inspected without time restraints, the quality criteria apparently tightened, even though no one had triggered a change in the criteria. Or maybe the inspectors just became more effective. Another possibility is that the inspectors felt that I was checking on their effectiveness in finding all the defects, so they were being extra conservative in interpreting the criteria. In any case, someone using data from the off-line inspection would get a defect rate almost double that seen on-line, from an equivalent production process. Therefore, if someone had implemented a change and was checking its effectiveness by checking for defects off-line, the change would have had to reduce the actual defects in half to even look equivalent to the historical data from on-line inspection. Obviously this would be problematic.

Time considerations are not the only influence on quality criteria interpretation. To check the optics on a parabolic reflector, an inspector would insert the reflector into a fixture that seated the reflector precisely over a light source. The inspector would then make a judgment on the quality of the resultant projected image. Too many "poor" readings would cause the product to be scrapped and the reflector-forming process to be reset.

As a test, on a day with an unusually high incidence of "good" optical readings, I collected the relatively few reflectors that had "poor" readings. On a later date, when the process was generating a lot of "poor" optical readings, I reintroduced the reflectors that had earlier been judged "poor." They were now judged as "good." Because of the qualitative nature of the criteria, the judgment of "good" or "poor" apparently became relative to the average optics that the inspector was currently seeing.

Sometimes people become very defensive (or maybe even offensive) when samples are taken from their process. In one of the case studies I relate later, employees of a manufacturing plant thought its defects were caused by bad raw materials. When a team began collecting defects on one of the plant's production lines and correlating them back to specific problems on that line, the line operator grieved to his union that he was being harassed, since the engineering team was not looking at the raw materials, which the operator was *sure* were causing the problem. Incidentally, the problems did prove to be related to the line and were not caused by raw materials.

CASE STUDY: OUTCOME BIAS

An engineer was automating a plant's production line with some in-line automatic inspection equipment. To validate the equipment, one of the Six Sigma test requirements was to see if there was a statistically significant difference between the products inspected by the automatic equipment and the products inspected by the people on-line.

The first test results showed that the packed products that had been inspected by the automatic inspection equipment had a significantly higher defect level than the products inspected by the people, so the automatic inspection equipment failed the test. This result surprised the engineer, because on previous tests with "master" defects, the automatic equipment had proven to be very good.

The tests comparing the automatic equipment and the manual on-line inspection involved comparing alternate intervals of ware inspected only by the equipment and ware inspected only by the people. In this way, the engineer felt that he was removing any variable related to the overall incoming quality of the product.

After failing this initial test, the engineer reviewed the sampling technique and the manner in which the two samples were compared and realized his methodology could be flawed. First, the people inspecting the product on-line did not want the automatic inspection equipment to work, since they felt that it might jeopardize their jobs. The engineer suspected that the inspectors were extra conservative in manually inspecting the product during the test. Second, the off-line people re-inspecting the samples of product also felt that their jobs could be possibly at risk, because their jobs were also classified as "inspector." The engineer suspected some bias in their judgment in what they were calling a "defect" when re-inspecting both groups of product. Third, the quality manager, who from the beginning had proclaimed that the automatic inspection equipment could never have the diverse inspection ability of a human, may have had some bias in any data outcome analysis.

To correct for these sampling and comparison deficiencies, the engineer running the tests changed his sampling and re-inspection procedures. He decided to gather his samples over a week's time period, on random shifts. Without prior notice, he would go out to the production line and collect samples of packed product that had just been inspected by the people. He would have them stop manually inspecting and he would start the automatic inspection equipment. Then he again collected packed product samples. Finally, he would turn off the inspection equipment and resume the manual standard inspection. He did not again collect samples; his samples were always taken just before and during automatic inspection, with no prior warning. These two groups of samples were numbered using a random number generator, so only he knew which of the samples came from the automatic inspection and which came from the on-line people. After collecting samples randomly over a week, he gave the samples to the quality department to inspect. He did not give the secret code for identifying the ware inspection method to the people re-inspecting the ware or to the quality manager. (Incidentally, this approach did not go over well with the quality manager. He put in a strong protest to the plant manager.)

Only after all the data on the re-inspected product were published was the code identifying the inspection method released. Then the statistical tests for change, which are covered later in the text, were applied. There was no statistically significant difference between the two groups of re-inspected product. The automatic inspection equipment passed its Six Sigma test requirements.

VARIABLES

There are many factors that can affect sampling. Here are a few to make you more aware of the complexity and difficulty of getting good data.

Sometimes an inspector "adjusts" data, truly believing that the adjustment gives a truer picture of the actual process. Here's an example.

I was watching an inspector who was inspecting product on a high-speed production line. On a regular basis, a random product was picked from the conveyor line and placed onto a fixture, which had several electronic gauges that took key measurements. These measurements were displayed on a computer screen and then automatically sent to the quality database, unless the inspector overrode the sending of the data. The override was intended only if the inspector saw a very specific problem, like the product not being seated properly in the fixture, necessitating a new reading on that product.

As I was observing, I saw the inspector periodically override the sending of the data, even though I saw no apparent problem with the seating. When I asked the inspector why the data were not being sent, she replied that the readings looked unusual and she didn't think they were representative of the majority of products being measured. She didn't want what she thought was erroneous data sent to the system, so she overrode the sending of the data and went to the next product. She didn't even reread the product.

She proudly told me that she had been doing that for years and that she had trained other inspectors accordingly. So much for using *those* data! Anyone running a test on this line, then taking his or her own quality samples, would likely find more variation in the self-inspected samples than the quality system historical data would show.

Attempting to get random samples from a conveyor belt is not always easy. Sometimes the production equipment has multiple heads that unload onto a conveyor belt in a non-random fashion. Some of the stations on the production machine may send all of their products down one side of the conveyor, so someone taking samples from the other side of the conveyor belt may never get any product from some of the production stations.

The start-up of any piece of equipment often generates an unusually high incidence of defects until it is debugged. After a shift change in multiple-shift plants, the new operator may take some time to get the machine running to his or her own parameters, during which time the quality may suffer. Absenteeism and vacations cause less experienced people to operate equipment, with generally lower quality. Maintenance schedules can often be sensed in product quality. Another influence on quality is scheduling—which production line is scheduled on which product. And, of course, there are variables of humidity, temperature, etc.

Certainly the overall quality is affected by the above variables and more. In fact, a case could be made that many of the quality issues come from these "exception" mini-populations. So, how can you possibly sample such that all these variables are taken into account?

First, you probably can't take samples to account for all of the possible combinations listed above. In fact, before you begin to take any samples, you have to go back to the first step in the DMAIC process and define the problem. Only with this better definition of the problem will you be able to ascertain what to sample.

PROCESS OFF-CENTER

Is the problem that the process is off-center? For example, are you worried about machined shaft diameters where the initial data indicate that on the average they run too large? Is the problem that all order takers are consistently making too many errors? Are almost all orders on a product being filled late? If a problem is of this nature, then you have a problem that perhaps is best addressed by improving the whole process, not focusing on the variation caused by the exception mini-populations. If this is the case, it makes collecting samples/data and measuring change a lot easier than if you had to gather samples/data on each peculiar part of the population.

When attempting to measure your success on centering a process or changing the process average, you want to collect samples or use data that represent a "normal" process, both before and after any process adjustment. You don't want samples from any of the temporary "mini-populations."

One of the ways to identify the "normal" population is to do a fishbone diagram where the head of the fish is "non-normal" populations. In this way the bones of the fish (the variables) will be all the variables that cause a population to be other than normal. You will then make sure that the time period in which you collect samples/data is free from any of the conditions listed on the fishbone.

Let's look at an example. Let's say the problem is the aforementioned issue, that machined shafts are generally running too large. Previously we did a fishbone diagram on shaft diameter error. Let's look at that fishbone again (Figure 8-1) in reference to this example.

Figure 8-1. Fishbone diagram of input variables affecting shaft diameter error

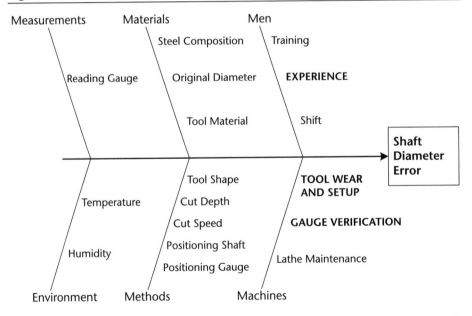

Let's look at the key process input variables (KPIVs) shown on this fishbone to determine which one(s) would likely cause the shaft diameters to run off-center, generally too large. The expert-picked KPIVs are experience of the operator, tool wear and setup, and gauge verification.

The experience of the operator would perhaps cause this problem for short periods, but the problem would not be ongoing; at times we would expect to have an experienced operator. Gauge setup and verification could account for the problem, since the gauge could be reading off-center such that the diameters would be generally too large. However, for this example, let's assume we check and are satisfied that the simplified gauge verifications (which will be covered in detail in the next chapter) have been done on schedule and correctly.

That leaves tool wear and setup. Tool wear would most likely cause the diameters to change as the tool wears, but then the cycle would start over as the tool is changed. However, if the tool setup is incorrect, it could position the tool incorrectly all the time. This could conceivably cause the diameters to be generally high. So, this is the variable we want to test.

We will want to run a test to see if having the operator set the tool up with a different nominal setting will make the process more on-center. We want to do random sampling during the process, with the tool setup being the only variable that we change.

Since the effect of tool setup is what we want to measure, we want to control all the other input variables. Per the above fishbone diagram, we especially want experienced people working on the process and want to be sure that the simplified gauge verification was done. These were the input variables that had been defined by the experts as being critical. We will also use a tool with "average" wear, so tool wear is not an issue. The test length for getting samples will be short enough that any additional tool wear during the test will be negligible.

We will use an experienced crew on day shift, verifying that the shaft material is correct and the lathe is set up correctly (cutter depth, cutter speed, position of shaft and gauge). We will make sure lathe maintenance has been done and that the person doing the measurements is experienced. We will minimize the effects of temperature and humidity by taking samples/data on the "normal" process and then immediately doing the test with the revised setup and taking the test samples/data. We will take samples/data only during these control periods.

Note that we used the fishbone to both show the KPIVs and to help pick the input variables we logically concluded could be causing the issue. Without this process of elimination, we would have had to test many more times. By limiting and controlling our tests, we can concentrate on getting the other variables under control, at least as much as possible.

If this test on tool setup did not solve the problem of diameters being too large, we would then go back and review our logic, perhaps picking another variable to test.

Getting Good Samples and Data
Use good problem definition, a fishbone diagram, and any of the other qualitative tools to minimize the number of variables you have to test. Then do a good job controlling the other variables during the test.

Sample sizes, needed statistical analysis, etc. will be covered in later chapters. In this chapter we are only emphasizing the non-numerical problems related to getting good data.

The example I just gave pertained to manufacturing. But what if the problem is in an office, like the earlier mentioned issue of almost all order takers making too many errors? Again, we would use a trusty fishbone diagram (Figure 8-2), with the head being "order errors." Let's assume that this is the fishbone completed by a group of "experts." These "experts" could have included experienced order takers, their managers, employees who pack the orders per the forms, billing staff, customer service personnel, and the customers.

Figure 8-2. Fishbone diagram of input variables affecting order error rate

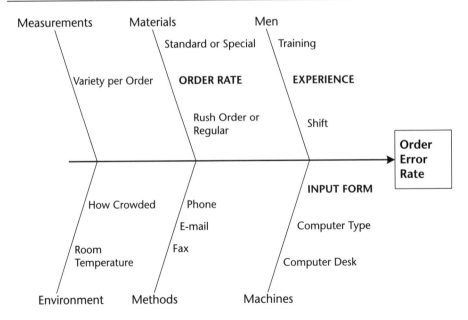

The KPIVs picked by the experts are order rate, experience, and input form. Let's see which of these KPIVs make sense as being the cause of the problem as defined.

The order rate would vary, with some time periods having a low order rate. This isn't consistent with our problem definition that the error rate is too high "consistently," so order rate is not the variable that we will test initially. Experience presumably varies among the order takers, so again that is not consistent with the problem definition that almost all the order takers were making too many errors. Only the input form looks like it would affect most order takers consistently.

So, we want to test if a redesign of the form that the order takers use can minimize these errors. Just as we did in the manufacturing example, we will want to control all of the variables except the one we wish to test and to collect our samples/data only during these controlled periods. Of special concern to control are the highlighted KPIVs, since these are the variables the "experts" identified as most likely to affect order error rate.

So, we will review only orders taken by experienced order takers during periods of time when the input of orders is at a somewhat average rate (i.e., not exceptionally high or low). We will do this on day shift, making sure the room temperature and number of people in the area are pretty much normal. To take out the effect of the different methods, we will evaluate only orders taken by phone. The base sample data to get the normal error rate will be taken one day; the test samples with the new form will be taken the following day.

CENTERING OR VARIATION?

The above examples were a way to get good samples/data when the problem definition indicated that the problem was related to a process not centered, so our emphasis was to improve the total process. As you will see later in the book, centering a process, or moving its average, is generally much easier than reducing its variation. Reducing process variation often involves a complete change in the process, not just a minor adjustment.

If the problem definition indicates that the problem is the variation and that the centering of the process is not the issue, then you would have no choice but to try to identify the individual causes of the variation and try to reduce their effect.

Again, you will save yourself a lot of trouble if you can make the problem definition more specific than just stating that the variation is too high. Does the problem happen on a regular or spaced frequency? Is it related to shift, machine, product, operator, or day? Any specific information will dramatically reduce the number of different mini-populations from which you will have to gather samples/data. This more specific problem definition will then be compared with the related fishbone diagram to try to isolate the conditions that you must sample.

PROCESS WITH TOO MUCH VARIATION

Suppose our earlier shaft diameter error problem had been defined as being periodic, affecting one machine at a time, and not being a process off-center problem. Let's revisit the fishbone diagram with this new problem definition in mind.

Figure 8-3. Fishbone diagram of input variables affecting shaft diameter periodic variation error

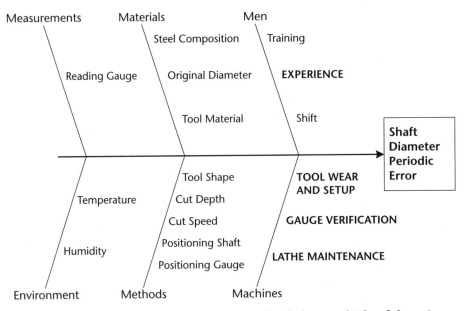

Since the problem was defined as periodic, let's see which of these input variables would likely be associated with a production line time period related to the problem. It appears that each KPIV (experience, tool wear and setup, gauge verification, and lathe maintenance) may have different periods. With this insight, go back and see if it is possible to get even better problem definition that will allow us to focus more sharply on the specific problem.

Assume that you go back to the customer or whoever triggered the issue and find that the problem occurs every several weeks on each line, but not on all lines at the same time. Let's look at our KPIVs with this in mind. Experience would be random, not every several weeks. The cutting tools are replaced every several days, so the time period doesn't match. Simplified gauge verifications are done monthly, so that cycle also doesn't fit. However, maintenance is done on a two-week cycle, one machine at a time. This variable fits the problem definition.

We want to control everything other than maintenance during our sample/data collection. We will change the cutting tool frequently, verifying its setup, to make sure that is not an issue. We will have experienced people working on the process and will be sure that simplified gauge verification was done. All of these input variables had been defined by the experts as being critical, so we want to be sure to have them in control.

We will use an experienced crew on day shift, verifying that the shaft material is correct and the lathe is set up correctly (cutter depth, cutter speed, position of shaft and gauge), and that an experienced person will be doing the measurements. We will minimize the effects of temperature and humidity by taking samples/data at the same time each day. Since we don't know if the problem is caused by not doing maintenance often enough or if the lathe takes some time to debug after maintenance, we probably want to take samples daily for at least two weeks to get a better idea of the actual cause.

As you can see in all the above examples, good problem definition combined with a fishbone diagram will focus us on which samples/data we need. The detail within the fishbone will further help us make sure that the other variables in the process being measured are as stable as possible, with the exception of the variable being evaluated.

Once a change is implemented, samples/data must be collected to verify that the improvement actually happened. The same care must be taken in collecting samples/data validating the improvement as was taken during the problem-solving process. You can use quality department data for validation if the means of collecting data stays consistent before and after the change. If you can't trust the quality department data, you will have to use data samples.

IMPORTANCE OF GETTING GOOD SAMPLES AND DATA

Minimum sample sizes, simplified gauge verification, and statistical tests to validate significant change all play a part. But the sample/data collection must be right to start with, so you have data to analyze that are truly representative of the process you are checking.

While testing, collecting data, and validating the process improvement, you and others must be alert for any event that makes your conclusions suspicious. When in doubt, don't believe the results. Redo the test!

The use of good problem definition and the fishbone diagram to help decide what to sample is valid for many applications.

Sales managers, store salespeople, distribution center employees, and others can assist in doing a fishbone diagram where the head of the fish is "inaccurate sales forecasts." Just as in manufacturing, there are probably many influencing variables. The problem definition and fishbone will help in deciding on the critical variables and in making sure your sampling and data are focused and minimally affected by input variables other than the one you are testing.

Marketing folks can get advertising experts from newspapers, TV, and magazines to assist in doing a fishbone where "ineffective advertising" is the head of the fish. Variables may be advertising style, media type, frequency, market, etc. This information helps determine what and how to sample.

Software developers can get users to help with the fishbone, with the head being "software crashes." Output can be used to identify which areas to focus on to get data on each key cause of software crashes.

Everyone from sales to accounting can contribute to a fishbone with "too many overdue receivables" as the head. Again, this is needed before determining what to sample to get good data on the problem.

Suppose an insurance company feels it has too many policies with only minor differences. A group of salesmen and customers can use a fishbone, with the head being the "excess of policies." Key causes will be identified and data can be collected based on this problem definition.

WHAT WE HAVE LEARNED IN CHAPTER 8

1. Getting valid samples and data is just as important as applying any statistical tool.
2. The people and methods used for taking the samples and data affect the randomness and accuracy of both. Also, the product population is changing as the process changes, sometimes quite radically and often.
3. It is generally not possible to sample all the mini-populations caused by the people and changes caused by the process.
4. Use the fishbone diagram to identify the key process input variables (KPIVs) that cause all these mini-populations. Use the problem definition and close analysis of the fishbone to limit your focus.
5. Generally, the easiest approach to improving a process's output quality is to center the total process or change the process average, rather than reducing the variation. For example, if a diameter of a product is running off center, it is generally easier to get the average back on center than to reduce the process variation.

6. If the variation is very high, you may have no choice but to attempt to reduce it. However, not only is improving the total process average easier, but the sampling process and valid data issues are minimized. In both cases, use a fishbone diagram to help identify the most stable process (day, shift, operator, product, etc.) to test.

7. Take a statistically valid sample before and after a change to be confident that the improvement was significant. The formulas for minimum sample size are covered later in the text.

8. Once the change is implemented, validate the effect on the total process. You can use quality department data for this validation, if the means of collecting data stays consistent before and after the change. If you can't trust the quality department data, you will have to take additional samples from the populations before and after the change to validate that the predicted improvement truly happened.

RELATED READING

Statistical Thinking: Improving Business Performance, Roger W. Hoerl and Ronald D. Snee (Pacific Grove, CA: Duxbury-Thomson Learning, 2002).

CHAPTER 9

Simplified Gauge Verification

What you will learn in this chapter is how to determine gauge error and how to correct this error if excessive. When a problem surfaces, one of the first things that must be done is to get good data/measurements related to the problem. The issue of gauge accuracy/repeatability/reproducibility applies everywhere a variables data measurement (decimals) is taken.

Before we use data, we must be satisfied that the data are accurate. One of the most frequent sources of error is the device used to measure the product or process. This device can be as simple as a ruler or as complex as a radiation sensor.

Data error can give us a false sense of security—we believe that the process is in control, that we are making acceptable product—or cause us to make erroneous changes to the process. These errors can be compounded by the difference between the gauges used by the supplier and those used by the customer or by variation among gauges within a manufacturing plant.

In Six Sigma projects, the use of this simplified gauge verification tool often gives an insight that allows for big gains with no additional efforts. In the DMAIC process, this tool can be used in the Define, Measure, Analyze, Improve, and Control steps.

MAXIMUM GAUGE ERROR

Ideally, a gauge should not "use up" more than 10% of the allowable tolerance. 30% is generally used as a maximum gauge error. If a gauge has a 30% error, then the supplier must keep the product measurements within 70% of the tolerance to ensure that the product is within specification.

Some plants discover that as many as half of their gauges will not meet the 30% criterion. Even after extensive rework, many gauges cannot pass the simplified gauge verification because the tolerance is too tight for the gauge design.

CASE STUDY: GAUGE ERROR ON MEASURING MOLDS

A complex mold was being sourced from an outside supplier, which had been supplying them for many years. There had been ongoing complaints about the dimensions of the products made from these molds; in response, the mold tolerances had been gradually tightened over the years.

The issue finally became severe enough that a project was undertaken to understand and rectify the problem. The supplier was insistent that his gauge showed that the molds were well within specifications and even sent the purchasing plant the measurement data. The purchasing plant had only a crude gauge that gave contradictory readings on the complex mold shape. The molds were finally sent out to a firm specializing in three-dimensional measurements to resolve the issue.

This firm specializing in 3-D measurements was able to demonstrate that most of the molds were out of specification, some dramatically. The gauge being used by the mold supplier was not capable of measuring the complex shape at the degree of accuracy required; tightening the tolerances had just made the gauge error worse without improving the molds.

Since most plants do not want to run with reduced in-house tolerances, a problem gauge must be upgraded to "use up" less of the tolerance.

The above case study is discussed further in the chapter on tolerances.

Checking for Gauge Error

There are many methods of checking for gauge error. The method discussed in this text is simple and emphasizes improving the gauge (when required) rather than retraining inspectors. The reason this approach is taken is that inspectors change frequently and it is nearly impossible to get someone to routinely follow a very critical procedure to get a gauge reading accurately. It is far better to have a robust gauge that is easy to use and not likely to be used incorrectly.

Gauge verification must include both *repeatability/reproducibility* and *accuracy*. In simple terms, it must check for variations in readings and for the correctness of the average reading.

Repeatability/Reproducibility

These are measurement concepts involving variations in readings. Repeatability is the consistency of measurements obtained when one person measures the same parts or items multiple times using the same instrument and techniques. Reproducibility is the consistency of average measurements obtained when two or more people measure the same parts or items using the same measuring technique.

Accuracy

Accuracy is a measurement concept involving the correctness of the average reading. It is the extent to which the average of the measurements taken agrees with a true value.

SIMPLIFIED GAUGE VERIFICATION INSTRUCTIONS

The first step in doing simplified gauge verification is to get several "master" products near the product specification center. The supplier and customer must agree on the dimensions of these masters.

Masters can be quantified either by using outside firms that have calibrated specialized measuring devices or by getting mutual agreement between the supplier and customer (Figure 9-1).

The reason the gauge error includes the ± accuracy is that the tolerance, which is the reference, also includes the ± variation from process center.

Using one of the randomly picked "masters," have three inspectors (or operators) measure the master seven times each. Have them take the readings as if they were taking them in normal production (amount of time, method, etc.). (The quality department should have already done its standard gauge setup independently of this verification.) Calculate the average $\bar{x}$ and standard deviation s of *all* 21 readings. If the standard deviation s in the formula below is calculated on a manual calculator, use the "n–1" option if available.

Just for reference, the reason the s is multiplied by 5 in the formula is that ±2.5 sigma represents 99% of the items on a normal distribution. If the effect of accuracy $(2*|\text{master} - \bar{x}|)$ is the predominant error (compared with the total gauge error), you should examine the setup procedure for the gauge. Accuracy error is normally easier to reduce than repeatability/reproducibility error.

Figure 9-1. Visual representation of simplified gauge verification

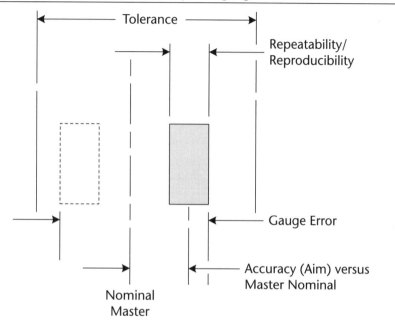

Simplified Gauge Verification, Variables Data

$$\% \text{ gauge error} = \frac{5s + 2 * |\text{master} - \bar{x}|}{\text{tolerance}} * 100 \quad (\text{ideally} < 10\%, \text{ maximum } 30\%)$$

$\bar{x}$ = average of *all* 21 readings of a master product
s = standard deviation of *all* 21 readings of the master product
master = standardized dimension of the master product
tolerance = allowable product tolerance (max − min)
$|\text{master} - \bar{x}|$ = difference between master and average $\bar{x}$, ignoring minus signs.

FORMULA

We chose to use a "master" that was close to the center of the specification, which is sufficient in most cases. However, for some types of gauges, you need to verify readings at both the center and an end of the specification. Some optical gauges need this verification because mechanical movement of the optics can cause them to read correctly at the center but not at the end; in this case, "masters" should be available at a specification end. In most cases, however, "masters" at the center are sufficient.

Gauge verification must be set up as a regular routine. The simplified gauge verification is in addition to (and independent of) any quality department gauge setup procedure, which is done separately by trained people taking whatever time is required.

TIP

Document Simplified Gauge Verification
Keep documentation of every gauge verification. Make verification and documentation a regular routine.

Example of Simplified Gauge Verification

We want to do the simplified gauge verification procedure on the gauge we are using to measure the diameter on machined shafts. We have established a "master" shaft, which is near nominal. We now have three inspectors (or operators) measure this shaft seven times each. Here are the results.

Master Shaft Standardized Reading = 1.0004
Allowable Shaft Dimensions: max = 1.0050,
min = 0.9960, so tolerance = 0.0090
(all dimensions in inches)

Inspector A	Reading #	Dimension
	1	1.0018
	2	1.0001
	3	0.9998
	4	1.0011
	5	0.9996
	6	1.0001
	7	1.0001
Inspector B	1	0.9992
	2	1.0011
	3	1.0002
	4	0.9991
	5	1.0004
	6	0.9988
	7	1.001
Inspector C	1	0.9997
	2	0.9988
	3	1.0008
	4	1.0015
	5	0.9998
	6	1.0006
	7	0.9996
Average $\bar{x}$ =		1.000152
Standard Deviation s =		0.000851
5s =		0.004253

$$\% \text{ gauge error} = \frac{5s + 2 * |master - \bar{x}|}{tolerance} * 100$$

$$\% \text{ gauge error} = \frac{0.0043 + 2 * |1.0004 - 1.0002|}{0.0090} * 100 = 52\%$$

Since the calculated gauge error of 52% exceeds the allowable 30%, we must go back and find ways to improve the gauge. Assume we do this. Here are the new results.

Gauge Readings after Rework		
Master Shaft Standardized Reading = 1.0004 Allowable Shaft Dimensions: max = 1.0050, min = 0.9960, so tolerance = 0.0090 (all dimensions in inches)		
Inspector A	Reading #	Dimension
	1	1.0008
	2	1.0006
	3	1.0001
	4	1.0011
	5	1.0004
	6	0.9998
	7	1.0007
Inspector B	1	0.9996
	2	0.9999
	3	1.001
	4	1.0005
	5	1.0001
	6	1.0003
	7	1.0002
Inspector C	1	1.0007
	2	1.0006
	3	0.9996
	4	0.9999
	5	1.0004
	6	1.0006
	7	1.0003
Average $\bar{x}$ =		1.000343
Standard Deviation s =		0.000426
5s =		0.002131

$$\% \text{ gauge error} = \frac{5s + 2 * |master - \bar{x}|}{tolerance} * 100$$

$$\% \text{ gauge error } = \frac{0.0021 + 0.0001}{0.0090} * 100 = 24.4\%$$

Although the calculated gauge error of 24.4% is not great, it is acceptable. Note that by just looking at the readings (before or after rework), it is not obvious whether the gauge is doing an acceptable job, even reading a master with a known diameter. That is why simplified gauge verification often has great payback, because it is a hidden problem (opportunity).

CASE STUDY: GAUGE DIFFERENCES BETWEEN CUSTOMER AND SUPPLIER

A customer was complaining about excursions on a product thickness. To address those concerns, the supplier monitored the next production run very closely, taking many measurements throughout the run. All the measurements showed that the product was well within specifications. The supplier called the customer and told him that he would be pleased with this production run. The supplier even sent the customer the measurements taken during the run.

Once the customer received the product, however, he found a large number of products to be clearly out of specification. The customer sent examples of the bad product back to the supplier so he could see for himself. Again, the supplier measured this returned product as being within specification.

At that point, both the supplier and the customer did simplified gauge verifications, using masters they agreed upon. The customer's gauge passed, whereas the supplier's gauge did not! The supplier found that his gauge, which was made to measure several similar products, did not readily allow this particular product to seat properly. A new gauge was built for this specific product and the problem of product out-of-specification was resolved.

It should be noted that when the supplier ran the simplified gauge verification, one of the inspectors *was* able to get the master to read properly. That inspector was aware of the difficulty of seating the product and was able to compensate. However, the supplier very wisely chose to make a new gauge rather than train all the inspectors to seat the product with such precision. Even though it may have been possible to get all the current inspectors to do that, absenteeism and personnel changes made that approach risky as a long-term solution.

GAUGE R&R

Most Six Sigma classes teach a process called gauge R&R, but the method taught addresses only repeatability and reproducibility, not accuracy (aim). Gauge R&R uses production products, rather than masters. To get valid results, the current production products must include the full range of process dimensions, which are not always readily available. If the test samples do not include the full range of process dimensions, the gauge R&R will often not pass.

The gauge R&R output is given as an ANOVA (analysis of variance), a rather sophisticated mathematical method that allows for the separation of gauge error into operator, gauge, and part contribution. The idea in gauge R&R is that, if the operator is the key contributor to the gauge error, then retraining or taking the person off the job will correct the problem. If the part is the biggest contributor to the error, it means that something about the physical part, such as distortion, is causing the issue; no direction is given for resolving this issue. If the gauge is the biggest contributor, than the gauge has to be replaced or repaired.

In gauge R&R, accuracy is tested separately, with no effort to check the combined error of repeatability and/or reproducibility and accuracy. In fact, gauge R&R doesn't directly address accuracy (aim) at all. It is up to the user of the gauge R&R method to find a way to estimate the total effect of any repeatability/reproducibility error and accuracy error.

The approach taken in this text combines repeatability/reproducibility and accuracy into one test and emphasizes total gauge error. This is based on much experience (frustration) with the difficulty of getting a changing group of inspectors to follow precise instructions for taking measurements. The gauge must be designed for ease of use, so operator error is minor and included as part of the total gauge error. Also, the part contribution of gauge error can't be addressed separately in any case, so why separate it?

Anyone choosing not to use this simplified gauge verification should consider the traditional gauge R&R, since both will give benefits. If gauge R&R is used, accuracy will have to be checked separately. Obviously, I believe that simplified gauge verification is a better choice.

WHAT WE HAVE LEARNED IN CHAPTER 9

1. In the DMAIC process, simplified gauge verification can be used in the Define, Measure, Analyze, Improve, and Control steps.
2. Ideally a gauge should not "use up" more than 10% of the allowable tolerance. The maximum is generally 30%.
3. The first step in simplified gauge verification is to get one or more "master" products near the specification center. The supplier and customer must agree on the dimensions of these masters. In some types of gauges (optical), you need to verify readings at both the center and an end of the specification. But, most gauges need "masters" only at the center of the tolerance.
4. Some production plants discover that as many as half of their gauges will not meet the criterion of maximum 30% of tolerance.
5. Emphasize improving the gauge (when required) rather than retraining inspectors. Inspectors come and go, so having them do a complex or detailed process is not a good long-term solution.
6. The simplified gauge verification formula includes both repeatability/ reproducibility (ability to duplicate a reading) and accuracy (aim or correctness of average reading).
7. Simplified gauge verification must be set up as a regular routine and documentation must be kept.
8. Gauge R&R, another approach to verifying that a gauge is not using excessive amounts of the tolerance, is an alternate method. However, it checks for repeatability/reproducibility only. It does not include error due to inaccuracy and the user must estimate the combined effect of repeatability/ reproducibility and accuracy error.

RELATED READING AND SOFTWARE

Rath & Strong's Six Sigma Pocket Guide, Rath & Strong Management Consultants (Lexington, MA: Rath & Strong/Aon Consulting Worldwide, 2000).

Basic Statistics: Tools for Continuous Improvement, Mark J. Kiemele, Stephen R. Schmidt, and Ronald J. Berdine, 4th edition (Colorado Springs, CO: Air Academy Press, 1997).

MINITAB 13, Minitab Inc., State College, PA, www.minitab.com.

CHAPTER 10

Probability

What you will learn in this chapter of the book is to let data drive problem solving. However, to interpret data, you need to make a judgment as to whether unusual results were due to random cause, like someone who flips a coin and gets an excessive number of heads by chance, or due to an assignable cause, like the coin having two heads. A knowledge of probability helps you make this determination with a minimum number of samples.

Much Six Sigma work can't be done without some understanding of probability statistics. Probability can be used in all the steps of DMAIC. You will be able to use these techniques to solve many problems in the workplace without using additional tools.

Probability

Manufacturing On any production line with multiple heads, compare defect levels from each head to see if they are significantly different. Compare two or more similar production lines, shifts, defects on different days of the week, etc. Often you will see significant differences that can be addressed at little cost.

Sales Compare salespeople. The criteria could include new customers, lost sales, etc. Cross training between the best and worst performers can often improve both! Also, through these careful comparisons, compensation can be made more equitable.

APPLICATIONS

Marketing Check if sales increased significantly in multiple markets after a marketing campaign.

Accounting and Software Development Compare error incidence to check for significant difference between groups.

Receivables Check the effect of increased or decreased monitoring of overdue receivables.

Insurance Compare the complaints at similar-sized treatment centers. The criteria could include patient care, billing errors, etc.

CASE STUDY: APPLICATION OF SIMPLE PROBABILITY

A production plant was in trouble. They were getting multiple defects in their product going out from every production line. They felt it was caused by a problem with the incoming raw material. They had given up on making good product and gave a panicked call for help to their home-office engineering group. A task force was assembled and began attacking the problems.

One of the first things an engineer did was collect defects from one line. He quickly concluded that one of the defects was coming from one set of tooling. (There were 20 tooling sets per line.) He had the tooling set taken out of production and found it had been assembled wrong. On looking at maintenance records on the machine, he found that the tooling set had been on the machine for two weeks. Since there were 20 tooling sets on the line, 5% of the product coming from the machine for two weeks was defective, since every product coming from this set of tooling was bad.

The engineer knew that raw materials would not cause this 100% defect on only one set of tooling without also affecting products off the other tooling sets. This is what triggered him to have the tooling set removed and inspected. Using this kind of systematic analysis of defect data and reacting accordingly, the plant was back to normal productivity within three days. There had been no problem with the raw materials.

Certainly this reasoning took only a rudimentary knowledge of probability, but no one in the plant, including the plant engineers, was analyzing the problem in this way. They just assumed, since they were having multiple problems throughout the plant, that the issue must be raw materials.

At the end of the third day, the task force received a call from their general manager who wanted an update on how the team was doing. When the team leader told the GM that the plant was now back to targeted production using the very basic analysis described, the GM did not initially believe it! It just seemed too simple. The task force went home.

By the beginning of the following week, the plant yields had again slipped dramatically. This time only one of the task force engineers returned and, with the same methods, was again able to get the plant back to targeted production within three days.

The net effect of all this was that the plant manager at the plant was taken out of his job and the plant began to pay more attention to the required detail of running production.

The above case study is typical in that the initial conclusion that the problem was caused by the raw materials was made without carefully analyzing data. In contrast, the engineer used specific data and an elementary knowledge of probability to reach his conclusions, since he knew that defects caused by raw materials would have been random and not specific to one of the sets of tools on a line. Although the other production lines did not have the identical problems, the same kind of careful analysis based on detailed data resolved the production problems.

USES OF PROBABILITY

This chapter on probability will help you problem-solve when the data aren't quite as obvious. The probability analysis included is not only the basis for many of the Six Sigma tools, but knowledge of probability can also be used independently on many problems.

We are frequently making estimates on the likelihood of an event, its probability—for example, the chance of rain, of winning the lottery, or of being in a plane crash. Some probabilities are easy to calculate and intuitive, like the chance of getting a head on a coin flip (one in two, or 0.5). Some probabilities are not easy to calculate nor intuitive, like the probability of an earthquake.

In Six Sigma we also need to estimate the probability of an event. In this way we can make some judgment as to whether something just happened due to random coincidence or if there is an assignable cause that we should address. Luckily the work you will be doing does *not* involve earthquakes!

We will start with problems where we know the mathematical probability of a single random event, verifying any answer with both the abbreviated binomial table (Figure 10-1) and Excel's BINOMDIST (binomial distribution) statistics option. Excel's BINOMDIST is the primary tool you will use to solve these problems, but if you use the Abbreviated Binomial Table first, you will get a more fundamental understanding of probability. This understanding will minimize the likelihood of an error when using any statistics software package.

Probability (BINOMDIST)

n = the number of independent trials, like the number of coin tosses, the number of parts measured, etc.

Probability p (or probability s) = the probability of a "success" on *each individual trial*, like the likelihood of a head on one coin flip or a defect on one part. This is always a proportion and generally shown as a decimal, like 0.0156.

Number s (or x successes) = the total number of "successes" that you are looking for, like getting exactly three heads.

Probability P = the probability of getting a given number of successes from *all the trials*, like the probability of three heads in five coin tosses or 14 defects in a shipment of parts. This is often the answer to the problem.

Cumulative = the sum of the probabilities of getting "the number of successes or fewer," like getting three *or fewer* heads on five flips of a coin. This option is used on "less-than" and "more-than" problems.

These definitions and their uses will become apparent as you solve the following problems.

Problem #1
What are the chances of getting three heads in three flips of a coin?

Using the above definitions, recognize that n (number of flips) = three. The probability of getting one head on any one flip is p = 0.5. The number of "successes" is three (three heads). P is the probability of getting exactly three heads on three coin flips, which is the desired answer to the problem.

We can make a table of all possible equally likely outcomes of the three coin flips:

Outcome	Flip #1	Flip #2	Flip #3
1.	head	head	head
2.	head	head	tail
3.	head	tail	head
4.	head	tail	tail
5.	tail	head	head
6.	tail	head	tail
7.	tail	tail	head
8.	tail	tail	tail

As you can see, only one of the eight equally likely outcomes of three coin flips is three heads. So, P = 1/8, or 0.125.

Logically (or mathematically) you can get the same answer. The chance of getting heads on the first flip is 50%, or p = 0.5. On each successive flip, the chances of a head are also 0.5. So, the chance of getting two heads on two coin flips is 0.5 x 0.5 = 0.25. Similarly, since each trial is independent (not affected by earlier tosses), we can multiply the probabilities on three flips: 0.5 x 0.5 x 0.5 = 0.125.

Verify this answer by using the following abbreviated binomial table (Figure 10-1). Note that more complete tables are available in most statistics books.

Figure 10-1. Abbreviated binomial table. Values within the table are the probability of getting exactly x successes on n trials.

n # of trials	x successes on n trials	p (each trial) =	0.125 (1/8)	0.167 (1/6)	0.250 (1/4)	0.500 (1/2)
2	0		0.7656	0.6944	0.5625	0.2500
2	1		0.2188	0.2778	0.3750	0.5000
2	2		0.0156	0.0278	0.0625	0.2500
		Sum of P:	1.0000	1.0000	1.0000	1.0000
3	0		0.6699	0.5787	0.4219	0.1250
3	1		0.2871	0.3472	0.4219	0.3750
3	2		0.0410	0.0694	0.1406	0.3750
3	3		0.0020	0.0046	0.0156	0.1250
		Sum of P:	1.0000	1.0000	1.0000	1.0000
4	0		0.5862	0.4823	0.3164	0.0625
4	1		0.3350	0.3858	0.4219	0.2500
4	2		0.0718	0.1157	0.2109	0.3750
4	3		0.0068	0.0154	0.0469	0.2500
4	4		0.0002	0.0008	0.0039	0.0625
		Sum of P:	1.0000	1.0000	1.0000	1.0000
5	0		0.5129	0.4019	0.2373	0.0313
5	1		0.3664	0.4019	0.3955	0.1563
5	2		0.1047	0.1608	0.2637	0.3125
5	3		0.0150	0.0322	0.0879	0.3125
5	4		0.0011	0.0032	0.0146	0.1563
5	5		0.0000	0.0001	0.0010	0.0313
		Sum of P:	1.0000	1.0000	1.0000	1.0000
10	0		0.2631	0.1615	0.0563	0.0010
10	1		0.3758	0.3230	0.1877	0.0098
10	2		0.2416	0.2907	0.2816	0.0439
10	3		0.0920	0.1550	0.2503	0.1172
10	4		0.0230	0.0543	0.1460	0.2051
10	5		0.0039	0.0130	0.0584	0.2461
10	6		0.0005	0.0022	0.0162	0.2051
10	7		0.0000	0.0002	0.0031	0.1172
10	8		0.0000	0.0000	0.0004	0.0439
10	9		0.0000	0.0000	0.0000	0.0098
10	10		0.0000	0.0000	0.0000	0.0010
		Sum of P:	1.0000	1.0000	1.0000	1.0000

Here's how to use the Abbreviated Binomial Table (Figure 10-1) on problem #1.

Find n = 3 in the leftmost column, which is the number of trials.

Find the # of successes (3 heads).

In the far column p = 0.500 (chance of a head on each flip), the value 0.1250 is P.

Now do it in Excel. After bringing up the Excel worksheet, click on [icon] in the toolbar. Under "category," click on "statistical." Then, under "function," click on "BINOMDIST."

In the first box, enter the "number of successes" (number of heads) you want in these trials, which is "3." The second box asks for the "number of trials," which is "3." The third box asks for the probability of a "success" (head) on each trial, which is "0.5."

The fourth box asks if the problem requires the cumulative probability. If you answer "true," you get the sum of the probabilities up to three (the probability of zero heads + the probability of one head + the probability of two heads + the probability of three heads), which is the probability of getting three or fewer heads. In this problem you do *not* want the cumulative probability, so answer "false." You then get our desired probability of exactly three heads, which is P = 0.125.

So, here is a summary of what we just did:

Excel BINOMDIST

successes = 3

trials = 3

probability = 0.5

cumulative: false

The result is P = 0.125.

Problem #2

What is the probability of getting two or fewer heads in three flips of a coin?

We will show five ways to get the answer to this problem.

You could look at the possible outcomes table (page 76) and add up the number of outcomes with zero heads (one outcome), one head (three outcomes), and two heads (three outcomes), for a total of seven outcomes (out of eight possible outcomes). This is a probability of 7/8, or 0.875.

The same answer can be found using the Abbreviated Binomial Table (Figure 10-1) by adding the probabilities of zero successes (0.125), one success (0.375), and two successes (0.375), for a total = 0.875.

Equally, using the BINOMDIST in Excel, you do it three times, adding the results of zero, one, and two successes (with cumulative: false), and you get 0.125 + 0.375 + 0.375 = 0.875.

Or you can recognize that the only outcome that has more than two heads is three heads, which has a probability of 0.125 (from problem #1). Since the sum of the probabilities of all possible outcomes always equals 1 (see the abbreviated binomial table, Figure 10-1), we can subtract the probability of three heads (.125) from 1 to get the answer = 0.875!

The following is the most direct way to the answer. Using Excel BINOMDIST, we can realize that the "cumulative true" gives the probability of getting two or fewer heads, which is what we want. So, here's how we can get the answer directly:

Excel BINOMDIST

successes = 2

trials = 3

probability = 0.5

cumulative: true

The result is P = 0.875.

Use the Sum of Probabilities = 1

Since the sum of the probabilities of all possible outcomes always equals 1, we can often use this knowledge to simplify a problem.

For example, if we want to know the probability of getting one or more heads on 10 coin tosses, we can find the probability of getting zero heads, then subtract this probability from 1. This is much easier than adding the probabilities of 1 head + 2 heads + 3 heads + 4 heads + 5 heads + 6 heads + 7 heads + 8 heads + 9 heads + 10 heads.

Using Excel's BINOMDIST Cumulative Function

Do not use the cumulative function for the probability of a single outcome/success, like three heads out of five coin tosses. Enter "false" in the box for cumulative function.

Use the cumulative function for "less-than," "equal-to-or-less-than," "equal-to-or-greater-than," or "greater-than" a given outcome or success, as follows.

For "less-than" a given outcome, like fewer than three heads out of eight coin tosses, use the cumulative function "true" with the success at one less than the given value (3 - 1 = 2).

success = 2

trials = 8

p = 0.5
cumulative: true
The result is P = 0.1445.

For "equal-to-or-less-than" a given outcome, like three heads or fewer out of eight coin tosses, use the cumulative function "true" with the success at the given value (3).

success = 3
trials = 8
p = 0.5
cumulative: true
The result is P = 0.3633.

For "greater-than" a given outcome, like more than three heads out of eight coin tosses, use the cumulative function "true" with the success at the given value (3), then subtract the result from 1.

success = 3
trials = 8
p = 0.5
cumulative: true
The result is 0.3633. P would then equal 1.0000 – 0.3633 = 0.6367.

For "equal-to-or-greater-than" a given outcome, like three or more heads out of eight coin tosses, use the cumulative function "true" with the success at one less than the given outcome (3 – 1 = 2), then subtract the result from 1.

success = 2
trials = 8
p = 0.5
cumulative: true
The result is 0.1445. P would then equal 1.0000 – 0.1445 = 0.8555.

You can satisfy yourself that the above cumulative function examples on eight coin tosses make sense by seeing that the probability of "less than three heads" plus the probability of "three or more heads" equals 1. The same is true for "three heads or fewer" plus "more than three heads."

Problem #3
What is the chance of getting eight or fewer tails on 10 flips of a coin?

Using the Abbreviated Binomial Table (Figure 10-1), we can add the probabilities of getting zero, one, two, three, four, five, six, seven, and eight tails. However, it is easier to add the probabilities of nine or 10 tails, then subtract from 1. The probability of nine tails is 0.0098 and the probability of 10 tails is 0.0010. Adding these and then subtracting the sum from 1 gives 1.0000 – 0.0108 = 0.9892. So, the P of getting eight or fewer tails on 10 coin flips is 0.9892, or 98.92%.

Or, here's the most direct way:

Excel BINOMDIST

successes = 8

trials = 10

probability = 0.5

cumulative: true

The result is P = 0.9893 (the slight difference from above is due to rounding error).

CASE STUDY: EXCESSIVE ACCIDENT RATE

A sales force had an accident rate that was excessive and the sales manager was under a lot of pressure to reduce it. One of the salespeople thought that the accidents were higher near the end of the year, so he looked at 100 random accidents from each of several years, calculating the average accident rate for each month. He found that December had the highest average of any month, at 15 accidents. The other months all had lower rates, more or less similar.

The sales manager determined that the chance of getting 15 or more accidents in December due to random causes alone was very unlikely. On analyzing further, he also noted that January was not high, so he doubted that weather was the cause.

The next year the sales manager dictated giving gifts to the customers during the holiday season, rather than partying with them, and the accident rate went down to the same as for the other months.

Let's verify the sales manager's finding that December's 15 accidents out of 100 for a year was "very unlikely." First, some interpretation as to *what* was "very unlikely." He wasn't surprised that the December accident average was *exactly* 15; he was surprised that it was that high. 16 or 17 would also have surprised him! So, that is why he checked against the likelihood of 15 *or more* accidents happening in December due to random cause. This approach is more conservative and made him less likely to erroneously find that something happened due to other than random cause. The likelihood of getting an *exact* number is generally small and will bias results to show that the result was not random.

Excel BINOMDIST
successes = 14
trials = 100
probability = 0.08333 (1/12, which is what would be expected for a random month)
cumulative: true
The result is 0.9814. P would then equal 1.0000 – 0.9814 = 0.0186 or 1.86%.

So the sales manager was correct in saying that 15 or more accidents in December was very unlikely, since it would be expected to happen randomly only 1.86% of the time. He would therefore be 98.14% (100% – 1.86%) confident that the December accident rate was not random.

Note that it was not sufficient just to find that the December accident rate was higher than the 100/12 = 8.33 he would have expected for a random month. It had to be determined with some confidence that the December results were high enough that they were probably not random.

The sales manager did not try to determine the "root cause" of December's higher accident rate. It could have been because of excessive drinking, more miles driving visiting customers, driving more at night, etc. He only saw the correlation between the month and the accident rate. His chance of success on implementing a solution would have been higher if he could have identified the root cause.

Independent Trials Are Not Affected by Earlier Results

The probability on an independent trial is *not* affected by results on earlier trials. For example, someone could flip 10 heads in a row, but the probability of a head on the next coin flip is still p = 0.5—assuming that both the coin and the person tossing it are honest, etc.

TIP

Problem #4
What are the chances of getting at least eight tails on 10 coin flips?

We could use either the abbreviated binomial table (Figure 10-1) or Excel BINOMDIST to find the P of eight, nine, and 10 tails. We would then add these to get the total probability P = 0.0439 + 0.0098 + 0.0010 = 0.0547.

Or, using the Excel BINOMDIST and realizing that the chance of at least eight tails (or eight or more tails) is the same as 1 minus the chance of seven or fewer tails, we solve as follows:
Excel BINOMDIST

successes = 7
trials = 10
p = 0.5
cumulative: true
The result is 0.9453. P would then equal 1.0000 - 0.9453 = 0.0547, or 5.47%.

Problem #5

A vendor is making 25% defective product. In a box of 10 random parts from this vendor, what is the probability of finding two or fewer defects?

If we use the abbreviated binomial table (Figure 10-1), with n = 10, successes = 2, 1, and 0, and p = 0.25, we get 0.282, 0.188, 0.056. We add these for P = 0.526, or 52.6%.

Or, using Excel BINOMDIST:
success = 2
trials = 10
p = 0.25
cumulative: true
The result is P = 0.526, or 52.6%.

Problem #6

A salesperson has been losing 25% of potential sales. In a study of 10 random sales contacts from this salesperson, what is the probability of finding three or more successful sales?

We must be careful that what we call a "success" (*successful* sales in this case) is consistent with the rest of the problem statement (which is currently stated as % *lost* sales). We can restate the question as "getting 75% of potential sales" so the success is measured in the same terms as rest of the problem statement. Then we have the following problem:

A salesperson has been successful in getting 75% of potential sales. In a study of 10 random sales contacts from this salesperson, what is the probability of finding three or more successful sales?

Again, to save work, we know that "three or more successful sales" is the same as 1 minus the probability of "two or fewer successful sales."
Excel BINOMDIST
success = 2
trials = 10
p = 0.75
cumulative: true

The result is 0.0004. P would then equal 1.0000 - 0.0004 = 0.9996, or 99.96%.

Or, we can restate the problem in terms of "lost sales":

A salesperson has been losing 25% of potential sales. In a study of 10 random sales contacts from this salesperson, what is the probability of finding seven or less lost sales?

Note that in the above problem restatement we had to recognize that three or more successful sales is the same as seven or less lost sales. If this is not obvious, consider that when you have three successes out of 10 potential sales, seven are lost; with four successes, six losses; with five successes, five losses; with six successes, four losses; and so on.

Excel BINOMDIST

success = 7

trials = 10

p = 0.25

cumulative: true

The result is P = 0.9996, or 99.96%, which is consistent with the answer above.

The above problem shows that if you think your problem through carefully and are careful that the definition you've chosen for "success" is consistent with the other values used in the solution, you will get a correct and consistent answer.

CASE STUDY: DEFECTS PRIMARILY IN ONE QUADRANT

A high-speed production line was making a small number of critical defects. A quality engineer randomly collected 100 defects. He examined them and found that 22 defects were from the first quadrant of the product, 36 from the second, 21 from the third, and 21 from the fourth. He concluded that there was less than a 1% chance that 36 or more defects out of 100 would be coming from the second quadrant due to random causes alone.

So he went looking for anything suspicious on the production line that was exclusive to the second quadrant. He found a cooling nozzle from which some of the spray hit the second quadrant of the product. Since the product was very hot at that point in the process, he suspected that stress was being introduced.

When he asked the operator why he had put the spray at that location, he was told that it was being used to cool the tooling that was adjacent to the product at this point. The engineer then designed a more directed spray method that missed the product but hit the tooling, which allowed adequate cooling and also solved the problem of excess defects in that quadrant.

Let's see if we agree with the engineer's conclusion that the higher number of defects in the second quadrant was probably not due to random causes alone. ("Random" would mean that there was nothing peculiar about this quadrant: he just happened to get a sample with more defects in this location.) Note that he checked the chances of 36 *or more* defects happening randomly, since there was nothing special about being *exactly* 36. So, we want to calculate the chances of 36 or more defects occurring in the second quadrant from random causes only.

Excel BINOMDIST

successes = 35

trials = 100

p = 0.25 (1/4, the probability of the defect randomly occurring in the second quadrant)

cumulative: true

The result is 0.9906. P would then equal 1.0000 – 0.9906 = 0.0094, or 0.94%.

So, there is only a 0.94% chance of getting 36 or more of the 100 defects in the second quadrant due to random results. So the engineer was right to be suspicious—and his conclusion enabled him to focus his attention on areas affecting only that quadrant, which minimized the areas in the process that he had to examine to identify the problem source.

Excel BINOMDIST Trials Max at 1000

Excel BINOMDIST allows a maximum of 1000 trials. So, if you have more than 1000 trials, proportion the trials and number of successes to 1000.

For example, if the data has 2000 trials and you are looking for 140 successes, use Excel BINOMDIST with 1000 trials and 70 successes. The p is not affected.

Problem #7

These are the results of 109 random erroneous orders processed by seven telephone operators, A through G:

Operator	Erroneous Orders
A	14
B	16
C	22
D	13
E	16
F	15
G	13

Is Operator C's performance worse than we should expect, since C's 22 error total is higher than that of any of the other six operators? We would want to be at least 95% confident that the performance was poor before we took any action. We want to check against the likelihood of getting 22 *or more* errors, rather than exactly 22. This will be more conservative and it's not important that there are *exactly* 22 order errors.

Excel BINOMDIST

successes = 21

trials =109

p = 1/7 = 0.14286 (random chance since there are seven operators)

cumulative: true

The result is 0.9429. P would then equal 1.0000 – 0.9429 = 0.0571, or 5.7%.

This means that there is a 5.7 % chance of this happening randomly without an assignable cause. The confidence level of the conclusion that this is not random would therefore be 100% – 5.7% = 94.3%, which is below the 95% test threshold.

Therefore, we can't conclude with a 95% confidence that Operator C is performing worse than any of the other operators.

Additional Practice Problems

Problem #8

What is the likelihood of getting four heads in seven flips of a coin?

Problem #9

What is the likelihood of getting at least four heads in seven flips of a coin?

Problem #10
What is the probability of getting three fives on six rolls of a die?

Problem #11
What is the probability of getting three or more fives rolling six dice one time?

Problem #12
An automaker entered the marketplace with a car to compete with two other brands already in that market. In the first month after introduction, the new entry got 355 sales of a random sample of 1000 sales from the total market. Can the automaker with the new entry say with a 95% confidence that he got more than the projected 1/3 of the sales due to other than random causes?

Problem #13
An automatic transmission repair shop had an established standard to do a certain type of repair. They hired a new mechanic. After six months, they sampled 12 of the new mechanic's repair times versus the standard repair. The new mechanic took more than the standard time on eight of the 12 samples. How confident would the repair shop be in judging that the higher times were due to performance rather than to random causes?

Solutions to Additional Practice Problems

Problem #8
What is the likelihood of getting four heads in seven flips of a coin?

> Excel BINOMDIST
> successes = 4
> trials = 7
> p = 0.5
> cumulative: false
> The result is P = 0.2734, or 27.34%.

Problem #9
What is the likelihood of getting at least four heads in seven flips of a coin?

> Excel BINOMDIST
> successes = 3
> trials = 7
> p = 0.5

cumulative: true

The result is 0.500. P would then equal 1.000 – 0.500 = 0.500, or 50.0%.

Problem #10

What is the probability of getting three fives on six rolls of a die?

Excel BINOMDIST

successes = 3

trials = 6

p = 1/6 = 0.1667

cumulative: false

The result is P = 0.0536, or 5.36%.

Problem #11

What is the probability of getting three or more fives rolling six dice one time?

Excel BINOMDIST

successes = 2

trials = 6

p = 1/6 = 0.1667

cumulative: true

The result is 0.9377. P would then equal 1.0000 – 0.9377 = 0.0623, or 6.23%.

(Note that rolling six dice at one time is the same as rolling one die six times. This is because in both cases the result on each die is independent of the results on the others.)

Problem #12

An automaker entered the marketplace with a car to compete with two other brands already in that market. In the first month after introduction, the new entry got 355 sales of a random sample of 1000 sales from the total market. Can the automaker with the new entry say with a 95% confidence that he got more than the projected 1/3 of the sales due to other than random causes?

We want to check against the likelihood of 355 *or more* sales, since getting *exactly* 355 is not what is important!

Excel BINOMDIST

successes = 354

trials =1000

p = 1/3 = 0.3333

cumulative: true

The result is 0.9220. P would then equal 1.0000 – 0.9220 = 0.0780, or 7.8%.

The automaker's confidence would therefore be 100.00% – 7.8% = 92.20%, which is below the 95% confidence target level the automaker wanted. Therefore, the automaker *can't* claim that the new entry gained more than 1/3 of the market due to other than random cause.

Note that if this problem had been done using *exactly* 355 as the test criterion, it would have shown that the automaker *did* get more than 1/3 of the market with a 99% confidence. This type of error occurs because it is unlikely to get *any* specific result randomly with this number of trials.

Problem #13

An automatic transmission repair shop had an established standard to do a certain type of repair. They hired a new mechanic. After six months, they sampled 12 of the new mechanic's repair times versus the standard repair. The new mechanic took more than the standard time on eight of the 12 samples. How confident would the repair shop be in judging that the higher times were due to performance rather than to random causes?

Assume that an average mechanic's repair times would be above standard 50% of the time, so p = 0.5. As in the problem above, we want to check versus eight *or more* repair times over the standard, since being *exactly* eight is not the issue.

Excel BINOMDIST
successes = 7
trials = 12
p = 1/2 = 0.5
cumulative: true
The result is 0.8062. P would then equal 1.0000 – 0.8062 = 0.1938, or 19.38%.

So, this result would happen randomly 19.38% of the time. So, the repair shop would be only 100% – 19.4% = 80.6% confident that the new mechanic was taking more time than the standard due to other than random causes.

WHAT WE HAVE LEARNED IN CHAPTER 10

1. Six Sigma work can't be done without some understanding of probability statistics.
2. Letting data drive your problem solving will often save work and lead to a condensed list of solution considerations.
3. Using basic probability techniques on the data will help separate random results from assignable causes.

4. Since the sum of the probabilities of all possible outcomes always equals 1, we can often use this knowledge to simplify a problem.

5. Excel BINOMDIST is sufficient for doing the probability calculations, using the cumulative function to save work in doing less-than or greater-than calculations.

6. Examine the data carefully to make sure they are truly independent.

7. Although probability techniques help to focus on solution options, usually additional analysis or trials are needed to identify a specific cause-effect relationship.

8. Because our confidence level is *never* 100%, any change must be verified with future tests or data. Past data can never validate a change.

9. You can already do real Six Sigma work by applying these basic probability techniques. Even if you read no further in this book, just applying this chapter will enable you to make substantial and meaningful improvements in diverse applications.

RELATED READING

Basic Statistics: Tools for Continuous Improvement, Mark J. Kiemele, Stephen R. Schmidt, and Ronald J. Berdine, 4th edition (Colorado Springs, CO: Air Academy Press, 1997).

Probability Through Problems, Marek Capinski and Tomasz Zastawniak (New York: Springer, 2001).

Statistics for Managers, Using Microsoft Excel (with CD-ROM), David M. Levine, David Stephan, Timothy C. Krehbiel, and Mark L. Berenson, 4th edition (Upper Saddle River, NJ: Prentice Hall, 2004).

CHAPTER 11

Data Plots and Distributions

W hat you will learn in this chapter of the book is to plot data and to spot opportunities from these plots. You will also learn what a "normal" distribution of data is and some terminology to describe this distribution. As in the previous section, this information will help you to solve many real problems and is needed for Six Sigma work. Plotting data is a necessary step in implementing many of the Six Sigma tools. It is used in all of the steps of the DMAIC methodology.

Receivables Plot the monthly receivables year over year and compare it with cash flow.

Insurance Compare surgeries done in comparable hospitals to spot cost differences.

CASE STUDY: COMPARING PLOTS OF TWO PRODUCTION LINES

A production plant had two similar lines producing containers. The wall thickness on these containers was critical to the customer, so measurements were taken regularly and entered into a computer file.

The customer had periodically expressed preference for containers from line #2 over containers from line #1, but the customer had no data to substantiate this preference. Since both lines made product within specifications, the container plant felt that any difference was imagined, since both lines were thought to be identical. Finally, an engineer plotted 1000 random wall thickness measurements from each line.

Figure 11-1 shows the histogram plots of the data from the two lines, with one histogram overlaying the other for ease of comparison.

Figure 11-1. Histogram of two production lines

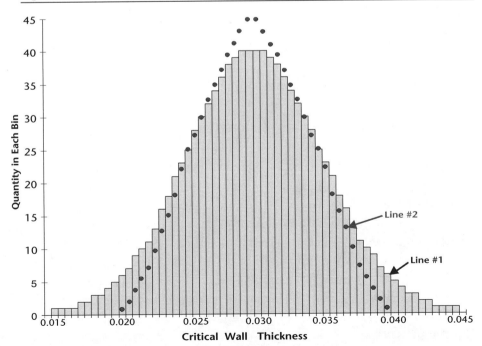

As you can see by looking at the above histograms, the wall thickness measurements from line #1 are more dispersed (more high and low values) than those from line #2. This is why the customer was happier with the containers from line #2.

Using the above data as a motivator, the engineer was able to find subtle differences between the two lines and then eliminate those differences. The wall thickness of containers from line #1 became nearly identical to the wall thickness of containers from line #2. The customer saw $25,000 per year savings from the resultant improved product and continuing plots of the data after the changes substantiated that the two lines were now making nearly identical product.

In this case study, there are several things of note. First, the customer's feelings on quality were ignored because there was no supportive data and both lines were making product within specification. Second, the data were already available in a database that no one had bothered to examine. Third, although both lines made product within specifications, the customer saw the improvement in the revised process. Fourth, without anyone realizing it, the two lines were not identical and over time small changes had been incorporated and had not been documented. Once someone decided to plot the data, it was obvious that the customer was correct and that the products from the two lines were not the same.

NORMAL DATA

A lathe is machining shafts to a 1.0000" nominal diameter. You carefully measure 100 diameters of these shafts. If you sort the diameters into 0.0005"-wide "bins" and plot this data, you will get a *histogram* similar to that shown below (Figure 11-2). In this illustration, the ends of the shafts are shown for clarity. This would not be shown in a regular histogram.

In a Histogram, Assume No Values Are on Bin "Edges"

When a value appears to be exactly on a bin "edge," convention is to put that value into the higher bin. In the example below, if a shaft were measured to be *exactly* 1.0000", it would be put into the 1.0000"-to-1.0005" bin.

Not having a value on the bin edge is not difficult to accept when you consider that with an accurate enough measurement system you would be able to see even the smallest difference from exactly 1.0000".

TIP

Figure 11-2. Histogram of 100 shafts

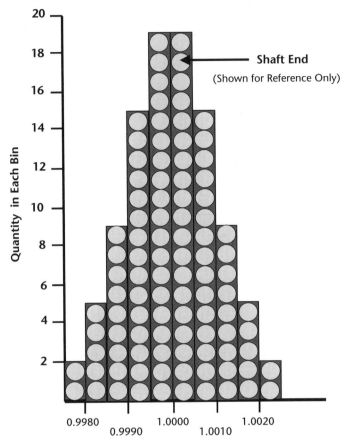

Shaft Diameter in Inches
(100) 1" Nominal Shafts Sorted into 0.0005" Bins

We must now interpret the data shown in this histogram.

First, notice that the process is centered and that the left half is a mirror image of the right. What percent of the shafts are within 0.001" of the 1.000" nominal diameter? Adding the bin quantities on both sides of the center ±0.001", we get 68, or 68% of the shafts. It will be shown later that on any process with a normal distribution, this 0.68 point (or 0.34 on either side of the center) is equal to ±1 sigma (or ±1 standard deviation).

For illustration purposes, 1 sigma in this case just happens to equal 0.001". Therefore, 2 sigma = 0.002". What % of the shafts is within ±2 sigma of the nominal diameter? Again, counting the bin quantities within ±0.002" on both sides of the center, we find that 96 shafts, or 96% of the shafts, are within 2 sigma of the nominal diameter.

Reference Data Within a Normal Distribution TIP

It is handy to remember that approximately 2/3 (68%) of the data points are within ±1 sigma of the center in a process with a normal distribution and that 95% are within ±2 sigma. Another good reference number is that 99.7% of the data points are within ±3 sigma of the center.

All of the above questions referred to data on both sides of the center. However, it is often important to know what is occurring on only one end of the data. For example, what percent of the shafts are at least 1 sigma greater than 1.0000" diameter? Adding the bin quantities to the right of +1 sigma (sigma in this case happens to be +0.0010"), we get 16, or 16%.

We will be using charts (and computer programs) that take the reference points either at the center or at either end of the data. You have to look carefully at the data and chart illustration to see what reference point is being used.

Now, using some of the techniques from the previous chapter on probability and assuming independence (assume that you put back the first shaft before picking the second), what is the likelihood of randomly picking two shafts that are above 1.0000" in diameter? Since the probability of each is 0.5, the probability of two in a row is $0.5 * 0.5 = 0.25$.

The above example used shafts, but other items could have been plotted with similar results. The height of adult men could have been plotted, with the bins representing 1" height increments. Multiple sales results could be shown as a histogram, with each bin increasing $10,000 dollars. Clerical errors could be displayed, with each bin being an increment of errors per 10,000 entries. Stock fund performance could be shown, with the bins being % annual gain. In all the above cases, you will probably get a normal distribution.

Let's now plot the same population of shaft data using 1000 shafts and breaking the data into 0.0001"-wide bins (Figure 11-3).

As we get more data from this process and use smaller bins, the shape of the histogram approaches a *normal* distribution. In fact it helps to think of a normal "curve" as a normal distribution with very small bins. This is the shape that will occur on many processes.

Below (Figure 11-4) is a normal distribution curve showing how it varies with different values of sigma.

As stated previously, on any plot of data from a normal process, approximately 2/3 (68%) of the data points are within ±1 sigma on either side of the center, 95% are within ±2 sigma on either side, and 99.7% are within ±3 sigma of the center. The use of normal curve standardized data allows us to make predictions on processes with normal distributions using small samples rather

Figure 11-3. Histogram of 1000 shafts

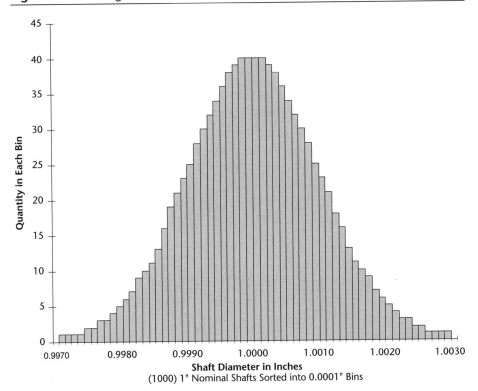

Shaft Diameter in Inches
(1000) 1" Nominal Shafts Sorted into 0.0001" Bins

Specifying a Normal Distribution

All that is needed to define a normal distributed set of data is the mean (average) and the standard deviation (sigma).

We could manually calculate the standard deviation (sigma) values; but since most $10 calculators and many computer programs do this so easily, we will not manually calculate these values. If you use a calculator to do this calculation, you may have your choice of using n or (n-1). Use (n-1).

Just for reference, here's the formula to solve for the standard deviation s on a set of n values, where $\bar{x}$ is the average of all the data points x:

$$s = \sqrt{\frac{(x_1 - \bar{x})^2 + (x_2 - \bar{x})^2 + \dots (x_n - \bar{x})^2}{n-1}}$$

The standard deviation is a measure of the spread of the normal curve. The greater the sigma, the more distributed the data, with more highs and lows.

Figure 11-4. Normal distribution with various sigma values

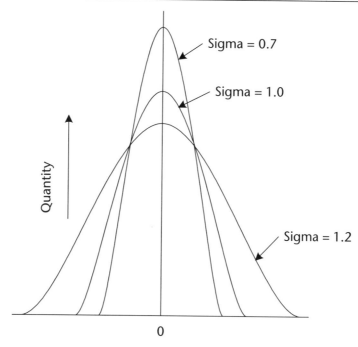

than collecting hundreds of data points on each process. As you will see later, once we establish that a process has a normal distribution, we can assume that this distribution will stay normal unless a major process change occurs.

We will be doing a lot of analysis based on the likelihood of randomly finding data beyond ±2 sigma, or outside of the expected 95% of the data. In the case of our 1000 shafts, below is our histogram (Figure 11-5) with this 5% area darkly shaded on the two ends below 0.9980" and above 1.0020".

To get a sense of what this kind of distribution would look like if it were distributed randomly, Figure 11-6 shows several hundred shafts with 5% of the shafts shaded.

If you randomly picked a shaft from the distribution in Figure 11-6, you would be unlikely to pick a shaded one. In fact, if you picked a shaded shaft very often, you would probably begin to wonder if the distribution really had only 5% shaded shafts. Much of the analysis we will be doing has similar logic.

Let's pursue this further. Suppose you had been led to believe that a distribution had 5% shaded shafts, but you suspected that this was not true. If you picked one shaft randomly and it was shaded, you would be suspicious, because you know that the chance of this happening randomly is only 5%. If you had picked two shaded shafts in a row (assuming that you had put the

Figure 11-5. Histogram of 1000 shafts with 5% shaded

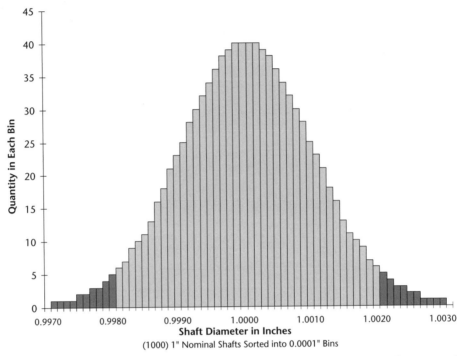

first shaft back, mixed the shafts, and then randomly picked the second shaft), then you would *really* wonder, since you know that the chance of randomly picking two shaded shafts in this manner is only 0.05 ∗ 0.05 = .0025, or only 0.25%! From this limited sample, you would suspect that the whole shaft population was more than 5% shaded.

Figure 11-6. Random shafts with 5% shaded

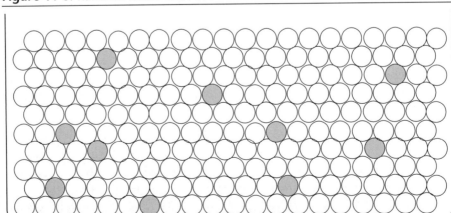

Z VALUE

The standardized normal distribution table (Figure 11-7) is one way to get probability values to use on any normal process or set of data. The Z in the table refers to the number of sigma to the right of the center. The probabilities refer to the area to the right of the Z point.

Figure 11-7. Standardized normal distribution table

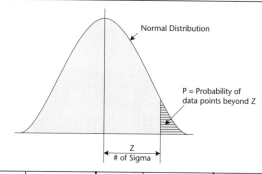

Z	P	Z	P	Z	P	Z	P
0.00	0.5000	0.05	0.4801	0.10	0.4602	0.15	0.4404
0.20	0.4207	0.25	0.4013	0.30	0.3821	0.35	0.3632
0.40	0.3446	0.45	0.3264	0.50	0.3085	0.55	0.2912
0.60	0.2743	0.65	0.2578	0.70	0.2420	0.75	0.2266
0.80	0.2119	0.85	0.1977	0.90	0.1841	0.95	0.1711
1.00	**0.1587**	1.05	0.1469	1.10	0.1357	1.15	0.1251
1.20	0.1151	1.25	0.1056	1.30	0.09680	1.35	0.08851
1.40	0.08076	1.45	0.07353	1.50	0.06681	1.55	0.06057
1.60	0.05480	1.65	0.04947	1.70	0.04457	1.75	0.04006
1.80	0.03593	1.85	0.03216	1.90	0.02872	1.95	0.02559
2.00	**0.02275**	2.05	0.02018	2.10	0.01786	2.15	0.01578
2.20	0.01390	2.25	0.01222	2.30	0.01072	2.35	0.009387
2.40	0.08198	2.45	0.007143	2.50	0.006210	2.55	0.005386
2.60	0.004661	2.65	0.004025	2.70	0.003467	2.75	0.002980
2.80	0.002555	2.85	0.002186	2.90	0.001866	2.95	0.001589
3.00	**0.001350**	3.05	0.001144	3.10	0.0009677	3.15	0.0008164
3.20	0.0006872	3.25	0.0005771	3.30	0.0004835	3.35	0.0004041
3.40	0.0003370	3.45	0.0002803	3.50	0.0002327	3.55	0.0001927
3.60	0.0001591	3.65	0.0001312	3.70	0.0001078	3.75	0.00008844
3.80	0.00007237	3.85	0.00005908	3.90	0.00004812	3.95	0.00003909
4.00	0.00003169	4.05	0.00002562	4.10	0.00002067	4.15	0.00001663
4.20	0.00001335	4.25	0.00001070	4.30	0.00000855	4.35	0.00000681
4.40	0.00000542	4.45	0.00000430	4.50	0.00000340	4.55	0.00000268
4.60	0.00000211	4.65	0.00000166	4.70	0.00000130	4.75	0.00000102
4.80	0.00000079	4.85	0.00000062	4.90	0.00000048	4.95	0.00000037

Be aware that some tables (and computer programs) use different reference points, so examine tables and computer programs carefully before using. Satisfy yourself that you can find data points on the standardized normal distribution table (Figure 11-7) relating to the previous shaft histogram with 0.0001" bins (Figure 11-5).

So there is no confusion reading this chart, let's be sure that it agrees with our reference number of 2/3 (68%) of data points being within ±1 sigma. Looking at the table, with a Z = 1.00 (which means a sigma of 1), we get P = 0.1587, or approximately 0.16. This is illustrated below (Figures 11-8 and 11-9).

Figure 11-8. Normal distribution

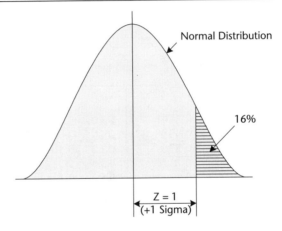

Since the left side is a mirror image of the right, this means:

Figure 11-9. Mirror image of normal distribution

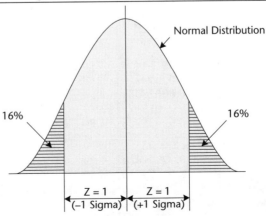

Given that the area under the curve always equals 1 (the sum of all the probabilities equals 1), we know that the lighter area under the curve = 1 – the shaded tails. This is 1 – (16% + 16%) = 1 – 32% = 68%. This confirms our reference number of 68% (or 2/3, which is easy to remember).

Problem #1

In the shaft process previously discussed, what is the probability of finding a shaft at least 2 sigma (0.0020") over 1.000" in diameter?

(The Z value is an indication of how many sigma, so in this case Z = 2.)

Looking at the standardized normal distribution table (Figure 11-7), Z = 2, P = 0.02275.

Answer: P = 0.02275, or 2.28%.

Problem #2

What is the probability of finding a shaft not greater than 1.002"?

We first must realize that 1.002" is 2 sigma above nominal (since sigma = 0.001"), so Z = 2. Using the standardized normal distribution table (Figure 11-7) to get the probability, looking at Z = 2 we see that P = 0.02275.

Looking at the normal distribution curve at the top of the table (Figure 11-7), we can see that this P is the probability of being *greater than* 1.002". Since we want *not greater than* 1.002", we must subtract 0.02275 from 1.0000. Again, we know to do this because the total area under the curve, which represents all probabilities, = 1. So, 1 – 0.02275 = 0.97725.

Answer: P = 0.97725, or 97.725%.

Assuming Normal Distribution TIP

Use plotted data to visually see if the data is normally distributed. When in doubt, plot more data. Unless the data is *dramatically* non-symmetrical (data extremely off to one side) or *dramatically* bimodal (two lobes), assume a normal distribution. The data must *clearly* show a different distribution or we assume it is normal. There are mathematical formulas to test whether data is normal, but optical inspection of the plotted data is generally sufficient. As you will see later, having a normal distribution allows you to directly use the absolute probability values in the Standardized Distribution Table. However, if the distributions are *not* normal, the table values can still be used for comparison purposes.

Chapter 14 will show that, as long as distributions have similar plots, they can be compared with each other even if their distributions are not normal.

For reference, below is a histogram example that I would consider borderline normal in that we can still use the standardized distribution table (Figure 11-7). The distribution, although not perfectly bell-shaped, is not skewed enough to be a concern.

Figure 11-10. Histogram—example

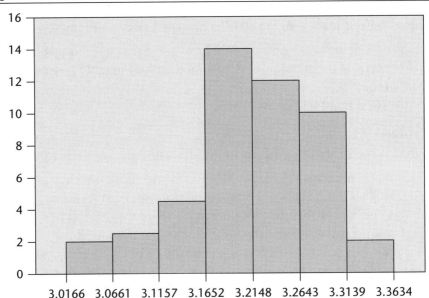

3.0166   3.0661   3.1157   3.1652   3.2148   3.2643   3.3139   3.3634

The plot above (Figure 11-10) is based on 48 data points. When in doubt, you can always plot more data.

As you will see in Chapter 14, most of the work we do in Six Sigma does not require a perfectly normal distribution, since we are generally looking for relative change.

CASE STUDY: INCUR GREAT COSTS RATHER THAN PLOTTING

A high-volume consumer product, with over $50,000,000 per year sales, had a historical increase of sales at 3% a year. This growth rate was expected to slowly decrease because of competing products having a longer life. To everyone's surprise, the sales actually increased 13% within a year.

Many people had different theories as to why this happened, but no one had any supporting data. The theories for the increased sales ranged from a sudden need by consumers for more of this specific product to an excellent marketing campaign. Plans were started to expand production facilities to support these sales, since the company was having great difficulty meeting this unexpected demand.

The marketing of this product was divided into two units, one of which handled large-volume outlets and the other handling mom-and-pop small stores. After over a year of the increased sales and almost $500,000 spent on expansion design, someone noticed that the increased sales had hit the large-volume outlets well before it had affected the low-volume outlets. Since both kinds of outlets served similar customers, this was mysterious. Finally, someone attributed the cause of the increased sales to a design change that had been implemented in the product sometime earlier. This design change inadvertently reduced average product life 10%. Since the large-volume outlets used just-in-time inventories, their customers experienced the effect of the shorter life far earlier than the small outlets, whose inventory usually covered many months of sales. So, the high-volume outlets felt the increased sales level well before the small outlets. The design change was reversed—and the unexpected sales increase disappeared.

If someone had just plotted the sales from these two marketing units when the sales increase first appeared, they would have spotted the difference between the two plots, which previously had shown the same 3% growth rate. This would have triggered a more extensive cause analysis one year earlier, prevented a $5,000,000 excessive cost to consumers, and a loss of some customers. Although the supplier had a short-term windfall from the increased sales, it lost much long-term business because it could not supply on a timely basis.

This case study shows how people are quick to react with solutions (expand facilities) at great costs, but will spend little time on plotting data and truly understanding a root cause.

Normal Distribution Symmetry

Remembering that each half of the normal distribution curve is a mirror image of the other, we can use data given for the plus side to solve problems related to both sides.

TIP

Problem #3

In the shaft process previously discussed, what is the probability of getting a shaft below 0.9978" in diameter?

This shaft diameter is 0.0022" below nominal (1 − 0.9978"). Since sigma = 0.0010", this is 2.2 sigma below nominal, so $Z = 2.2$. Looking at the standardized normal distribution table (Figure 11-7), $Z = 2.2$, we see that $P = 0.0139$. 1.39% of the data points would occur above a positive 2.2 sigma.

Since the negative side of the probability table is a mirror image of the positive side, the probability also applies to a negative 2.2 sigma.

Answer: P = .0139, or 1.39%.

No Values Occur Exactly at a Z Point

In using a standardized normal distribution curve, all values are assumed to be above or below a Z point. For example, if you wanted to know what percent of values are "above Z = 2," it would be the same as the percent of values "at or above Z = 2."

TIP

For simplicity, the previous shaft data had a sigma = 0.0010". This was to make calculations and understanding easier. Usually the sigma doesn't correlate with the bin edges, nor is it such an even number. This in no way changes the logic or diminishes the value of the standardized normal distribution table (Figure 11-7), as illustrated below.

Problem #4

Using the shaft example, let's assume that the customer has complained that the amount of variation in the shafts is causing him process problems. The customer is especially critical of shafts less than 0.9980" and greater than 1.0020" (more than 0.0020" from nominal). In response, the lathe is overhauled. On taking another 1000 measurements, it is determined that the average has stayed at 1.0000", but the sigma has been reduced from 0.0010" to 0.0007".

The reduced sigma means that the variation among shafts is less than before the overhaul. We want to communicate to the customer what improvement he can expect in future shipments, specifically what reduction he will see in shafts more than 0.0020" above or below the nominal 1.0000" diameter.

Before the overhaul (Problem #1, sigma = 0.0010"), we found that the probability of finding a shaft at least 0.0020" above 1.0000" in diameter was 0.02275. Given that both sides of the curve are mirror images, we double that number to calculate the chances of being at least 0.0020" ± nominal.

P = 0.02275 * 2 = 0.0455, or 4.55% (P *before* the overhaul).

We must now calculate the P with the new reduced sigma (0.0007"). First, we see how many sigma "fit" between nominal and 0.0020". We use the plus side first, since that is the data given to us in the standardized normal distribution table (Figure 11-7).

0.0020" / 0.0007" = 2.86 sigma fit! This gives us the Z to use in the standardized normal distribution table (Figure 11-7).

Using the standardized normal distribution table (Figure 11-7), looking at Z = 2.85 (the closest table data point), the P value we read from the table is 0.002186. So, 0.2186% of the shafts will be at least 0.0020" above nominal. We double this to include those at least 0.0020" below 1.0000" diameter.

$$2 * 0.002186 = 0.004372$$

The total P is 0.004372, or 0.4372% (P *after* the overhaul).

Answer: Since the process had been making 4.55% at 0.0020" above or below 1.0000" and it is now making 0.4372%, the customer can expect to see 9.6% (0.437 / 4.55) of the former problem shafts.

Problem #5
Let's change the above problem again to make it even more "real." After the overhaul, the lathe sigma is reduced to 0.0007" (same as above), but the average shaft diameter is now 1.0005". The process plot is still normal. Will the customer be receiving fewer problem shafts than before the overhaul?

Since the process average is no longer centered at the 1.0000" nominal, the amount of product outside the 0.9980"-to-1.0020" target is different for the large diameters than for the small diameters, so calculate each independently.

First, we will calculate the P for the too-large shafts. As before, we see how many sigma (0.0007") "fit" between the new process average (1.0005") and the +1.0020" upper limit.

This calculation is (1.0020" − 1.0005") / 0.0007" = 2.143 sigma fit.

Looking at the standardized normal distribution table (Figure 11-7), we see that the P at a Z of 2.15 (closest value to 2.143) is 0.01578. That means that 1.578% of the shafts will be 1.0020" in diameter or larger.

Looking at the too-small shafts, we do a similar calculation. First, find the value for the difference between the process average and the lower end of the target. (The process average is 1.0005" and the lower target value is 0.9980".) The difference is 1.0005" − 0.9980" = 0.0025".

We then see how many sigma (0.0007") "fit": 0.0025" / 0.0007" = 3.57 sigma. Although we must use the data on the positive end of the curve, we know that the mirror image would be identical. Looking at the P value for a Z of 3.55, we get P = .0001927. So, 0.019% of the shafts will be .9980" or smaller.

Answer: When we add the too-large and too-small diameter shafts, we get 1.578% + 0.019% = 1.60% of the shafts will be at least 0.0020" off the 1.0000" nominal. 1.60% is less than the 4.45% the customer was receiving before the overhaul, so the customer will be receiving a better product. Note, however, that 1.60% is much higher than the 0.4372% (Problem #4) the customer would receive if the process were centered.

This change in both the average and the sigma is not unusual in a process change. However, it is usually not difficult to get the process mean back to the target center (in this case, 1.0000" diameter). If the process center is put back to nominal, we get the 10-fold improvement we saw in the earlier problem.

Adjusting a Process's Mean Versus Reducing Its Sigma

Normally moving a process's mean is easier than trying to reduce its sigma.

A mean change is often just choosing the center around which the process will be run; it requires no major process change. A sigma reduction often requires a significant change in the process itself, like dramatically slowing the process or changing the equipment being used.

TIP

Note that in the above cases, the standardized normal distribution table (Figure 11-7) Z values that were used were those closest to the calculated values of Z. There was no attempt to extrapolate or go to another table or computer program for greater accuracy. Either would have been possible, but if you look at the relative values obtained versus the changes being noted, the greater accuracy was not required. Often the calculation accuracy far exceeds the requirements of the output results.

Using Excel to Get Normal Distribution Values

TIP

Those wishing to use the computer to get the probability values for various values of Z can use Excel. After bringing up the Excel worksheet, click on f_x in the toolbar. Under "category," click on "statistical." Then, under "function," click on "NORMSDIST." When you enter a Z value, it gives you the probability values using the left end of the distribution as the reference zero, whereas the standardized normal distribution table (Figure 11-7) uses the right end of the distribution as zero. To convert either one to the other, simply subtract the value from 1.

For example, if you enter Z = 2 in the Excel NORMSDIST, you get a probability value of 0.97725. This is the probability of being less than the Z value. 1.00000 − 0.97725 = 0.02275 is the probability of being greater than Z, which matches the probability given for Z = 2 on the standardized normal distribution table (Figure 11-7).

Just for information purposes, the 6-sigma process is sometimes referred to as three defects per million. If you look at the standardized normal distribution table (Figure 11-7) you will see that three defects per million is 4.65 sigma, not 6 sigma. The 6-sigma short-term target is tighter than 4.65 sigma, because it assumed a process drift would take place over time. If you started with a process that was 6 sigma short term, the goal was to have a 4.65-sigma process when the long-term drift was included.

PLOTTING DATA

There are hundreds of computer programs available that will plot data and do some degree of statistical analysis. Some of these are quite good; many are somewhat confusing. Generally the more ambitious the program (three-dimensional plots in various colors, every type of plot imaginable, esoteric statistical analysis), the more chances of getting an output that doesn't tell the desired story. This problem is caused by incomplete or confusing directions or help screens, the user not taking the time to understand the details of the program, or even errors within the program.

CASE STUDY: NOT TESTING A GRAPH FOR REASONABLENESS

In a large corporation there was a review of Six Sigma projects. In attendance were many black belts and green belts. The presenter was displaying what he described as "normal" data consisting of one hundred individual data points, with the ±3 sigma lines shown on the graph (Figure 11-11).

Figure 11-11. Graph: normal data

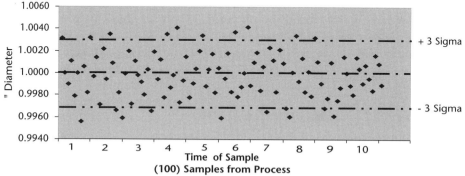

During the presentation, no one questioned this chart or the resultant conclusions. At the end of the presentation, one person asked how approximately 20% of the data points could be beyond the 3-sigma limits, since the limits were supposedly calculated from the data points displayed. (If you will recall, one of the rules of thumb is that 99.7% of the data points in a normal distribution are within the ±3-sigma limits.) This triggered some negative comments toward the questioner, inquiring whether he thought he was smarter than the person who wrote the software program. There also was general confusion, since the program used was the designated statistical program for the whole corporation. Only later did someone discover that within the program was a default that used the last 10 data points entered to calculate the 3-sigma limits.

This case study is problematic for several reasons. First, other than the questioner, no one else demonstrated a basic understanding of what the 3-sigma limits meant; no one tested the graph for reasonableness. Second, it's troublesome that the default in the computer program would use only the last 10 points entered to calculate the 3-sigma limits. (You will learn later that a *minimum* of 11 points is needed to get a decent estimate of sigma, with 30 points preferred.) Third, almost no one using this program had bothered to understand how the program worked (or its defaults) or what was the basis of its output.

Many programs are so forbidding that the user is just relieved to get an output. There is also a feeling that a graph output is some verification that the input is correct and that the output is meaningful. Many of these programs are powerful, but require care to use.

Any users of a statistical program not completely familiar to them should do some manual work with the data before using the program. They should then input a very simplified set of data for which they already know the outcome. Finally, they should test the output carefully for reasonableness.

In this manual we use Excel to generate our graphs. This is *not* because Excel is the best program for graphs (it isn't), but because I'm assuming that most users of this text will have Microsoft's Excel on their computers. Details of other programs must be left to individual users.

Using Excel's Graphing Program

I will go into more detail than you probably need in case you are less Excel-oriented. If you are completely familiar with graphing with Excel, you can quickly glance over this section.

First, make sure Excel's Data Analysis program is loaded into Tools on your computer. Bring up Microsoft Excel. On the header on the top of the screen, go to Tools. See if "Data Analysis" is one of the options available. If not, under Tools go to "Add-ins." Check the boxes opposite Analysis ToolPak and Analysis ToolPak VBA, then "OK." If it is not available, you will have to insert the Microsoft Office Professional disk and install. You may have to close Excel and then reopen it to see "Data Analysis" as one of the options. For now, go back out of Tools.

Copy the following 50 numbers into an Excel worksheet, column A.

1.0004	0.9994	1.0008	1.0013
0.9991	0.9978	1.0005	0.9984
1.0001	0.9982	1	0.9996
0.9995	1.0015	0.9996	1.0009
1.0012	1.001	0.9997	0.9998
0.9998	1.0016	0.9985	0.9998
0.9986	0.999	0.9991	0.9989
0.9999	0.9989	1.0004	0.9993
1	1.0001	0.9993	1.0003
0.9996	0.9972	1.0006	1.0019
1.0002	1.0009	0.9991	0.9996
0.9988	1.0024	1.0002	
1.0009	0.9996	1.0014	

These numbers represent 50 shaft diameter readings we may expect from the previously discussed shaft process. After copying these numbers, highlight then "order" these numbers using the AZ down arrow option in the second row header at the top of the screen. (If this option doesn't show, go into Data on the toolbar and you will see the AZ down arrow opposite "Sort." Click on "ascending.") After ordering these, the top number will be 0.9972 and the bottom number will be 1.0024.

In column B, row one, enter the formula "= (bottom or maximum number) – (top or minimum number)," which in this case will be "= A50 – A1." This will give the difference between the largest and smallest shaft diameter, which will be 0.0052.

In that same column B, second row, insert the formula "= 1.02 * B1 / 7." This gives us bin sizes for seven bins. (See the following Tip for calculating the number of bins.) The "1.02" makes the total bin widths slightly wider than the data range. If we have more data, we can use more bins by changing the denominator from 7 to the higher bin quantity. With seven bins, the bin width shown in B2 will be 0.0007577.

Now we have to show the specific bin edges. In C1, insert the formula "= A1 – 0.01 * B1." In this example it will put a value of 0.99715 in C1. This gives the left bin edge, which is slightly less than the minimum data value. Then, in C2 insert the formula "= C1 + B2." This determines that the next bin edge will be the number in C1 plus the bin width. C2 in this example will then be 0.99791. The $'s in this case "freeze" the bin width B2 for use in the next steps.

Under Edit, copy C2. Highlight C3 through C8. (You would highlight more if you had more bins.) Edit > Paste Special > Formulas. This gives you the edge values for each of the remaining bins. In this example C8 should show bin value 1.00245, the right edge of the last bin. This value is slightly higher than the maximum data number.

Now, go to Tools in the top header, then Data Analysis > Histogram. When this screen comes up, highlight column A (your data) and enter it as the Input Range. Then, click on the second box (Bin Range) and enter the highlighted bin ranges from column C. The options "New Worksheet Ply" and "Chart Output" should be chosen, then OK. The histogram will come up. Drag down the right bottom corner to extend the vertical axis.

The histogram should look similar to the one in Figure 11-12.

Figure 11-12. Histogram

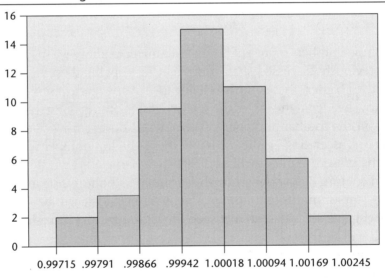

0.99715 .99791   .99866   .99942 1.00018 1.00094 1.00169 1.00245

The bottom horizontal X-axis, as labeled in Excel, makes it look like the bin values are in the middle of the bins rather than on the right edges. This was modified for the above illustration. Also, if you get more (or less) label digits than shown above, you can modify them to match the above (or whatever you desire) by formatting the bin-edge column in the Excel spreadsheet. You may want to add definition to the wording on the axis. However, in this book we are more interested in the histogram shape than the labels.

Rule of Thumb for the Number of Bins to Use in a Histogram

$$\#\text{of Bins} = \sqrt{\#\text{of Data Points}}$$

Note: This is only a general guideline. Feel free to experiment.

Additional Practice Problems

Use the following information and the standardized normal distribution table (Figure 11-7) on the following additional problems.

An insurance company has plotted hospital bills for delivering a baby when there are no complications and has found that the distribution is normal. In a specific city, the average delivery cost is $3020, with a standard deviation of $280.

Problem #6
What is the probability of the hospital bill for a normal delivery in this city being greater than $3380?

Problem #7
What is the range (high and low) of hospital bills that 95% of people would expect for a normal delivery in this city?

Problem #8
The insurance company has found that delivery costs in this city are greater than in other similar cities. Should the insurance company emphasize reducing the average cost or the variation in costs within this city?

Problem #9
The insurance company makes a concerted effort to reduce delivery costs in this city. After a year they find that they have reduced the average cost from $3020 to $2910. The sigma stayed the same at $280. What reduction (%) can they expect in the number of bills over $3200?

Problem #10
As above, the insurance company reduces the average delivery cost from $3020 to $2910, but the standard deviation goes from $280 to $305. What reduction (%) can they expect in bills over $3200?

Problem #11
Using Excel and the following 48 numbers, create a histogram.

3.24	3.25	3.25	3.29
3.21	3.36	3.26	3.28
3.29	3.28	3.3	3.18
3.28	3.18	3.18	3.22
3.32	3.21	3.19	3.24
3.21	3.25	3.1	3.17
3.25	3.18	3.11	3.16
3.13	3.29	3.18	3.06
3.14	3.1	3.14	3.31
3.26	3.22	3.19	3.31
3.22	3.02	3.21	3.27
3.2	3.19	3.12	3.25

Solutions to Additional Practice Problems

An insurance company has plotted hospital bills for delivering a baby when there are no complications, and has found that the distribution is normal. In a specific city the average delivery cost is $3020, with a standard deviation of $280.

Problem #6

What is the probability of the hospital bill for a normal delivery in this city being greater than $3380?

$3380 – $3020 = $360

$360 / $280 = 1.2857, so Z = 1.286.

Looking at the standardized normal distribution table (Figure 11-7), Z = 1.30 (the closest to 1.286), P = 0.09680.

So, the chance of getting a bill greater than $3380 is approximately 9.7%.

Problem #7

What is the range (high and low) of hospital bills that 95% of people would expect for a normal delivery in this city?

We first solve for the high end of the range, since the standardized normal distribution table (Figure 11-7) shows that end.

95% / 2 = 47.5% of the bills are on the upper half.

50.0% – 47.5% = 2.5% is the probability of a bill higher than expected.

Looking within the standardized normal distribution table (Figure 11-7), P = 0.025 (2.5%): Z = 1.95 (the closest Z).

Multiply the Z times the sigma value to calculate how much higher the upper end of the range is versus the average:

1.95 * $280 = $546.
Adding this to the mean gives us the high end of the range:
$3020 + $546 = $3566.

Since we know that a normal distribution is symmetrical, we know that the low end of the range will be an equal amount below the average:
$3020 – $546 = $2474.

So, 95% of the people in this city can expect to pay between $2474 and $3566 for a normal delivery.

Problem #8

The insurance company has found that delivery costs in this city are greater than in other similar cities. Should the insurance company emphasize reducing the average cost or the variation in costs within this city?

In general, the average is easier to change than the variation. The insurance company has a better chance of reducing its average costs (by putting out general guidelines, encouraging the use of generic drugs, etc.) than of reducing the variation among all doctors and hospitals. Of course, some reduction in variation may also come as a secondary benefit.

Problem #9

The insurance company makes a concerted effort to reduce delivery costs in this city. After a year they find that they have reduced the average cost from $3020 to $2910. The sigma stayed the same at $280. What reduction (%) can they expect in the number of bills over $3200?

First let's calculate the number of bills over $3200 at the initial $3020 average cost, with the sigma of $280. We need to get the Z value:
$$Z = (\$3200 – \$3020) / \$280 = 0.643$$

From the standardized normal distribution table (Figure 11-7), $P = 0.2578$ (25.78%).

So, at the initial $3020 average, 25.78% of the bills were over $3200.

Now calculate the number of bills over $3200 at the $2910 average cost, with the sigma of $280. We need to get the Z value:
$$Z = (\$3200 – \$2910) / \$280 = 1.0357$$

From the standardized normal distribution table (Figure 11-7), $P = 0.1469$ (14.69%).

So, at the lower $2910 average, 14.69% of the bills are over $3200.
The difference is 25.78% – 14.69% = 11.09%. 11.09% / 25.78% = 0.430.
So, they will see an approximate 43% reduction in bills over $3200.

Problem #10

As above, the insurance company reduces the average delivery cost from $3020 to $2910, but the standard deviation goes from $280 to $305. What reduction (%) can they expect in bills over $3200?

Again, first calculate the number of bills over $3200 at the initial $3020 average cost, with the sigma of $280. We need to get the Z value:

Z = ($3200 – $3020) / $280 = 0.643

From the standardized normal distribution table (Figure 11-7), P = 0.2578 (25.78%).

So, at the initial $3020 average, 25.78% of the bills were over $3200.

Now calculate the number of bills over $3200 at the $2910 average cost, with the sigma of $305. We need to get the Z value:

Z = ($3200 – $2910) / $305 = 0.951

From the standardized normal distribution table (Figure 11-7), P = 0.1711 (17.11%).

So, at the lower $2910 average, 17.11% of the bills were over $3200.

The difference is 25.78% – 17.11% = 8.67%. 8.67% / 25.78% = 0.336.

So, they will see an approximate 34% reduction in bills over $3200.

Problem #11

Using Excel and the following 48 numbers, create a histogram.

3.24	3.25	3.25	3.29
3.21	3.36	3.26	3.28
3.29	3.28	3.3	3.18
3.28	3.18	3.18	3.22
3.32	3.21	3.19	3.24
3.21	3.25	3.1	3.17
3.25	3.18	3.11	3.16
3.13	3.29	3.18	3.06
3.14	3.1	3.14	3.31
3.26	3.22	3.19	3.31
3.22	3.02	3.21	3.27
3.2	3.19	3.12	3.25

After copying the numbers into an Excel file in column A and with them highlighted, "order" these highlighted numbers using the AZ down arrow option in the second row header at the top of the screen. (If this option doesn't show, go into Data on the toolbar and you will see the AZ down arrow opposite "Sort." Click on "ascending.") After ordering these, the top number will be 3.02 and the bottom number will be 3.36.

In column B, row one, enter the formula "= (bottom or maximum number) – (top or minimum number)," which in this case is "= A48 – A1." This is the difference between the largest and smallest diameter, which is 0.34.

In that same column B, second row, insert a formula "= 1.02 * B1 / 7." This gives us bin sizes for seven bins, per the Tip on bin number. With seven bins, the bin width shown in B2 will be 0.049543.

Now we have to show the specific bin edges. In C1, insert the formula "= A1 – 0.01 * B1." In this example it will put a value of 3.0166 in C1. This gives the left bin edge, which is slightly less than the minimum data value. Then, in C2 insert the formula "= C1 + B2." This determines that the next bin edge will be the number in C1 plus the bin width. C2 in this example will then be 3.0661. The $'s in this case "freeze" the bin width B2 for use in the next steps.

Under Edit, copy C2. Highlight C3 through C8. (You would highlight more if you had more bins.) Edit > Paste Special > Formulas. This gives you the edge values for each of the remaining bins. In this example C8 should show bin value 3.3634, the right edge of the last bin. This value is slightly higher than the maximum data number.

Now, go to Tools in the top header, then Data Analysis > Histogram. When this screen comes up, highlight column A (your data) and enter it as the Input Range. Then, click on the second box (Bin Range) and enter the highlighted bin ranges from column C. The options "New Worksheet Ply" and "Chart Output" should be chosen, then OK. The histogram (Figure 11-13) will come up. Drag down the right bottom corner to extend the vertical axis.

Figure 11-13. Histogram

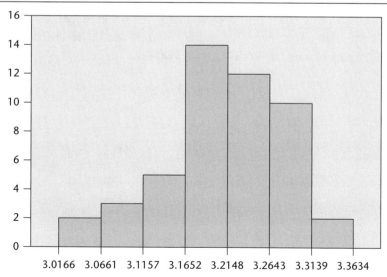

WHAT WE HAVE LEARNED IN CHAPTER 11

1. Plotting data is a step needed in implementing many of the Six Sigma tools.
2. Data needed for histograms and standardized normal distribution table analysis are often readily available.
3. Using histograms to compare supposedly similar areas or year-to-year performance helps spot unexpected differences and areas of opportunity. Using the standardized normal distribution table (Figure 11-7) to evaluate data on a normal distribution or to compare two processes with similarly shaped histograms can often help quantify a problem.
4. Excel can be used to make histograms or get normal distribution values.
5. A graphing program may be powerful, but the user needs to fully understand it.
6. You can do real Six Sigma work by using histograms and the normal distribution table.

RELATED READING

Basic Statistics: Tools for Continuous Improvement, Mark J. Kiemele, Stephen R. Schmidt, and Ronald J. Berdine, 4th edition (Colorado Springs, CO: Air Academy Press, 1997).

Excel Charts (with CD-ROM), John Walkenbach (Indianapolis, IN: John Wiley & Sons, 2003).

Data Analysis with Microsoft Excel, Kenneth N. Berk and Patrick Carey (Southbank, Australia; Belmont, CA: Brooks/Cole, 2004).

Statistics for Managers, Using Microsoft Excel (with CD-ROM), David M. Levine, David Stephan, Timothy C. Krehbiel, and Mark L. Berenson, 4th edition (Upper Saddle River, NJ: Prentice Hall, 2004).

PART IV

Six Sigma Tools to Test for Statistically Significant Change

CHAPTER 12

Testing for Statistically Significant Change Using Variables Data

W hat you will learn in this chapter is how to use limited samples of variables (measurable) data to make judgments on whether a population or process has changed. We will be comparing samples with the population and samples with other samples. We first want to determine the minimum sample size required. This is very important, because taking too small a sample can cause invalid estimates, but excessive samples are costly. This chapter is used for the Define, Measure, Analysis, Improve, and Control steps in the DMAIC process.

Changes in Real Processes, Variables Data

Manufacturing Compare dimensional samples from two similar production lines or compare shift samples on one line to look for significant differences. Verify the results of a test by comparing a sample against the population or against another sample.

Sales Compare samples from different salespeople on sales dollars generated using samples from many random days.

Marketing Compare samples of advertising dollars spent in a city over a period of time versus the sales generated in that city to see if advertising dollars makes a significant difference in sales.

Accounting and Software Development Sample error rates and look for differences among people or departments doing similarly complex work, using samples from many individual days.

Receivables Sample delinquent receivables to check for a correlation with company size or D&B rating. Use data from many individual days.

Insurance Sample costs among treatment centers on similar procedures, using data from many individual days.

In the chapter on probability, we learned to judge whether an event was due to random or assignable cause. In all cases we knew the specific odds of the random event, like 0.5 on a coin flip or 1/6 on rolling a die. If an event were non-random, it hinted at a problem or an opportunity.

In the chapter on data plots and distributions, we plotted a large quantity of data from a sample or population to see trends or changes. We would use the plot to see the distribution of data. We used a Standardized Normal Distribution Table to do further analysis. As in the probability chapter, once we had an identified distribution, we used this knowledge to judge whether an event was due to random or assignable cause.

Variables Data

Variables data are measurable, generally in decimal form. Theoretically, you could look at enough decimal places to find that no two values are exactly the same. *Continuous* data is another term used for this type of data.

DEFINITION

Sample Size Rule of Thumb on Variables Data

To calculate sigma on variables data, a rule-of-thumb minimum sample size n of 11 is needed, with a preferable sample size n of 30 or more.

To calculate an average, the sample size n can be as low as 6. But, since we normally must calculate sigma at the same time, the minimum n of 11 and preferable n of 30 are the standard.

This rule of thumb should be used only when it is not possible to calculate a specific minimum sample size. This would be where we don't know the population sigma or are not sure of the accuracy we need.

TIP

CASE STUDY: OBSCENE SCRAP CALL

In a process that ran 24 hours per day, an inspector took product readings continuously. Every time seven pieces were measured, a computer program calculated an average and sigma from these seven pieces. Using that average and sigma, the computer projected the percentage of the product that was out-side specifications. The results of these calculations were then displayed in the operator's booth, which was at the other end of the manufacturing plant. If the projected percentage of the product that was outside specifications was too high, the product was put into "scrap" and remained there until the calculations on another seven-piece sample showed an acceptable defect projection.

The "scrap" decision was communicated back to the machine operator, who was supposed to make adjustments to bring the product back to acceptable levels. The operator had learned from experience, however, that these "scrap" decisions were sometimes invalid and that the "scrap" would often cancel out on the next sample without any process adjustments being made. Therefore, the operator would delay adjusting the process until several "scrap" calls occurred in a row.

The result was that scrap time was excessive, bad product was shipped (the erroneous "scrap" calls also missed some bad product), and the plant production people had no faith in the quality system. The machine operators had even coined an obscene phrase for the basis of the scrap decision. The first half of this phrase was "sigma," which I am not sure they fully understood. But they certainly knew what the last half of the coined phrase meant!

Per the earlier Tip on sample size, the rule of thumb for the minimum sample size for a valid sigma estimate is 11. The quality system in this example was using a sample size of seven! The quality manager was very hesitant to increase the sample size, because he thought the system reaction time would then be too slow. It took much convincing for him to even try a larger sample size.

When the sample size was increased to 15, the erroneous "scrap" calls were substantially reduced (this was verified by data taken before and after the change), the outgoing quality was improved, scrap time was reduced, and faith in the quality system was restored. The reaction time of the system never became an issue, since having valid scrap calls was far more important. The scrap time reduction alone was worth over $100,000 per year and there was negligible cost for implementation.

Almost any formal or informal quality system has a sample size that is used to make decisions and to give feedback to the people involved. Even where there are no formal rules, someone makes a judgment on how many items should be reviewed before making a determination. This is true in reviewing office staff output, incoming product, medical errors, accounting errors, programming mistakes, etc. If too many examples are required, a decision is delayed and poor performance is missed. If judgment is made on too small a sample, then erroneous calls are often made.

Labeling Averages and Standard Deviations

The average of a population is labeled $\overline{X}$, whereas the sample averages are labeled $\overline{x}$.

Similarly, the standard deviation (sigma) of the population is labeled S and the sample standard deviations are labeled s.

We will use $\overline{X}$, S, $\overline{x}$, and s in this book rather than the Greek letters used in some texts. Both are in use and acceptable. The feeling of the author is that the Greek letters are sometimes intimidating and give no real benefit except to appear esoteric. Statistics has enough of a stigma without unnecessary intimidation.

Population vs. Sample

We seldom have *all* the data on a population, but make an estimate about the population based on large or multiple samples.

ESTIMATING A POPULATION AVERAGE $\overline{X}$ AND SIGMA S

Here are two ways of determining the population $\overline{X}$ and S. You can estimate a population average $\overline{X}$ and sigma S from the $\overline{x}$ and s of a large sample with a minimum sample size of n = 30. Assume that the population average and sigma are the same as that of the large sample.

You can also estimate the population sigma if you have two or more samples of similar size n. The formula is shown in the box.

Estimating Population $\overline{X}$ and S from Multiple Samples of Similar-Size n

$$\overline{X} = \frac{\overline{x}_1 + \overline{x}_2}{2}$$

$\overline{X}$ is the population average
$\overline{x}_1$ is the average from the #1 sample
$\overline{x}_2$ is the average from the #2 sample

$$S = \sqrt{\frac{s_1^2 + s_2^2}{2}}$$

S is the population sigma
s_1 is the sigma of the #1 sample
s_2 is the sigma of the #2 sample

If you have three or more samples, modify the formulas accordingly, with more sample sigma or averages in the numerator and dividing by the total number of samples.

Example: If you have $s_1 = 16$ and $s_2 = 12$, then

$$S = \sqrt{\frac{s_1^2 + s_2^2}{2}} = \sqrt{\frac{16^2 + 12^2}{2}} = 14.14$$

If the sample sizes are substantially different, use the s from the larger sample for the estimate of S, since the confidence related to a small sample is suspect. You can also use a computer program that will compensate for different sample sizes, but this is not normally necessary.

Problem #1

You have data from two samples taken from a stable process, with no other knowledge of the process population.

Sample #1	Sample #2
n = 16	n = 36
x̄ = 14.96	x̄ = 15.03
s = 1.52	s = 1.48

What is the estimate for the population average $\overline{X}$ and sigma S?

Since the sample sizes n are quite different from each other, use the larger sample. Also, since the sample size of #2 is over 30, we feel comfortable that it is a reasonable estimate. So, the estimate for the population is:

$\overline{X} = 15.03$
$S = 1.48$

Problem #2

You have data from three samples taken from a stable process, with no other knowledge of the process population.

Sample #1	Sample #2	Sample #3
n = 16	n = 18	n = 15
x̄ = 14.96	x̄ = 15.05	x̄ = 15.04
s_1 = 1.52	s_2 = 1.49	s_3 = 1.53

What is the estimate for the population average $\overline{X}$ and sigma S?

Since all three samples have a similar sample size n, we will use the above formulas to calculate our estimate for the population.

$$\overline{X} = \frac{\overline{X}_1 + \overline{X}_2 + \overline{X}_3}{3}$$

$$\overline{X} = \frac{14.96 + 15.05 + 15.04}{3} = 15.017$$

$$S = \sqrt{\frac{s_1^2 + s_2^2 + s_3^2}{3}}$$

$$S = \sqrt{\frac{1.52^2 + 1.49^2 + 1.53^2}{3}}$$

$$S = \sqrt{\frac{6.8714}{3}} = 1.513$$

Maximize Sample Size to Estimate the Population Average and Sigma

TIP

The greater the sample size n ("n is your friend"), the better your estimate of the population average and standard deviation!

Calculating Minimum Sample Size and Sensitivity, Variables Data

FORMULA

$n = \left(\frac{Z*S}{h}\right)^2$ to calculate minimum sample size on variables data

n = minimum sample size on variables data (Always round up.)
Z = confidence level. (When in doubt use Z = 1.96, per the following Tip.)
S = the population standard deviation
h = the smallest change we want to be able to sense
(When in doubt, use h = total tolerance / 10, or h = 0.6S.)

Note that the formula shown above can be rewritten as:

$$h = \sqrt{\frac{Z^2 * S^2}{n}}$$

This allows us to see what sensitivity h (change) we can expect to see with a given sample size and confidence level.

There is a lot of judgment that goes into calculating sample size. Often the final sample size will be a compromise between cost (both product and inspection) and customer need. The formulas allow you to make sample size a knowledge-based decision rather than just a guess.

Looking at the components of the sample-size formula, we see that the sample size n is influenced not only by the sensitivity (h) required, but also by the process sigma. Sometimes this formula will point out that the sample size requirement is so excessive that only a process improvement (reduced sigma) or a loosening of the customer's requirements (increased h) will make sampling viable. The alternatives to sampling include automatic inspection or 100% process sorting. This use of sample size formulas is a very productive use of the Six Sigma process.

Z, Confidence of Results

Z relates to the probability, or confidence, we are looking for. For one-tailed questions (like greater-than), use Z = 1.64 for a 95% confidence. On two-tailed problems (like greater-than *or* less-than), use Z = 1.96 for 95% confidence.

We normally test to a 95% confidence.

Assume two-tailed unless it is specifically given as one-tailed. *So, the Z will normally be 1.96.*

Here are some important notes with regard to confidence testing. First, you can find countless tables and computer programs that will test significance at many different confidence levels. If you look at a low enough confidence level, you may find differences that are significant that were *not* significant at a 95% confidence level. But at lower confidence levels, you are increasing the chance of erroneous conclusions. Also, using higher confidence levels will make little difference since you usually have to rerun any test to see if the results hold. If you recall from the probability chapter, running two tests at a 0.95 probability minimizes "chance" to p = 0.05 * 0.05 = 0.0025! There is normally no reason to test to a higher confidence than 95%, since you may miss real opportunity.

CASE STUDY: ENFORCING MINIMUM SAMPLE SIZE

A company had calculated the minimum sample size to be used for inspecting a skid of product. They assigned an inspector to randomly measure product as it was being put on the skid. The product measurements were entered into a computer and the program then made a determination to ship or to hold each skid for re-inspection.

The product was produced 24 hours per day, seven days per week. Supervision was minimal. Besides the four inspectors assigned to this line, there were relief inspectors and people who covered for vacations and illness.

Despite the incorporation of the minimum sample size instruction, the customer was still seeing skids that contained an excessive amount of defects. After several complaints, the supplier looked at past records of the quality checks and found that, at times, the quantity checked was far less than the calculated minimum sample size.

The company then changed the quality system to hold a skid when the sample size was too low, put a message on the inspector's computer screen that this was being done, and send an exception report to the quality manager. Instantly, the problem with low sample sizes stopped and the customer stopped seeing the defect excursions.

Sample Size Verification
Determining minimum sample size for a quality system is not enough. Some system for verifying sample size is also required.

TIP

Problem #3
Administrators of a high school had just gotten the results from a national achievement test, and they wanted to know how many random results they would have to review before deciding, with a 95% confidence, if the performance of the students had *changed*. The historical sigma on this test was 1.24. They wanted to be able to sense a change of 0.6S, which is 0.744.

$$n = \left(\frac{Z*S}{h}\right)^2$$

$$n = \left(\frac{1.96*1.24}{0.744}\right)^2$$

$$n = 10.67$$

So, they would have to look at the results from at least 11 tests to see if the performance had changed 0.744, with a 95% confidence.

Problem #4
Administrators of a high school had just gotten the results from a national achievement test and they wanted to know how many random results they would have to review before deciding, with a 95% confidence, if the performance of the students had *improved*. The historical sigma on this test was 1.24. They wanted to be able to sense an improvement of 0.6S, which is 0.744.

Note that this problem is now one-tailed, because they want to see only if the students improved. This changes the value of Z to 1.64.

$$n = \left(\frac{Z*S}{h}\right)^2$$

$$n = \left(\frac{1.64*1.24}{0.744}\right)^2$$

$$n = 7.47$$

So, they would have to look at the results from at least eight tests to see if the performance had improved 0.744, with a 95% confidence.

Note that by only looking for "improved" scores, the minimum sample size is reduced from 11 to 8. However, knowing if change occurred only on the "up" side is usually not sufficient, since the school would at some point be concerned about change on both the "up" and "down" sides. Because of this, the sample size is usually determined by a two-tailed $Z = 1.96$, as in problem #3, giving a minimum sample size of 11.

Problem #5
Before doing the above calculations, someone had already tabulated the results from 20 tests. At a 95% confidence, what change in results (h) could be sensed from reviewing this many results versus the minimum 0.744 change target? The historical sigma on this test was 1.24.

$$h = \sqrt{\frac{Z^2*S^2}{n}}$$

$$h = \sqrt{\frac{1.96^2*1.24^2}{20}}$$

$$h = 0.543$$

So, the sensitivity on 20 results is 0.543 vs. the 0.744 target. The school officials would be able to sense a smaller change. This shows the benefit of a larger sample size, n = 20 versus n = 11.

USING A SAMPLE TO CHECK FOR A CHANGE VERSUS A POPULATION

We will use a three-step process:

1. Check the distributions to see if the data histogram shapes (population versus sample) are substantially different.

2. If the distribution shapes are not substantially different, then see if the sigmas are significantly different.

3. If neither of the above tests shows a difference, then check if the averages are significantly different.

If we sense a significant difference at any point in the above steps, we stop and try to find the cause. Any significant difference is potentially important since it can affect costs, quality, etc.

Don't Use Data Analysis Alone to Drive Decisions

The following formulas will give you the ability to detect change. The reaction to any analytical finding should be tempered by common sense and expert knowledge. This should not keep you from pursuing a finding that violates common sense and expert knowledge because it is not uncommon to discover that some preconceptions are invalid. However, tread softly, because the analysis could also be wrong.

Remember:, we are testing to a 95% confidence level, which means that 5% of the time you could be wrong!

TIP

1. Checking the Distributions

First, it may be necessary to plot a large number of individual measurements to verify that the sample distribution shape is similar to that of the earlier population. Although a process distribution will normally be similar over time, it is important to verify this, especially when running a test after a policy change, machine wreck, personnel change, etc. We are only concerned about gross differences, like one plot being very strongly skewed or bimodal versus the other. If plotting is required, it will need a sample size of at least 36. If there is a substantial change in the distribution shape, there is no reason to do further tests, because we know the process has changed and we should be trying to understand the change cause and ramifications.

If there are outliers (data values clearly separate from the general distribution), the causes of those data points must be determined before doing any quantitative statistics on the data. If you can confidently determine that the questionable data points are due to an error in collecting or entering data and they don't reflect the process, then the data points should be removed. If the wild data points are *not* an input error, then you have found a potential problem that must be resolved.

Examining Plotted Data
Visually examining plotted data will often give insights that can't be seen with any quantitative method.

TIP

2. Checking the Sigmas

If the process distribution has not changed qualitatively (looking at the plots), then you can do some quantitative tests. The first thing to check is if the sigma has changed significantly. The sigma on a process does not normally change unless a basic change in the process has occurred. To see if the sigma has changed, we calculate a *chi-squared test value* (Chi_t^2) (see Figure 12-1, page 130).

Chi-Squared Test Value of a Sample Sigma s Versus a Population Sigma S

FORMULA

$$Chi_t^2 = \frac{(n-1)s^2}{S^2}$$

n = sample size
s = sample sigma
S = population sigma

We compare the calculated Chi_t^2 results with the values in the following simplified chi-squared distribution table (Figure 12-1). If the Chi_t^2 test value we calculated is less than the table low value, or greater than the table high value, we are 95% confident that the sample sigma s is different from the sigma S of the population.

If there had been a significant change in the sigma, there would be no reason to do further tests and we should be trying to understand the change cause and ramifications.

3. Checking the Averages

If in 1) and 2) we did not find that either the distribution or the sigma had changed significantly, we are now free to test whether the sample average is significantly different from the population average. We will have to calculate a *t-test value* (t_t) to compare to a value in the simplified t distribution table (Figure 12-2).

Problem #6

We have made a process change on our infamous lathe that is machining shafts. We want to know, with a 95% confidence, if the "before" process, with an average $\overline{X}$ of 1.0003" and a sigma S of 0.00170", has changed.

Figure 12-1. Simplified chi-squared distribution table to test a sample sigma s (with sample size n) versus a population sigma S

	95% Confident They Are Different if Chi_t^2 Is				95% Confident They Are Different if Chi_t^2 Is		
	< Low	Or	> High		< Low	Or	> High
n	Low Test		High Test	n	Low Test		High Test
6	0.831209		12.83249	36	20.56938		53.20331
7	1.237342		14.44935	37	21.33587		54.43726
8	1.689864		16.01277	38	22.10562		55.66798
9	2.179725		17.53454	39	22.87849		56.89549
10	2.700389		19.02278	40	23.65430		58.12005
11	3.246963		20.48320	41	24.43306		59.34168
12	3.815742		21.92002	42	25.21452		60.56055
13	4.403778		23.33666	43	25.99866		61.77672
14	5.008738		24.73558	44	26.78537		62.99031
15	5.628724		26.11893	45	27.57454		64.20141
16	6.262123		27.48836	46	28.36618		65.41013
17	6.907664		28.84532	47	29.16002		66.61647
18	7.564179		30.19098	48	29.95616		67.82064
19	8.230737		31.52641	49	30.75450		69.02257
20	8.906514		32.85234	50	31.55493		70.22236
21	9.590772		34.16958	55	35.58633		76.19206
22	10.28291		35.47886				
23	10.98233		36.78068	60	39.66185		82.11737
24	11.68853		38.07561	65	43.77594		88.00398
25	12.40115		39.36406				
26	13.11971		40.64650	70	47.92412		93.85648
27	13.84388		41.92314	80	56.30887		105.4727
28	14.57337		43.19452				
29	15.30785		44.46079	90	64.79339		116.989
30	16.04705		45.72228				
				100	73.3611		128.4219
31	16.79076		46.97922				
32	17.53872		48.23192				
33	18.29079		49.48044				
34	19.04666		50.72510				
35	19.80624		51.96602				

t Test of a Population Average X̄ Versus a Sample Average x̄

$$t_t = \frac{|\bar{x} - \bar{X}|}{\frac{s}{\sqrt{n}}}$$

FORMULA

$\bar{X}$ = population average
$\bar{x}$ = sample average
s = sample sigma
n = sample size
$|\bar{x} - \bar{X}|$ is the absolute value of the difference of the averages, so ignore a minus sign in the difference.

We then compare this calculated t-test (t_t) value against the value in the following Simplified t Table (Figure 12-2). If our calculated t-test (t_t) value is greater than the value in the table, then we are 95% confident that the sample average is significantly different from the population average.

Figure 12-2. Simplified t distribution table to compare a sample average (size = n) with a population average or to compare two samples of size n_1 and n_2, using n = ($n_1 + n_2 - 1$). 95% confidence (assumes two-tailed). If the calculated t_t test value exceeds the table t value, then the two averages being compared are different.

n	t value	n	t value	n	t value
6	2.571	26	2.060	45	2.015
7	2.447	27	2.056		
8	2.365	28	2.052	50	2.010
9	2.306	29	2.048		
10	2.262	30	2.045	60	2.001
11	2.228	31	2.042	70	1.995
12	2.201	32	2.040		
13	2.179	33	2.037	80	1.990
14	2.160	34	2.035		
15	2.145	35	2.032	90	1.987
16	2.131	36	2.030	100+	1.984
17	2.120	37	2.028		
18	2.110	38	2.026		
19	2.101	39	2.024		
20	2.093	40	2.023		
21	2.086				
22	2.080				
23	2.074				
24	2.069				
25	2.064				

We use our three-step process to look for change. Assume that we first plotted some data from after the change and compared it with a plot of "before" data and saw no large differences in the shape of the two distributions. We must now compare the sigma before and after the change.

What is the minimum sample size we need, assuming we want to be able to see a change h of 0.6S?

h = 0.6S = 0.6 * 0.00170" = 0.00102"

Z = 1.96

S = 0.00170"

$$n = \left(\frac{Z * S}{h}\right)^2$$

$$n = \left(\frac{1.96 * 0.00170"}{0.00102"}\right)^2$$

n = 11 (rounding up)

Now that we know the minimum sample size, we can take the sample.

We want to know if the sample sigma is significantly different from the "before" population sigma. From the sample, we calculate s = 0.00173".

n = 11

s = 0.00173"

S = 0.00170"

$$Chi_t^2 = \frac{(n-1)s^2}{S^2} = \frac{(11-1)0.00173"^2}{0.00170"^2} = 10.356$$

Looking at the simplified chi-square distribution table (Figure 12-1), with an n = 11, the low value is 3.24696 and the high value is 20.4832. Since our test value (10.356) is not outside that range, we can't say that the sigma of the sample is different (at a 95% confidence) from the population sigma.

Since we were not able to see a difference in the distribution or the sigma, we will now see if the averages are significantly different. Assume that the after-change sample (n = 11) had an average $\bar{x}$ of 0.9991".

$\bar{x} = 0.9991"$

$\bar{X} = 1.0003"$

s = 0.00173"

n = 11

$$t_t = \frac{|\bar{x} - \bar{X}|}{\frac{s}{\sqrt{n}}}$$

$$t_t = \frac{\left|0.9991" - 1.0003"\right|}{\dfrac{0.00173"}{\sqrt{11}}} = 2.3005$$

Looking at the simplified t distribution table (Figure 12-2), with an n = 11, our calculated t-test value (2.3005) is greater than the table value (opposite n = 11: 2.228). We therefore assume with a 95% confidence, that the sample average *is* significantly different from the population.

The average has significantly changed from what it was before. We should therefore decide whether the process change was detrimental and should be reversed. Here is where judgment must be used, but you have data to help.

CHECKING FOR A CHANGE BETWEEN TWO SAMPLES

We sometimes want to compare samples from two similar processes or from one process at different times. As in comparing a sample with a population, we do three steps in checking for a change between two samples.

1. Check the distributions to see if they are substantially different.
2. If the distribution shapes are not substantially different, then see if the sigmas are significantly different.
3. If neither of the above tests shows a difference, then check if the averages are significantly different.

If we see a difference at any of the above steps, it is important to know, since it affects costs, quality, etc.

1. Checking the Distributions

First, it may be necessary to plot a large number of individual measurements to verify that the sample distribution shapes are similar. Although a process distribution will normally be similar over time, it is important to verify this, especially when running a test after a policy change, machine wreck, personnel change, etc. We are concerned only about gross differences, like one plot being very strongly skewed or bimodal versus the other. If plotting is required, it will need a sample size of at least 36. If there is a substantial change in the distribution, we know the process has changed and we should be trying to understand the change cause and ramifications.

2. Checking the Sigmas

If the sample distributions have not changed qualitatively (looking at the plots), then you can do some quantitative tests. The first thing to check is if the sigma has changed significantly. The sigma on a process does not nor-

FORMULA

F Test Comparing Two Sample's Sigma s

$F_t = \dfrac{s_1^2}{s_2^2}$ (put the larger s on top, as the numerator)

s_1 = sample with the larger sigma
s_2 = sample with the smaller sigma

The sample sizes n should be within 20% of each other. There are tables and programs that allow for greater differences, but since you control sample sizes and get more reliable results with similar sample sizes, these other tables and programs are generally not needed.

Compare this F_t with the value in the following simplified F table (Figure 12-3). If the F_t value exceeds the table F value, then the sigmas are significantly different.

Figure 12-3. Simplified F table (95% confidence) for comparing sigma from two samples (sizes = n_1 and n_2) (sample sizes equal within 20%)

$$n = \frac{n_1 + n_2}{2}$$

If the calculated F_t value exceeds the table value, assume a difference.

n	F	n	F	n	F
6	5.05	26	1.96	60	1.54
7	4.28	27	1.93	70	1.49
8	3.79	28	1.90	80	1.45
9	3.44	29	1.88	100	1.39
10	3.18	30	1.86	120	1.35
11	2.98	31	1.84	150	1.31
12	2.82	32	1.82	200	1.26
13	2.69	33	1.80	300	1.21
14	2.58	34	1.79	400	1.18
15	2.48	35	1.77	500	1.16
16	2.40	36	1.76	750	1.13
17	2.33	37	1.74	1000	1.11
18	2.27	38	1.73	2000	1.08
19	2.22	39	1.72		
20	2.17	40	1.70		
21	2.12	42	1.68		
22	2.08	44	1.66		
23	2.05	46	1.64		
24	2.01	48	1.62		
25	1.98	50	1.61		

mally change unless a substantial basic change in the process has occurred. To see if the sigma has changed, we do an F test.

Problem #7

Suppose that in our now-familiar shaft example we take two samples. (They could be from one lathe, or from two different lathes doing the same job.) We have already plotted the samples and found that the shape of the distributions were not substantially different. We now want to know if the sample sigmas are significantly different with a 95% confidence.

Sample 1
$\bar{x}_1 = 0.9982"$
$s_1 = 0.00273"$
$n_1 = 21$

Sample 2
$\bar{x}_2 = 1.0006"$
$s_2 = 0.00162"$
$n_2 = 19$

As before, we must first check the sigma to see if the two processes are significantly different. We therefore calculate the F test value and compare this with the value in the simplified F table (Figure 12-3).

Since our sample sizes are within 20% of each other, we can use the previous formula.

$$F_t = \frac{s_1{}^2}{s_2{}^2} = \frac{0.00273"^2}{0.00162"^2} = 2.840$$

We now compare 2.840 with the value in the simplified F table (Figure 12-3). Use the average n = 20 to find the table value, which is 2.17. Since our calculated value is greater than the table value, we can say with a 95% confidence that the two processes' sigmas are different. We must now decide what the cause and ramifications are of this change in the sigma.

Problem #8

Suppose that in our shaft example we take two samples. (They could be from one lathe or from two different lathes doing the same job.)

We have already plotted samples and found that the distributions are not substantially different. We now want to know if the sample sigmas are significantly different with a 95% confidence.

Sample 1
$\bar{x}_1 = 0.9982"$
$s_1 = 0.00193"$
$n_1 = 21$

Sample 2
$\bar{x}_2 = 1.0006"$
$s_2 = 0.00162"$
$n_2 = 19$

Calculating an F_t:

$$F_t = \frac{s_1^2}{s_2^2} = \frac{0.001932^2}{0.00162^2} = 1.42$$

We now compare 1.42 to the value in the Simplified F Table (Figure 12-3). Use the average n = 20 to find the table value, which is 2.17. Since 1.42 is less than the table value of 2.17, we can't say with a 95% confidence that the processes are different (with regard to their sigmas).

We now test to see if the two sample averages are significantly different.

3. Checking the Averages

Since we did *not* find that either the distribution shape or sigma had changed, we now test whether the two sample averages are significantly different. We calculate a *t-test value* (t_t) to compare with a value in the Simplified t Distribution Table (Figure 12-2).

FORMULA

t Test of Two Sample Averages $\bar{x}_1$ and $\bar{x}_2$

$$t_t = \frac{|\bar{x}_1 - \bar{x}_2|}{\sqrt{\left(\frac{n_1 s_1^2 + n_2 s_2^2}{n_1 + n_2}\right)\left(\frac{1}{n_1} + \frac{1}{n_2}\right)}}$$

$\bar{x}_1$ and $\bar{x}_2$ are two sample averages.
s_1 and s_2 are the sigmas on the two samples.
n_1 and n_2 are the two sample sizes.
$|\bar{x}_1 - \bar{x}_2|$ is the absolute difference between the averages, ignoring a minus sign in the difference.

We then compare this calculated t-test value against the value in the simplified t distribution table (Figure 12-2). If our calculated t-test number is greater than the value in the table, then we are 95% confident that the sample averages are significantly different.

Returning to problem #8, we must calculate our test t_t:

$\bar{x}_1 = 0.9982"$ $\bar{x}_2 = 1.0006"$
$s_1 = 0.00193"$ $s_2 = 0.00162"$
$n_1 = 21$ $n_2 = 19$

$$t_t = \frac{|\bar{x}_1 - \bar{x}_2|}{\sqrt{\left(\frac{n_1 s_1^2 + n_2 s_2^2}{n_1 + n_2}\right)\left(\frac{1}{n_1} + \frac{1}{n_2}\right)}}$$

$$t_t = \frac{\left|0.9982" - 1.0006"\right|}{\sqrt{\left(\dfrac{21(0.00193")^2 + 19(.00162")^2}{21+19}\right)\left(\dfrac{1}{21} + \dfrac{1}{19}\right)}} = 4.24$$

We now compare this 4.24 with the value from the simplified t distribution table (Figure 12-2). (Use $n = n_1 + n_2 - 1 = 39$.) Since the calculated 4.24 is greater than the table value of 2.024, we can conclude with a 95% confidence that the two process means are significantly different.

We would normally want to find out why and decide what we are going to do with this knowledge.

Tests on Averages and Sigmas Never Prove "Sameness"
The chi-squared, F, and t tests test only for significant difference. If these tests do not show a significant difference, it does not prove that the two samples or the sample and population are identical. It just means that with the amount of data we have we can't conclude with a 95% confidence that they are different. Confidence tests never prove that two things are the same!

TIP

INCIDENTAL STATISTICS TERMINOLOGY NOT USED IN ABOVE TESTS

You will not find the term *null-hypothesis* used in the above confidence tests, but it is implied by the way the tests are done. Null -hypothesis is a term that is often used in statistics books to mean that your base assumption is that nothing (null) changed. (An analogy is someone being assumed innocent until proven guilty.)

This assumption is included in the above tests and it is the basis for the above Tip that the hypothesis tests never prove "sameness." (Again, just because a person is not proven guilty does not necessarily mean that he or she is innocent.) There is no need to add the complexity of the term "null -hypothesis" when the nature of the tests implies it.

Several of the tables used in this book are titled as "simplified." This includes the chi-squared, F, and t tables. The main simplification relates to the column showing sample size n. In most other statistics books, the equivalent chi-squared, F, and t tables label this column as "degrees of freedom." One statistics book states that "degrees of freedom" is one of the most difficult terms in statistics to describe. The statistics book then goes on to show that, in almost all cases, "degrees of freedom" is equivalent to n – 1. This therefore becomes the knee-jerk translation (n – 1 = "degrees of freedom") of almost everyone using tables with degrees of freedom.

The chi-squared, F, and t tables in this book are shown with the n – 1 equivalency built in. This was done to make life easier. In the extremely rare cases where "degrees of freedom" is not equivalent to n – 1, the resultant error will be trivial in comparison with the accuracy requirements of the results. The validity of your Six Sigma test results will not be compromised.

You may need this (n – 1 = "degrees of freedom") equivalency if you refer to other tables or use software with "degrees of freedom" requested.

Additional Practice Problems

Problem #9
An insurance company wants to see if costs on a certain medical procedure have changed in the last three months. They have much historical data showing that the distribution shape stayed the same over the years even when costs changed. They are not aware of anything that would have influenced a change in the distribution. The historical average price for this procedure was $387.61, with a sigma of $12.76. They want to be able to identify a cost change as low as $4.00 and be 95% confident of the answer (so they know whether to change rates).

a. Will they have to plot data to compare distributions?

b. What is the minimum number of random procedure costs they will have to sample?

Using the sample number n obtained above, the recent sample cost data on this procedure indicate an average price of $391.04 and a sigma of $14.23.

c. Does the sigma change indicate that the cost variation is no longer the same as historical?

d. If the above test does not show a significant sigma change, is the average change significantly different?

Problem #10
After analyzing the above sample, the insurance company decides to take a similar sample from a separate district to see if the two district sample costs are different. The two districts have much historical data showing that the distribution shapes are similar and have stayed the same over the years even when costs changed. They are not aware of anything that

would have influenced a change in the distributions. As given above, the first district sample had an average price of $391.04 and a sigma of $14.23. The second district sample had an average price of $384.97 with a sigma of $16.06. Are the two districts different at a 95% confidence?

Solutions to Additional Practice Problems

Problem #9

An insurance company wants to see if costs on a certain medical procedure have changed in the last three months. They have much historical data showing that the distribution shape stayed the same over the years even when costs changed. They are not aware of anything that would have influenced a change in the distribution. The historical average price for this procedure was $387.61, with a sigma of $12.76. They want to be able to identify a cost change as low as $4.00 and be 95% confident of the answer (so they know whether to change rates).

a. Will they have to plot data to compare distributions?

Technically no, because they have historical plots showing that the distributions are stable and no knowledge of anything that would have affected the distribution (like a change in the procedure). However, it never hurts to do an additional plot and, since the data are being collected anyway, it seems like a prudent thing to do.

b. What is the minimum number of random procedure costs they will have to sample?

$$n = \left(\frac{Z * S}{h}\right)^2$$

Z = 1.96
S = $12.76
h = $4.00

$$n = \left(\frac{1.96 * \$12.76}{\$4.00}\right)^2$$

n = 39.09

So, the insurance company will have to sample a minimum of 40 procedure costs.

Using the sample number n obtained above, the recent sample cost data on this procedure indicate an average price of $391.04 and a sigma of $14.23.

c. **Does the sigma change indicate that the cost variation is no longer the same as historical?**

$$\text{Chi}_t^2 = \frac{(n-1)s^2}{S^2}$$

n = 40

s = \$14.23

S = \$12.76

$$\text{Chi}_t^2 = \frac{(40-1)(\$14.23)^2}{(\$12.76)^2}$$

$$\text{Chi}_t^2 = 48.50$$

Looking at the simplified chi-squared distribution table (Figure 12-1), n = 40, the low-test value is 23.6543, and the high-test value is 58.12005. Since our calculated Chi_t^2 value of 48.50 is between these two numbers, we can't say with a 95% confidence that the sigma has changed.

d. **If the above test does not show a significant sigma change, is the average change significantly different?**

Since we did not find that the sigma has changed, we check the average.

$$t_t = \frac{|\bar{x} - \bar{X}|}{\dfrac{s}{\sqrt{n}}}$$

$\bar{X}$ = \$387.61

$\bar{x}$ = \$391.04

s = \$14.23

n = 40

$$t_t = \frac{|\$391.04 - \$387.61|}{\dfrac{\$14.23}{\sqrt{40}}}$$

$$t_t = 1.524$$

The simplified t table (Figure 12-2), n = 40, shows that the t value is 2.023. Since the calculated $t_t = 1.524$ is not greater than 2.023, we can't say with a 95% confidence that the average has changed.

Problem #10

After analyzing the above sample, the insurance company decides to take a similar sample from a separate district to see if the two district sample costs are different. The two districts have much historical data showing that the distribution shapes are similar and have stayed the same over the years even when costs changed. They are not aware of anything that would have influenced a change in the distributions. As given above, the first district sample had an average price of $391.04 and a sigma of $14.23. The second district sample had an average price of $384.97 with a sigma of $16.06. Are the two districts different at a 95% confidence?

We do not have to plot the distributions and, as calculated in the above problem, the sample size for both samples is 40.

Checking the sigma:

$$F_t = \frac{s_1^2}{s_2^2} \text{ (put the larger s on top, as the numerator)}$$

$s_1 = \$16.06$

$s_2 = \$14.23$

$$F_t = \frac{(\$16.06)^2}{(\$14.23)^2}$$

$F_t = 1.274$

The simplified F table (Figure 12-3), n = 40, shows that F = 1.7. Since our calculated F_t value of 1.274 does not exceed 1.7, we can't say with a 95% confidence that the two samples' sigmas are different.

We can now check to see if the two sample averages are significantly different.

$$t_t = \frac{\left| \overline{x}_1 - \overline{x}_2 \right|}{\sqrt{\left(\frac{n_1 s_1^2 + n_2 s_2^2}{n_1 + n_2} \right) \left(\frac{1}{n_1} + \frac{1}{n_2} \right)}}$$

$\left| \overline{x}_1 - \overline{x}_1 \right| = \$6.07$

$s_1 = \$16.06$

$s_2 = \$14.23$

$n_1 = 40$

$n_2 = 40$

$t_t = 1.79$

The simplified t table (Figure 12-2), n = 80 (the closest table value to $n_1 + n_2 - 1 = 79$), shows that the t value is 1.99. Since the calculated $t_t = 1.79$ is not greater than 1.99, we can't say with a 95% confidence that the two district averages are different.

Note that in this problem another approach would have been to compare the second district sample with the first district population. The problem statement, however, specified comparing the two samples.

WHAT WE HAVE LEARNED IN CHAPTER 12

1. Valid sampling and analysis of variables data are needed for the Define, Measurement, Analysis, and Control steps in the DMAIC process.
2. Variables data are usually in decimal form, with no discrete "steps."
3. 11 is the rule-of-thumb minimum sample size on variables data.
4. When possible, use the formulas to determine minimum sample size.
5. We seldom have complete data on a population, but use samples to estimate its composition.
6. The greater the sample size, the better the estimate on the population.
7. Sample size is usually a compromise between cost and desire for accuracy.
8. We normally work to a 95% confidence test level.
9. Assume two-tailed (high *and* low) problems unless specifically indicated as one-tailed.
10. We normally want to sense a change equal to 10% of the tolerance, or 0.6S.
11. When checking for a change, we can compare a sample with earlier population data or compare two samples with each other.
12. We follow a three-step process when analyzing for change. Compare distribution shapes first, then sigmas, and then averages. If significant change is identified at any step in the process we stop. We then must decide what to do with the knowledge that the process changed.
13. Change analysis is useful on any process or population where data are available.

RELATED READING AND SOFTWARE

Statistics for the Utterly Confused, Lloyd R. Jaisingh (New York: McGraw-Hill, 2000).

Statistics at Square One, T.D.V. Swinscow and M.J. Cambell, 10th edition (London: BMJ Books, 2001).

Basic Statistics: Tools for Continuous Improvement, Mark J. Kiemele, Stephen R. Schmidt, and Ronald J. Berdine, 4th edition (Colorado Springs, CO: Air Academy Press, 1997).

MINITAB 13, Minitab Inc., State College, PA, www.minitab.com.

Testing for Statistically Significant Change Using Proportional Data

W hat you will learn in this chapter is to use limited samples on proportional data. This chapter will parallel the last chapter, in which we learned to use limited samples on variables data. Valid sampling and analysis of proportional data may be needed in all steps in the DMAIC process.

Changes in Real Processes, Proportional Data

Manufacturing Use samples of scrap parts to calculate proportions on shifts or similar production lines. Look for statistically significant differences in scrap rate.

Sales Sample and compare proportions of successful sales by different salespeople.

Marketing Use polls to prioritize where advertising dollars should be spent.

Accounting and Software Development Use samples to compare error rates of groups or individuals.

Receivables Sample overdue receivables, then compare proportions and due dates on different product lines. Adjust prices on products with statistically significant different overdue receivables.

APPLICATIONS

Insurance Sample challenged claims versus total claims in different groups, then compare proportions. Adjust group prices accordingly.

Proportional Data
Proportional data are based on attribute inputs, such as "good" or "bad," "yes" or "no," etc. Examples are the proportion of defects in a process, the proportion of "yes" votes for a candidate, and the proportion of students failing a test.

DEFINITION

Data Type
Because of the large sample sizes required when using proportional data, if possible use variables data instead.

TIP

When people are interviewed on their preferences in an upcoming election, the outcome of the sampling is proportional data. The interviewer asks whether a person is intending to vote for a candidate, "yes" or "no." After polling many people, the pollsters tabulate the proportion of "yes" (or "no") results versus the total of people surveyed. This kind of data requires very large sample sizes. That is why pollsters state that, based on polling over 1000 people, the predictions are accurate within 3% or ±3% (with a 95% confidence). We will be able to validate this with the following sample size formula (at 95% confidence).

Calculating Minimum Sample Size and Sensitivity, Proportional Data

FORMULA

$$n = \left(\frac{1.96\sqrt{(p)(1-p)}}{h} \right)^2$$

n = sample size of attribute data, like "good" or "bad" (95% confidence)
p = probability of an event (the proportion of defects in a sample, chance of getting elected, etc.) (When in doubt use p = 0.5, the most conservative.)
h = sensitivity, or accuracy required
   (For example, for predicting elections it may be ±3%, or h = 0.03. Another guideline is to be able to sense 10% of the tolerance or difference between the proportions.)

Note that the formula shown above can be rewritten as:

$$h = 1.96\sqrt{\frac{(p)(1-p)}{n}}$$

   This allows us to see what sensitivity h we will be able to sense at a given sample size and probability.

Let's do an election example. If the most recent polls show that a candidate has a 20% chance of getting elected, we may use p = 0.2. We will want an accuracy of +/-3% of the total vote, so h = 0.03.

p = 0.2

h = 0.03

$$n = \left(\frac{1.96\sqrt{(p)(1-p)}}{h}\right)^2$$

$$n = \left(\frac{1.96\sqrt{(0.2)(1-0.2)}}{.03}\right)^2$$

n = 682.95

So, we would have to poll 683 (round up) people to get an updated probability on someone whose estimated chance of being elected was 20% in earlier polls. However, if we had no polls to estimate a candidate's chances or we wanted to be the most conservative, we would use p = 0.5.

p = 0.5

h = 0.03

$$n = \left(\frac{1.96\sqrt{(p)(1-p)}}{h}\right)^2$$

$$n = \left(\frac{1.96\sqrt{(0.5)(1-0.5)}}{.03}\right)^2$$

n = 1067.1

In this case, with a p = 0.5, we would need to poll 1068 (round up) people to be within 3% in estimating the chance of the candidate being elected.

As you can see, the sample size of 683, with p = 0.2, is quite a bit less than the 1068 required with p = 0.5. Since earlier polls may no longer be valid, most pollsters use the 1068 as a standard. Using this formula, we have verified the pollsters requiring over 1000 inputs on a close election to be within 3% on forecasting the election outcome with a 95% confidence.

Equally, because the forecast has only a 95% confidence, the prediction can be wrong 5% of the time!

Here is an example showing how, in everyday life, conclusions are regularly made on sample sizes that are too small. Calculate how many baseball games are needed, based on their win/loss records, before you can state with a 95% confidence that one team is 20% different from the others. At the start of the season, we will assume that all teams are equal, so we use the most conservative p = 0.5. h would then be 20% of p (0.2 * 0.5 = 0.1 = h).

$$p = 0.5$$

$$h = 0.1$$

$$n = \left(\frac{1.96\sqrt{(p)(1-p)}}{h}\right)^2$$

$$n = \left(\frac{1.96\sqrt{(0.5)(1-0.5)}}{0.10}\right)^2$$

$$n = 97$$

As you can see, they need to have played 97 games. Watch how early in the season fans talk about one team being far better or worse than the others and compare how many games have been played of the calculated 97 games required.

In some cases we have a choice of getting variables or attribute data.

Many companies choose to use go/no-go gauges for checking parts. This choice is made because go/no-go gauges are often easier to use than a variables gauge that gives measurement data. However, a go/no-go gauge checks only whether a part is within tolerance, either good or bad, and gives no indication as to how good or how bad. This generates attribute data that are then used to calculate proportions.

Any process improvement with proportions is far more difficult, because it requires much larger sample sizes than the variables data used in the examples in the previous chapter. Using a gauge that gives variables (measurement) data output is a better choice!

With proportional data, comparing samples or a sample versus the population involves comparing proportions stated as decimals. These comparisons can be "defects per hundred" or of any other criteria that is consistent with both the sample and the population. Although these proportions can be stated as decimals, the individual inputs are still attributes.

Using Proportional Data as Variables Data
TIP
If you have multiple periods (at least 11) and you have calculated proportions for each period (using the minimum sample size formulas), you can calculate an average and a sigma of these periods and treat the resulting values as you would treat variables data. This is valid because each of the 11-plus multiple periods has decimal (continuous) values.

FORMULA

Comparing a Proportional Sample with the Population (95% Confidence)

First, we must calculate a test value Z_t.

$$Z_t = \frac{|p-P|}{\sqrt{\dfrac{P(1-P)}{n}}}$$

P = proportion of defects (or whatever) in the population (historical)
p = proportion of defects (or same as above) in the sample
|p − P| = absolute proportion difference (no minus sign in difference)
n = sample size
If $Z_t > 1.96$, then we can say with a 95% confidence that the sample is different from the population.

The following is the formula for comparing two proportion data samples with each other. We will then show a case study that incorporates the formulas for proportional data sample size, comparing a proportion sample with the population and comparing two proportion samples with each other.

FORMULA

Comparing Two Proportional Data Samples (95% Confidence)

Again, we must calculate a test value Z_t.

$$Z_t = \frac{\left|\dfrac{x_1}{n_1} - \dfrac{x_2}{n_2}\right|}{\sqrt{\left(\dfrac{x_1+x_2}{n_1+n_2}\right)\left(1-\dfrac{x_1+x_2}{n_1+n_2}\right)\left(\dfrac{1}{n_1}+\dfrac{1}{n_2}\right)}}$$

x_1 = number of defects (or whatever) in sample #1
x_2 = number of defects (or same as above) in sample #2

$\left|\dfrac{x_1}{n_1} - \dfrac{x_2}{n_2}\right|$ = absolute proportion difference (no minus sign in difference)

n_1 = size of sample #1
n_2 = size of sample #2
If $Z_t > 1.96$, then we can say with a 95% confidence that the two samples are significantly different.

CASE STUDY: TESTING IF AN AUTOMATIC PACKER DAMAGED PRODUCT

A fragile component was automatically packed using a high-speed packing machine. The component was then shipped to another plant, where it was assembled into a final consumer product. This assembly took place in a complex machine that would jam if a component broke.

The assembly machine was experiencing excessive downtime, because 0.1% of the fragile components were breaking during assembly. The assembly plant suspected that the components were being cracked during the automatic packing process at the component plant. This crack would then break during assembly, causing downtime.

In order to test this theory, a test would be run in which half the product would be packed manually while the other half was being packed automatically. This randomness would make the populations of the automatically packed components and the manually packed components the same, other than any cracks resulting from the packing process.

The original goal was to use a minimum sample size able to sense a 10% difference between the two test samples (manual and auto pack). However, this sample was found to be extremely large, exceeding the realities of being able to run a good test.

As a compromise, it was decided to use a test sensitivity of 50% for the difference between the two samples. This approach was thought to be reasonable, since many felt that the automatic packer was the dominant source of the cracks and that the difference between the two samples would therefore be dramatic. Even with the reduced sensitivity, the calculated minimum sample size was 15,352 manually packed components!

The tests were run, with 15,500 components being manually packed and 15,500 components being auto packed. This was to be used to verify that the 0.1% breakage historical baseline had not changed.

The results were that 12 of the automatically packed components and four of the manually packed components broke when assembled. It was determined that this difference was statistically significant. Because of the costs involved of rebuilding the packer, the test was rerun and the results were similar.

The automatic packer was rebuilt and the problem of components breaking in the assembly operation was no longer an issue.

Since the above case study incorporates all of the formulas we have covered in the use of samples on proportion data, we will use a series of problems to review in detail how the case study decisions were reached. Note that in the above study they not only checked the manual sample against the historical population defect level, but also collected a current auto-packed sample in order to verify that the defect level did not just happen to be lower (or higher) during the test.

Problem #1

Assuming we wish to be able to sense a 10% defect difference between a proportional data sample of components and an earlier population (or another proportional sample) and the historical defect level is 0.1%, what is the minimum number of samples we must study? Assume 95% confidence.

$p = 0.001$

$h = 0.0001$ (which is 10% of p)

$$n = \left(\frac{1.96\sqrt{(p)(1-p)}}{h}\right)^2$$

$$n = \left(\frac{1.96\sqrt{(0.001)(1-0.001)}}{0.0001}\right)^2$$

$n = 383{,}776$

Answer: We would have to check 383,776 components to have a 95% confidence that we could see a change of 0.01%.

You can see why they concluded that this was an excessive number of components to test.

Problem #2

Assuming we wish to be able to sense a 50% defect difference between a proportional data sample of components and an earlier population (or another proportional sample) and the historical defect level is 0.1%, what is the minimum number of samples we must study? Assume 95% confidence.

$p = 0.001$

$h = 0.0005$ (which is 50% of p)

$$n = \left(\frac{1.96\sqrt{(p)(1-p)}}{h}\right)^2$$

$$n = \left(\frac{1.96\sqrt{(0.001)(1-0.001)}}{0.0005}\right)^2$$

$n = 15{,}352$ (round up)

Answer: We would have to check 15,352 components to have a 95% confidence that we could see a change of 0.05%.

Although this is still a high number to test, it is only 4% of the 383,776 we calculated were needed to see a change of 0.0001. The minimum sample size changes dramatically with a change in sensitivity h.

Problem #3

12 of 15,500 (0.0774%) automatically packed components broke. This was less than the 0.1% that historically broke. Is the difference between this test sample with 12 defects and the historical 0.1% statistically significant?

P = 0.001
p = 0.000774
n = 15,500

$$Z_t = \frac{|p-P|}{\sqrt{\frac{P(1-P)}{n}}}$$

$$Z_t = \frac{|0.000774 - 0.001|}{\sqrt{\frac{0.001(1-0.001)}{15500}}}$$

$Z_t = 0.89$

Answer: Since 0.89 is less than the test value of 1.96, we can't say with a 95% confidence that the sample is different from the population. So, the test sample with the 12 defects is not significantly different from the historical 0.1% defect rate.

Problem #4

4 of 15,500 (0.0258%) manually packed components broke during assembly. Is this significantly different from the 0.1% that historically broke?

P = 0.001
p = 0.000258
n = 15,500

$$Z_t = \frac{|p-P|}{\sqrt{\frac{P(1-P)}{n}}}$$

$$Z_t = \frac{|0.000258 - 0.001|}{\sqrt{\frac{0.001(1-0.001)}{15500}}}$$

$Z_t = 2.92$

Answer: Since 2.92 is greater than the test value of 1.96, we can say with a 95% confidence that the sample is different from the population. So, the manual pack test is significantly different from the historical 0.1% breakage.

Problem #5

A baseline sample was collected during the test; in this baseline sample, 12 of 15,500 automatically packed components were broken. 4 of 15,500 manually packed test components broke during assembly. Is the manually packed sample breakage statistically significantly different from the breakage in the baseline sample?

$x_1 = 12$

$x_2 = 4$

$n_1 = 15,500$

$n_2 = 15,500$

$$Z_t = \frac{\left| \dfrac{x_1}{n_1} - \dfrac{x_2}{n_2} \right|}{\sqrt{\left(\dfrac{x_1 + x_2}{n_1 + n_2} \right)\left(1 - \dfrac{x_1 + x_2}{n_1 + n_2} \right)\left(\dfrac{1}{n_1} + \dfrac{1}{n_2} \right)}}$$

$$Z_t = \frac{\left| \dfrac{12}{15500} - \dfrac{4}{15500} \right|}{\sqrt{\left(\dfrac{12 + 4}{15500 + 15500} \right)\left(1 - \dfrac{12 + 4}{15500 + 15500} \right)\left(\dfrac{1}{15500} + \dfrac{1}{15500} \right)}}$$

$Z_t = 2.001$

Answer: Since 2.001 is greater than the test value of 1.96, we can say with a 95% confidence that the manual pack test sample is significantly different from the baseline sample.

The reason we checked the manual packed sample against both the historical population and the baseline sample is that, even though the baseline was not statistically different from the historical breakage, the baseline sample had a lower defect result that could have been different enough to have it pass the sample/population test but fail the sample/sample test. If this conflicting result had occurred, we would have had to make a decision whether or not to rerun the test.

As it was, because of the cost of rebuilding the packer, the test was rerun anyway, with similar results. The decision was then made to rebuild the packer.

Just for interest, after the packer was rebuilt the test was run a third time. This time the automatic packer had zero defects, whereas the manual pack still had some defects. Apparently the manual pack was not as gentle as assumed and it was causing some cracks.

CASE STUDY: ISOLATING BAD PRODUCT!

A factory producing a glass component had a process that wasn't very robust. It produced, on the average, 15% bad product and the outgoing quality relied on an inspector who was on-line to reject bad product before the components were packed by an automatic packing machine. This inspector sat in front of a conveyor belt, where the product went by in a single line at 50 pieces per minute, and the inspector looked at each piece, without picking it up. If the inspector saw a defect, he or she picked it up and discarded it.

The components were shipped to an assembly plant, where they were unpacked manually and loaded into an assembly machine. Since the components were unloaded manually, the assembly plant was able to do some incoming inspection, so they had agreed to accept product with a defect rate as high as 3%. Their experience was that when the rate was higher than 3% their incoming inspection was not capable of segregating the defective components, so some got into the assembly machine. The defects would then cause a machine wreck or, even worse, cause the finished product to be defective.

The assembly plant had complained for many months that they were often seeing skids of components arrive with well over the 3% allowable defects. Since they didn't see the manufacturer taking any measurable corrective action, they began taking samples from the top layer of each incoming skid of glass components. They would inspect 250 pieces: if they found 15 or more defects, they would reject the whole skid, which was in excess of 3000 components.

The manufacturer protested vehemently, saying that the sample was invalid since it came from only the top layer of parts and so, they argued, it was not representative of the whole skid. The customer didn't want to hear it! They were seeing fewer machine wrecks since they had started sampling incoming components and rejecting "bad" skids, so they were going to continue. The assembly plant was rejecting 20% of the incoming product and, to add insult to injury, subtracting the labor cost of this incoming sampling from their payment for the glass components. This cost was in addition to the costs for the resultant re-inspection and for product losses due to the 20% returned product.

The management of the component plant asked its home-office engineering team to get involved and find a more cost-effective solution to the ongoing conflict over component quality. Obviously the ideal solution was to fix the root cause, a non-robust process. But the plant had put a lot of time, hours, and money into this process over the years and the engineering team, although confident, was not going to bet on being able to fix this process within three months, which was the time target they were given to resolve the problem.

The company was just beginning to implement the Six Sigma process, so the engineers decided to start using some of the tools. First, they defined the problem better. They had a meeting with representatives from both plants, including several operators and inspectors from the glass plant. After getting through some initial emotional outbursts, they were able to develop a realistic problem definition.

The first part of the problem definition was that, when the glass process was producing an unusually high level of defects, the on-line inspector was unable to effectively segregate the defective components. The second part of the problem definition was that, when defective components were returned several weeks after production, the operator did not know when these incidents of higher defects had occurred, which made it more difficult to tweak the process to an acceptable defect level. The operator needed quicker feedback about when the quality was declining. Even though the operator regularly looked at product as it was being produced, the sample size was too small and the inspection was not rigorous enough to allow a valid judgment on defect level.

So, here was the project as a result of the project definition. The goal was to isolate incidents when the glass process was producing excessive defects and to notify the operator. This isolated product should be held for re-inspection before being sent to the assembly plant. The problem was that there was no current measure of the process defect level by which to ascertain when it reached an excessive level, since it had already been demonstrated that the on-line inspector was not effective in finding defects at high levels. What was needed was an additional quality sample of the product before inspection.

Of course, management had told the engineering team to solve this problem without additional plant labor. The team had some money for some minor on-line physical changes and computers, but the "no extra labor" directive was firm.

They met with the plant on-line inspectors and it was agreed that the inspectors could periodically pick up a random product, inspect it, and key the inspection result into the computer system. The rate agreed upon to not impede the current inspection efficiency was one product every 15 seconds. The thought was that the packed components would be held in a queue on a conveyor line coming out of the packing machine while the samples pulled from production were being gathered. Once the sample was large enough to make a statistically valid decision on its quality, then all of the packed components would either be released for shipment to the customer or be set aside for another inspection.

The team now had a means of collecting samples of the components as they were produced. However, what interested the customer was the quality of the product *after* it was inspected on-line. So, the team had to figure some way to "predict" the outgoing quality (after the on-line inspection) based on the quality of the product coming to the inspector.

The team took samples of the product going to the inspector, immediately returning components to the production line after sampling them. They again sampled the same product after the on-line inspection. In this way they were able to ascertain the effectiveness of the inspector on each type of defect. They found that the on-line inspection was approximately 90% effective on large defects, like chips, and only 30% effective on small defects, like small cracks in the rim of the product.

Since the samples pulled from the line for inspection every 15 seconds were going to be keyed into the computer in terms of defect type, this proportion of effectiveness was applied to each defect type to predict what level of defect would go on to the customer. For example, for every 10 large defects found by the inspector in the 15-second samples, it was assumed that one would get to the customer and that seven out of 10 small defects would get through to the customer. With the "effectiveness" correction applied to each defect, it was possible to predict the outgoing quality after the on-line inspection.

The customer had been inspecting incoming components in samples of 250 pieces, rejecting any skid that had 15 or more defects out of the 250. The sensitivity (h) on this sample size was 3%, so the actual defect level was between 3% and 9%, with a 95% confidence. The glass plant decided to use the same sampling based on the predicted outgoing defect level. This wasn't very selective, but proportional data made any sampling difficult. The sample size could be increased, but then the hold time made the queue of held components too large for the conveyor coming out of the packing machine. As it was, at one sample every 15 seconds, it took 75 minutes to get the sample size of 250 components and up to 3750 pieces were in hold. (The actual time required to get the 250 samples was 62.5 minutes, but some allowance was made for missed samples.)

The customer had been rejecting 20% of the product. The engineering team had set a goal that not more than 10% of the product would be held for re-inspection at the glass plant. This would save half the re-inspection cost, plus the costs the customer was billing the plant for incoming sampling and shipping costs to return components labeled defective. The 10% re-inspection goal was felt to be reasonable, because the new sampling plan included a provision to send the defect information to the operator. This information would be displayed on a computer monitor as simplified control charts (which we will cover in a later chapter). In the early meetings, the operators had indicated that these control charts would enable them to address process issues far sooner than they could without this information.

To ensure that the inspector would pick up a random product sample every 15 seconds, a photocell, a timer, and a small air cylinder were installed upstream of the inspector. Every 15 seconds, the next product that came in front of the photocell was displaced slightly by the air cylinder. The inspector was to pick this product up as the sample to inspect. If the inspector found a defect, he or she keyed the defect type into the computer. To save the inspector unnecessary work, no keyboard entry was required when no defect was found. The inspector then set aside the sample, defective or good. To ensure that the inspector had picked up the sample, additional photocells downstream from the inspector verified that there was a space on the conveyor belt where the selected sample had been. If there was a space and no defect had been entered into the computer by the inspector, then the inspected product was counted as "good." If there was no space, it was assumed that the inspector had not taken the selected sample. If, after 75 minutes of holding, there were not at least 250 samples that had been inspected, then the held components were put into re-inspection because the sample size was insufficient. (An interesting note on this feature was that it was self-policing. If an operator's product was put into re-inspection because the inspector had not taken sufficient samples, the operators were able to address the problem themselves. No action was required by supervisors.)

As this project was unfolding, there was quite a lot of negativity expressed in both plants. Many at the supplier plant, including the quality manager and production manager, felt that the system would just put all the products into re-inspection. These people had no faith in the statistical procedures that were being applied and did not believe the operator would do better with the simplified control chart information on defects. As stated earlier, they were just starting with Six Sigma and they were not yet comfortable with the methodology. Meanwhile, many people at the customer plant also had little faith in this approach to the problem. They felt that the supplier should either go after the root cause (the non-robust process) or add more inspection labor.

Once the project was implemented, everyone was anxious to see how it did. Well, it exceeded all expectations. The customers were so satisfied with the incoming product that they stopped sampling. The components being held for re-inspection at the glass plant were 6%—less than the 10% team goal.

The management of the glass plant was so happy with the project that, in the year following the project, it implemented a similar system on all similar production lines.

As was noted, when this project was implemented, Six Sigma was just being introduced. If this project were to be done now, more Six Sigma tools would be used. If a QFD and FMEA had been used on this project, it probably would have reduced some of the negativity of the people, since more of them would have felt involved and their input would have been considered early in the project. Also, if they had been fully trained in Six Sigma, they would have had more faith in the power of the statistical methods applied.

Additional Practice Problems

Problem #6

A software company has a development group of 10 people whose primary job is to write code. However, on a rotating basis, they also answer user questions related to past programs. Since many of the code-writers would prefer just writing code, the company wants to know if the time spent answering these questions justifies assigning a person whose sole function would be to answer questions, not write code. Since the new position would involve taking a person away from the development group, management wants to make sure it would be freeing up at least 10% (one person) of the time of the current group. Although the manager is not sure what percentage of time is being spent on answering questions, he is reasonably sure it isn't over 20%.

To get an estimate of the time spent on answering questions, the manager decides that, from time to time, at random, he will survey the 10 members of the development group to find out whether they are working on a customer question at that given time. So, each time he surveys he gets a sample of 10 inputs. Assume the total hours worked by the group in a day to be 80 and that the program questions come in at a constant and uniform level.

How many times must the manager survey to get a group accuracy of two hours/day at a 95% confidence level? Assuming he randomly surveys 10 times per day, how many days will it take him to get an answer?

Problem #7

Assume that in the above survey the manager finds that the group is spending seven hours a day answering questions, so he decides not to reassign a person just to answer questions.

Six months later, an identical survey finds that the group is spending nine hours answering questions. Is the result of this second survey statistically different from the result of the first survey?

What are the minimum results that the manager should see on the survey before he assigns a person to answer questions full time? Again, assume that the program questions come in at a constant and uniform level.

Solutions to Additional Practice Problems

Problem #6

A software company has a development group of 10 people whose primary job is to write code. However, on a rotating basis, they also answer user questions related to past programs. Since many of the code-writers would prefer just writing code, the company wants to know if the time spent answering these questions justifies assigning a person whose sole function would be to answer questions, not write code. Since the new position would involve taking a person away from the development group, management wants to make sure it would be freeing up at least 10% (one person) of the time of the current group. Although the manager is not sure what percentage of time is being spent on answering questions, he is reasonably sure it isn't over 20%.

To get an estimate of the time spent on answering questions, the manager decides that, from time to time, at random, he will survey the 10 members of the development group to find out whether they are working on a customer question at that given time. So, each time he surveys he gets a sample of 10 inputs. Assume the total hours worked by the group in a day to be 80 and that the program questions come in at a constant and uniform level.

How many times must the manager survey to get a group accuracy of two hours/day at a 95% confidence level? Assuming he randomly surveys 10 times per day, how many days will it take him to get an answer?

First, realize that two hours/day is 2/80, or 0.025 of the group's day. So, h will be 0.025.

p = 0.2 (Since the manager is sure that the time spent is not over 20%, 0.2 is the most conservative p value.)

h = 0.025 (to get an accuracy of two hours/day)

$$n = \left(\frac{1.96\sqrt{(p)(1-p)}}{h}\right)^2$$

$$n = \left(\frac{1.96\sqrt{(0.2)(1-0.2)}}{0.025}\right)^2$$

n = 984

Answer: Since the manager gets 10 replies every time he surveys, he must survey 99 times and get 990 replies. If he does this 10 times per day, he will have his answer in slightly less than 10 days.

Problem #7

Assume that in the above survey the manager finds that the group is spending seven hours a day answering questions, so he decides not to reassign a person just to answer questions.

Six months later, an identical survey finds that the group is spending nine hours answering questions. Is the result of this second survey statistically different from the result of the first survey?

What are the minimum results that the manager should see on the survey before he assigns a person to answer questions full time? Again, assume that the program questions come in at a constant and uniform level.

We must calculate a test value Z_t.

First, we must identify the values for the inputs to the equation:

n_1 = 990 (the manager asks 99 times and gets 10 replies each time)

n_2 = 990 (the manager asks 99 times and gets 10 replies each time)

x_1 = the number of times in the first survey that the developers were working on a customer problem

(Since seven hours is 7/80, or 0.0875, of the group's daily hours, the developers must have replied that they were working on customer problems 0.0875 * 990 = 87 times.)

x_1 = 87

x_2 = the number of times in the second survey that the developers were working on a customer problem

(Since nine hours is 9/80, or 0.1125, of the group's daily hours, the developers must have replied that they were working on customer problems 0.1125 * 990 = 111 times.)

$X_2 = 111$

$$Z_t = \frac{\left| \dfrac{X_1}{n_1} - \dfrac{X_2}{n_2} \right|}{\sqrt{\left(\dfrac{X_1 + X_2}{n_1 + n_2} \right) \left(1 - \dfrac{X_1 + X_2}{n_1 + n_2} \right) \left(\dfrac{1}{n_1} + \dfrac{1}{n_2} \right)}}$$

$$Z_t = \frac{\left| \dfrac{87}{990} - \dfrac{111}{990} \right|}{\sqrt{\left(\dfrac{87 + 111}{990 + 990} \right) \left(1 - \dfrac{87 + 111}{990 + 990} \right) \left(\dfrac{1}{990} + \dfrac{1}{990} \right)}}$$

$Z_t = 1.798$

Answer: Since 1.798 is not greater than the test value 1.96, we can't say with a 95% confidence that the nine-hour survey result is significantly different from the seven-hour survey result.

As for assigning someone to just answer customer questions, the manager wants to be confident that the survey shows the need to be significantly greater than eight hours a day. In this way he would be sure that the dedicated position would be full time.

To test this, set as the baseline that the population requires eight hours a day from the group for answering questions and see what survey result is required to be significantly different from that baseline. We will try a survey result of 10 hours for answering questions, since this is the eight-hour baseline plus the two hours we used for sensitivity h.

We must use the formula for comparing a sample with a population.

We first determine the value of the inputs to the equation:

$p = 0.125$ (10/80 of the group hours, our assumption to test)

$P = 0.1$ (8/80 of the group hours, our baseline)

$n = 990$ (from the previous calculation)

$$Z_t = \frac{|p-P|}{\sqrt{\dfrac{P(1-P)}{n}}}$$

$$Z_t = \frac{|0.125-0.1|}{\sqrt{\dfrac{0.1(1-0.1)}{990}}}$$

$$Z_t = 2.62$$

Answer: Since 2.62 is greater than the 1.96 test value, we can say with a 95% confidence that, with a survey answer of 10 hours, the loading is significantly different from the eight-hour baseline loading, so the assigned person would be loaded in terms of time.

When checking a sample versus a population, "P + sensitivity h" and "P – sensitivity h" will always show significance. This is because we set up the test to check for a 95% confidence at the h sensitivity.

WHAT WE HAVE LEARNED IN CHAPTER 13

1. Valid sampling and analysis of proportional data may be needed for all the steps in the DMAIC process.
2. Proportional data are generated from attribute inputs such as yes/no and go/no-go.
3. Testing for statistically significant change with proportional data involves comparing proportions stated as decimals.
4. Proportional data require much larger sample sizes than variables data.
5. Sample size is usually a compromise between cost and desire for accuracy.
6. We normally work to a 95% confidence level.
7. We generally want to be able to sense a change of 10% of the difference between the proportions or 10% of the tolerance.
8. When checking for a change, we can compare a sample with earlier population data or compare two samples with each other.
9. Change analysis using proportional data is useful anywhere we have proportions but don't have variables data.
10. Proportional data can be compared the same as variables data if we have a large number of periods with calculated proportions for each.

RELATED READING AND SOFTWARE

Statistics for the Utterly Confused, Lloyd R. Jaisingh (New York: McGraw-Hill, 2000).

Statistics at Square One, T.D.V. Swinscow and M.J. Cambell, 10th edition (London: BMJ Books, 2001).

Basic Statistics: Tools for Continuous Improvement, Mark J. Kiemele, Stephen R. Schmidt, and Ronald J. Berdine, 4th edition (Colorado Springs, CO: Air Academy Press, 1997).

MINITAB 13, Minitab Inc., State College, PA, www.minitab.com.

Testing for Statistically Significant Change Using Non-Normal Distributions

W hat we will learn in this chapter is that many distributions are non-normal and occur in many places, but that we can use the formulas and tables we have already reviewed to get meaningful information on any changes in the processes that generated these distributions. We often do Six Sigma work on non-normal processes.

Non-Normal Distributions

Manufacturing Any process having a zero at one end of the data is likely to have a skewed distribution. An example would be data representing distortion on a product.

Sales If your salespeople tend to be made up of two distinct groups, one experienced and the other inexperienced, the data distribution showing sales versus age is likely to be bimodal.

Marketing The data showing dollars spent in different markets may be non-normal because of a focus on specific markets.

Accounting and Software Development Error rate data may be strongly skewed based on the complexity or uniqueness of a program or accounting procedure.

APPLICATIONS

Receivables Delinquent receivables may be skewed based on the product or service.

Insurance Costs at treatment centers in different cities may be non-normal because of varying labor rates.

In the real world, non-normal distributions are commonplace. Below are some examples. Note that these are plots of the individual parts measurements.

Figure 14-1. Non-normal distribution examples

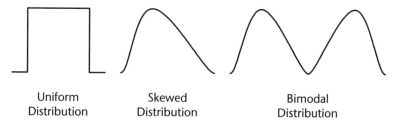

| Uniform | Skewed | Bimodal |
| Distribution | Distribution | Distribution |

Examples of where these would occur:

- The *uniform distribution* would occur if you plotted the numbers occurring on a roulette wheel or from rolling a single die.
- The *skewed distribution* would be typical of a one-sided process, like the non-flatness or positive warp on a machined part. Zero may be one end of the chart.
- The *bimodal distribution* can occur when there is play in a piece of equipment or where a process has a self-correcting feedback loop. This could also indicate that there are two independent processes involved.

In most classes on Six Sigma, one of the statistical tests is to check the plotted data to see if it is "normal." However, it often seems that, no matter what the outcome of this test, the analysis of the data proceeds as if the data were completely normal. For most Six Sigma work this is not a serious problem. Here is why.

If the population is not "normal," then the "absolute" probabilities generated from using computer programs or from tables may be somewhat in error. This would include results obtained from using the standardized normal distribution table (Figure 11-7). If we want to have good estimates of the absolute probabilities, the population must be normal to use any computer program or table based on a normal distribution.

However, since most of the work we do in Six Sigma involves comparing similar processes relatively (before and after or between two similar processes) to see if we have made a significant change, these relative comparisons are valid even if the data we are using are non-normal.

There are esoteric statistics based on non-normal distributions and software packages that will give more accurate estimates of actual probabilities, but they require substantial knowledge of statistics. This added degree of accuracy is not required for most Six Sigma work, where we are looking for significant change, not absolute defect values.

Statistical Tests on Variables, Non-Normal Data

TIP

You can use the included statistical tests for change, including referencing the numbers in the standardized normal distribution table (Figure 11-7), to compare a process before and after or to compare processes with similarly shaped non-normal distributions. However, it is important to know that, although the relative qualitative comparison is valid, the absolute probability values on each process may be somewhat inaccurate.

As in checking processes with normal distributions, the distributions that are non-normal must be periodically plotted to verify that the shapes of the distributions are still similar. If a distribution shape has changed dramatically, you can't use the formulas or charts in this book for before/after comparisons. It would be the proverbial apples vs. oranges thing! However, similar processes usually have and keep similarly shaped distributions.

CASE STUDY: TESTING FOR CHANGE ON NON-NORMAL DATA

A production plant made a product that was not flat enough. The customer wanted product with a maximum 0.020" non-flatness, a criterion that the production plant regularly exceeded. A plant engineer was assigned to solve this problem and came up with a new process that he felt would greatly reduce the non-flatness. The engineer had discovered that the non-flatness was directional, so he built into the process a "reverse non-flatness" to reduce the problem.

The production plant had non-flatness data (mean and sigma) from before the process change and the engineer got similar measurements after the process change. He then used the before/after data to support a claimed 95% reduction in product that exceeded the 0.020" maximum.

The customer questioned this conclusion, since the data were obviously skewed. (Since zero was the one end of the non-flatness data, there were many low values and a few higher values.) To calculate his 95% reduction, the engineer had used tables based on a normal distribution; the customer took issue with that. The engineer defended his approach, since he was looking at differences between the before/after data on similarly shaped distributions. He was using the absolute defect rates from before and after only for calculating the relative reduction in defects between the two.

The customer then took the raw data the engineer had used and redid the analysis using Crystal Ball 2000. This is a software package that enables users to fit the data to a skewed curve to get more accurate absolute defect levels. The percentage reduction that the customer calculated with the more difficult method was almost identical to the percentage reduction that the engineer had calculated.

As stated previously, the important thing to remember when comparing groups of data is that the two distributions can't have totally different shapes. It is critical for them to have a normal distribution only when we want to use absolute values for other than change comparisons.

Another important thing to know about non-normal distributions is that you should understand the reason why the distribution is non-normal. We have already mentioned some underlying causes, like having a zero at one end of the data. This would be the case when measuring the non-flatness of a plate. You would expect the data to be skewed, with many data points near zero and fewer points at the higher readings. If you get a non-normal distribution when you don't expect it, it should set off an alarm for you to identify the cause.

WHAT WE HAVE LEARNED IN CHAPTER 14

1. We often do Six Sigma work on non-normal processes.
2. You can use the included statistical tests for calculating differences on similarly shaped non-normal distributions.
3. The absolute probability values obtained may be someone inaccurate, but comparing probabilities to determine qualitative change on a process or on similar processes is valid.
4. As in checking processes with "normal" distributions, the distributions that are non-normal must be periodically plotted to verify that the shapes of the distributions are still similar. You cannot use standard statistical tests to compare differently shaped distributions.

5. Any distribution with a non-normal shape should be analyzed for cause. If the cause is not obvious, then an investigation should follow. Often large gains come from these surprise observations.

RELATED SOFTWARE

MINITAB 13, Minitab Inc., State College, PA, www.minitab.com.

Crystal Ball 2000, Decisioneering Inc., Denver, CO, www.decisioneering.com.

PART V

Additional
Six Sigma Tools

CHAPTER 15

Simplified Design of Experiments

What you will learn in this chapter is how to run a simplified Design of Experiments (DOE). The intent of a DOE is to optimize a process by finding the right settings for a set of key process input variables (KPIVs). This chapter applies to the Improve step in the DMAIC process. This chapter is primarily for those involved in manufacturing or process work.

Some Six Sigma practitioners feel that DOEs do not belong in a text for green belts, because DOEs are too complicated. Also, since there are whole books written just on this subject, these people don't believe that DOEs can properly be covered in a relatively few pages. These concerns may be valid for traditional DOEs, but the simplified DOE presented here has been used many times by green belts, with successful results.

First, some discussion on what a DOE entails. It is a controlled test of KPIVs, usually done right in the production environment using the actual production equipment. It attempts to measure all possible combinations of KPIVs, rather than taking a standard setup and modifying one variable at a time, one after the other. In this way the DOE attempts to find any interaction among variables and includes this interaction in identifying the optimum settings. Many dedicated DOE software programs attempt to predict the optimum settings even if they are in between the actual test settings.

That sounds good, right? It is, but here are some of the challenges:

1. It is difficult to identify a limited list of KPIVs to test. After all, if the process were all that well understood, you would not have to run the DOE!

2. It is difficult to keep in control the variables *not* being tested. These could include temperature, humidity, operator skill, etc.

3. A large number of test variables requires many trial iterations and setups. There are many reduced-iteration DOEs, but these all sacrifice statistical confidence.

4. One way a DOE can reduce the number of trials is to run with KPIV settings far outside normal ranges. The problem with this approach is that many processes become non-linear and any conclusions become suspect. Some processes can't even be run outside their normal settings because of process limitations.

5. The results of the DOE must then be tested under controlled conditions, since the real test of a process change is its ability to predict future results.

6. What to use as an output goal is not trivial. What if product variation is reduced, but so is product output? What if the process settings give an excellent product, but require more operator skill? Most software programs limit optimization to one output measurement.

Now that we have listed all the reasons a DOE may scare you, here is an effective way to run a simplified DOE that will minimize these difficulties and drive process improvement.

Note: The results of any DOE are usually *not* the key that drives the process improvement. Instead, it is the disciplined process of setting up and running the test that gives process insight. Observations made during the DOE often trigger process breakthroughs. *Serendipity* becomes dominant in this kind of test.

SIMPLIFIED DOE STEPS

Here are the steps to run an effective simplified DOE.

1. Hold a meeting with a representative from every group familiar with the process. These people may include a process operator, engineer, quality representative, and even someone from a supplier and a customer. Have them develop the list of key process input variables (KPIVs) and prioritize them. Use the fishbone diagram, correlation check, and process flow diagram in this process. Pick no more than three variables to test. If, after running the first simplified DOE, you feel you may not have picked the critical three, have the same group reprioritize the variables and run another simplified DOE.

2. Test combinations of variables. To test two variables (A and B), each at two values (1 and 2), there are four possible combinations: A1/B1, A2/B1, A1/B2, A2/B2. To test three variables, each at two values, there are eight combinations: A1/B1/C1, A2/B1/C1, A1/B2/C1, A1/B1/C2, A2/B2/C1, A2/B1/C2, A1/B2/C2, A2/B2/C2.

What makes a DOE difficult to run is that each of the combinations should be run a minimum of five times to get a valid statistical average for each iteration. This means that a test of two variables should have a minimum of 4 * 5 = 20 setups and a test of three variables should have a minimum of 8 * 5 = 40 setups. This assumes that the settings are run at the edge of, but within, the normal process window on each variable.

3. Do each setup independently of the earlier one. It is not valid to count multiple readings in one setup as the same as individual setups. Also, each setup should be in random order to reduce any influences of setup order.

Example of a Simplified DOE

Here is a simplified DOE to optimize the machining of a shaft so the average diameter is as close as possible to 1.0000", which is critical to the customer. After each setup, the lathe will be reset at the nominal 1.0000" using a standardized setup gauge. Assume the historical sigma = 0.0010".

The first thing to do is calculate the minimum number of shaft diameter readings that must be taken at each setup. This will determine the length of time each setup must be run. Using the equation from Chapter 12:

$n = \left(\dfrac{Z*S}{h}\right)^2$ to calculate minimum sample size on variables data

n = minimum sample size on variables data (always round up)

Z = confidence level (use Z = 1.96)

S = the population standard deviation (historically 0.0010")

h = the smallest change we want to be able to sense (h = 0.6S = 0.0006")

n = 11

We know from past runs that if we run 0.5 hour at each setup we will get at least 11 shafts during that 0.5 hour. So, for the simplified DOE, we will schedule the setup run length to be 0.5 hour.

Assume that, using a fishbone diagram, a knowledgeable group of people determined that machine tool design—rounded (R) or pointed (P)—and machining speed—fast (F) or slow (S)—are the two critical variables to test. The runs will each be 0.5 hour long. The test will be run seven hours per day for two days.

The four test combinations are R/F, R/S, P/F, and P/S. Each combination will be run seven times on a random basis, which is more than the five minimum required. This means there will be 4 * 7 = 28 setups. At each setup we will measure 11 shafts per our calculations on minimum sample size. So, we will have 28 * 11 = 308 individual shaft measurements being taken.

Figure 15-1 shows the results from the simplified DOE. The values within the table are the average and sigma of the 11 readings in each setup (in inches on the diameters). At the bottom of the table is the total of averages and sigmas for the seven runs, calculated using the Chapter 12 formulas.

Figure 15-1. Results from example simplified DOE

Run #	R/F Avg	R/F s	R/S Avg	R/S s	P/F Avg	P/F s	P/S Avg	P/S s
1	1.0005	0.00087	1.0003	0.00021	1.0007	0.00091	1.0002	0.00022
2	0.9991	0.00102	1.0001	0.00034	0.9998	0.00099	0.9996	0.00032
3	0.9996	0.00090	0.9995	0.00031	0.9999	0.00082	0.9994	0.00037
4	0.9997	0.00094	1.0003	0.00028	0.9997	0.00097	0.9989	0.00042
5	0.9991	0.00076	1.0001	0.00027	1.0011	0.00081	1.0004	0.00027
6	1.0005	0.00111	1.0006	0.00032	1.0005	0.00101	0.9995	0.00039
7	0.9999	0.00089	0.9997	0.00023	1.0009	0.00088	1.0006	0.00025
Total Avg	0.99977		1.00009		1.00037		0.99980	
Total s		0.00093		0.00028		0.00092		0.00033

Since the goal of the simplified DOE is to minimize the difference from a nominal 1.0000" diameter, the above results are restated below as to how much they deviated (delta) from 1.0000":

Group	R/F	R/S	P/F	P/S
Delta Avg from 1.0000"	0.00023"	0.00009"	0.00037"	0.00020"
Sigma S on reading	0.00093"	0.00028"	0.00092"	0.00033"

We can see from the results that the R/S (rounded tool, slow machining speed) resulted in the shafts closest to the nominal diameter, being off only 0.00009". This group also had the lowest sigma at 0.00028".

However, we must now check if this group is significantly different from the next closest group, which is P/S.

We use the three-step procedure to test for a change between two samples, from Chapter 12.

The first step is to plot the data from the two groups to see if the two distributions are substantially different. If they are dramatically different, we will know that we have two totally different processes and will not be able to use the following formulas to check for differences between the two groups. Then we would just use the raw data to make some judgment on which is preferred or decide to run more tests at the two settings.

Since we ran each combination seven times and had 11 measurements each time, we had 77 readings from each to plot, which is more than sufficient. Assume that these plots show that the distribution shapes are not substantially different.

We now do the second step, which is to compare the *sigma* of each group. Again, from Chapter 12:

F Test Comparing Two Sample Sigma s

$F_t = \dfrac{s_1^2}{s_2^2}$ (put the larger s on top, in the numerator)

$s_1 = 0.00033$

$s_2 = 0.00028$

$F_t = 1.389$

The sample sizes are both 77.

We now compare 1.389 with the value in the simplified F table (Figure 12-3). Use the average n = 80 (the closest value to 77 in the table) to find the table value, which is 1.45. Since 1.389 is less than the table value of 1.45, we can't say with a 95% confidence that the processes are different (with regard to their sigmas).

We should now see if this R/S *average* is significantly different from the average of the next-best results (P/S). In Chapter 12 we learned the formula for comparing two sample averages:

t Test of Two Sample Averages $\bar{x}_1$ and $\bar{x}_2$

$$t_t = \frac{\left| \bar{x}_1 - \bar{x}_2 \right|}{\sqrt{\left(\dfrac{n_1 s_1^2 + n_2 s_2^2}{n_1 + n_2} \right) \left(\dfrac{1}{n_1} + \dfrac{1}{n_2} \right)}}$$

$\bar{x}_1 = 0.00009"$

$\bar{x}_2 = 0.00020"$

$n_1 = 77$

$n_2 = 77$

$s_1 = 0.00028"$

$s_2 = 0.00033"$

$t_t = 2.230$

Compare $t_t = 2.230$ with the t value from the simplified t distribution table (Figure 12-2, n = 100+, t = 1.984). Since 2.230 > 1.984, we know that the two group averages are different with a 95% confidence.

Comparing the R/S group and the P/S group, we were not able to show that the sigmas were different at a 95% confidence level. The significant difference was in the average. However, if the setup gauge were modified to account for the 0.00020" the P/S group was off the 1.0000" nominal, the P/S group may have performed as well as the R/S group. So, if there was any advantage in using the pointed tool (like lower tool cost), then using the P/S setup should be considered.

Note that the fast speed (F) was worse with both tools. It would be advisable to run another test with the rounded tool with speed as the only variable, testing slightly faster and slightly slower than the first test slow speed (S). Once the speed is bracketed, then it is necessary to retest at the final tool/speed combination to verify that the results replicate.

Some items of note! First, everyone involved should be present at the simplified DOE, observing and taking notes. For example, it may have been noted that the lathe vibrated at the higher speed. In that case a lathe overhaul may have allowed the shaft to be machined at the higher speed with no loss of diameter consistency. This kind of observation during a DOE would not be unusual.

Pay Attention During Simplified Design of Experiments

As many people as possible with knowledge of the process should participate in a simplified DOE. They should be focused and not spend their time worrying about other problems. The reason this is important is that a DOE is a rare opportunity to observe a process under controlled conditions, and unexpected observations often trigger process breakthroughs. You need the best computers (brains) and the best sensors (eyes and ears).

TIP

Multiple simplified DOEs are often required, both to optimize results and to test the findings.

There are other considerations on reviewing the results of a simplified DOE. In the above example a slower machining speed caused less variation. But would the lower speed then raise costs? Maybe the most cost-effective option is to keep running at a higher speed, but add some inspection device to reject exceptionally large shafts.

In the chapter on simplified QFDs, there was a case study that described designing a test in-line tubing cutter. Here is what happened during the DOE using this piece of test equipment.

CASE STUDY: SIMPLIFIED DOE ON A TEST TUBING CUTTER

A simplified DOE was being run on a test in-line tubing cutter. The design of this machine was dictated by the output of a QFD done some months earlier. One of the setups involved testing a support spring that was added at the operators' insistence during the QFD. This involved a support wheel under the tubing that was to be supported with a spring.

The support spring initially picked to be run in the simplified DOE proved to be too weak to support the wheel. Someone had gone to get a stronger spring. Meanwhile, the manager went over to the wheel and supported it manually so the process could run while they were waiting. This brought the normal jokes about the manager now being a critical part of the process, etc.

The manager suggested that, rather than making jokes, they should be paying attention and taking every process reading possible. Holding the wheel up with minimum force enabled the tubing to be cut perfectly. Minimum force supporting the wheel was critical. If the manager had not been observant, this would not have been noticed and the KPIV would probably not have been discovered.

As you can see, carefully observing the simplified DOE and determining what to do with the results are as critical as setting up the simplified DOE with a correct procedure. The input from the operators during the QFD had caused the team to put the spring under the support wheel. But, the discovery that this spring had to be of minimum force came accidentally as the manager was supporting the wheel while someone was getting a stronger spring. The manager had played with the force as he was observing that he had a good cut and he had gotten a sense that it was critical to use minimal force.

For those choosing to run a traditional DOE, there are many task-specific software programs available and many versions of DOEs. These include screening DOEs that help limit the number of input variables to run in a full DOE. Although these programs are powerful, they must be understood completely and care must be taken when they are run. Screening DOEs sacrifice confidence and reduced-iteration DOEs often test outside normal parameters. As stated previously, testing outside normal parameters can cause a process to be extremely non-linear, making the predictions for optimum settings suspect. There is also a very real chance of damage to the equipment as a result of running at these unusual settings. There probably is a very good reason that the "normal" parameter limits are where they are; these reasons should be understood before ignoring them.

Use a Simplified DOE to Optimize a Machine or Process
If you have any machine or process with adjustments, the settings are probably not optimal unless someone has run a DOE. This is especially an opportunity for those machines or processes with product complaints from customers.

TIP

WHAT WE HAVE LEARNED IN CHAPTER 15

1. This chapter applies to the Improve step in the DMAIC process.
2. Simplified DOEs can give valuable process knowledge.
3. The benefit from any DOE often comes from the discipline of running a controlled test, rather than from the direct output of the DOE.
4. It is important to limit the test variables to three or fewer. Use a fishbone diagram to assist in identifying the variables to be tested.
5. The output goal to be optimized is limited to one.
6. It may require two runs of the simplified DOE to optimize and verify.
7. Everyone involved in a simplified DOE should spend close attention to detail, looking for any surprises.
8. DOEs with abbreviated setups or runs always sacrifice statistical confidence in the results.
9. The formulas covered in previous chapters are sufficient to run a simplified DOE. There are software packages that are specifically designed for traditional DOEs; however the user *must* take the time to understand all their quirks!

RELATED READING

Basic Statistics: Tools for Continuous Improvement, Mark J. Kiemele, Stephen R. Schmidt, and Ronald J. Berdine, 4th edition (Colorado Springs, CO: Air Academy Press, 1997).

Design and Analysis of Experiments, Douglas C. Montgomery, 5th edition (New York: John Wiley, 2001).

Understanding Industrial Designed Experiments (with CD-ROM), Stephen R. Schmidt and Robert G. Launsby, 4th edition (Colorado Springs, CO: Air Academy Press, 1997).

CHAPTER 16

Simplified
Control Charts

What you will learn in this chapter is how to make simplified control charts that are intuitive and improve process stability. This tool is used in the Improve and Control steps of the DMAIC process. This tool is primarily for those involved in manufacturing or process work.

Control charts have a chaotic history. In the 1960s, when Japan was showing the United States what quality really meant, some people here tried to implement some quick fixes, which included control charts. Few understood control charts and control charts were never used enough to realize their full potential.

Now with Six Sigma control charts are getting a second look and have had some impressive successes. However, in a society that is geared to make product within tolerances and with a workforce that generally thinks "sigma" is a health insurance company, control charts are a hard sell. But their potential has been proven and there is a way to implement them that people will more readily accept and use. That way is the simplified control chart.

Traditional control charts use two graphs. The simplified control chart has one graph. The rationale for this simplification is covered throughout the chapter.

In most cases, if a supplier can reduce defect excursions (incidents of higher-than-normal quality issues), the customers will be happy with the product. This does not necessarily mean that all products will be within specification. It means the customers have designed their processes to work with the normal incoming product. So, the emphasis should be on reducing defect excursions, which is the reason control charts were designed.

TRADITIONAL CONTROL CHARTS

Traditional control charts have two graphs.

The top graph is based on the process average, with statistically based control rules and limits telling the operator when the process is in or out of control. This graph cannot have any reference to the product tolerance because it displays product averages. By definition, a tolerance is for individual parts and is meaningless on averages. When tolerances are displayed on traditional control charts, which people sometimes try to do, they make no sense and can give an erroneous message that a process is running well when it isn't.

Displaying Tolerances on Control Charts
A tolerance, or specification limit, can't be displayed on a chart that is displaying averages and not the individual data values. It is not valid. Specifications refer to measurements of individual parts, not averages.

TIP

The second graph on traditional control charts is based on the process variation (or sigma), also with rules and limits.

If either of these graphs shows an out-of-control situation (based on a myriad of statistical rules), the operator is supposed to work on the process. However, the charts are somewhat confusing to the operators. Often the control chart shows an out-of-control situation while quality checks do not show product out-of-specification. Also, one graph can show the process in control while the other is showing it out of control.

SIMPLIFIED CONTROL CHARTS

A single chart, as used on the simplified control chart, can give the operator process feedback in a format that's understandable and intuitive and that encourages him or her to react before product is out of specification. It is intuitive because it shows the average and the predicted data spread on one bar. This is the way an operator actually thinks of his or her process.

Here is how it works.

Assume that the operator or an inspector is regularly getting variables data on a critical dimension. Without regular variables data that are entered into some kind of computer or network, control charts are not effective.

Sometimes people use control charts on proportional data based on attributes (example: defect/total), but if you look at the formulas in this book you will see that the error is generally huge because of the large sample size required on proportional data to get a statistically valid view of the population.

Setting the control limits on a simplified control chart should not be done in a vacuum. Data should be gathered on the process for a period of time before the control chart is implemented. Identify a time period when the process is running acceptable product for an extended period and the process is reasonably stable. You will want a period with at least 100 data points. Use the data in that stable time period to calculate the initial control limits. Remember: these are only the initial control limits. They will be reviewed later.

The initial control limits should not be tighter than needed to eliminate excursions. The intent is to run the current process the best it reasonably can, not to put undue (or unfair) stress on the operator. Figure 16-1 shows an example of how the initial control limits should be established.

> **Calculating Initial Control Limits**   **TIP**
> You should use at least 100 individual data points from an apparently in-control time period to calculate the initial control limits. Identify a time when the process is running acceptable product for an extended period and the process appears stable, as in Figure 16-1.

Calculate the average $\overline{X}$ and sigma S of the 100-plus data points in the chosen data group.

We now have to assess whether the process is capable of running product within the specifications. Subtract the average $\overline{X}$ you just calculated from the nearest specification limit. Divide the result by the sigma S you just calculated to get the number of sigma that "fit." This number indicates how well the process runs when in control.

Figure 16-1. Example for establishing initial control limits

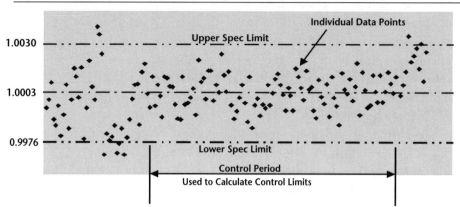

Ideally this "fit" number will be greater than 3. ±3 sigma would give 99.7% product within specification, per the standardized normal distribution table, Figure 11-7. A fit of 2.5 sigma is 99% within tolerance. A fit of 2.0 sigma is 95% in specification. Without a process change, this is the best you can do! We will first assume that the fit is better than 3 sigma.

We will now set up the control chart (Figure 16-2). The initial upper control limit will be midway between the upper spec limit (upper tolerance) and $(\overline{X} + 3S)$. The initial lower control limit will be midway between the lower spec limit and $(\overline{X} - 3S)$. This will give some "early warning" to the operator that he or she is getting close to running product out of specification, while minimizing "false alarms" that cause needless process adjustment.

Each vertical feedback bar to the operator will be based on the data from the previous 11 product readings. The average $\overline{x}$ and sigma s will be calculated on these 11 readings. The vertical bar will have a small horizontal dash representing the average $\overline{x}$ and be ±3 sigma in height from the horizontal average dash. If the ends of the bar cross a *control* limit, the vertical bar will be yellow (light gray in this book). This is the trigger for the operator to review the process and adjust as necessary. If a vertical bar crosses a *spec* limit, it will be red (dark gray on this graph). This indicates that some of the product is predicted to be out of specification.

Setting up this graph will require some computer skills. Figure 16-2 gives an example of this type of simplified control chart.

For reference, Figure 16-2 assumed an $\overline{X} = 1.0002$ and an $S = 0.0006$. This determined that the upper control limit to be 1.0025, which is midway between the +3-sigma value of 1.0020 and the upper spec limit of 1.0030. The lower control limit of 0.9980 is midway between the −3-sigma value of 0.9984 and the lower spec limit of 0.9976.

Figure 16-2. Simplified control chart

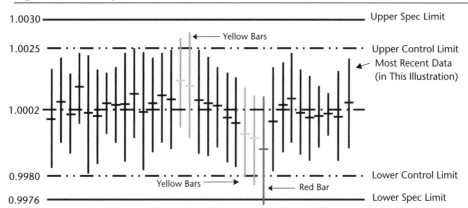

A tolerance limit *can* be shown on this chart because each vertical line represents the projected ±3-sigma measurement spread of an individual part. This is equivalent to displaying individual data points. However, this chart also displays a control limit, to which the operator has to learn to respond. Note that the control limits must be *inside* the tolerance limits or you are asking the operator to do the impossible with the process! If the control limits are *outside* the tolerance limits, the target to which you are asking the operator to run is beyond the current consistent capability of the process.

Every time a simplified control chart is implemented, there will be many who protest that specific process instructions must be given to the operator on how to bring the process back into control if it goes out. Emphatically no! They know how. It may take them some time, but they will do it. They already react when the parts get out of specification; you just want them to respond somewhat sooner. This quicker reaction often saves them work, because it will require only tweaks rather than major process changes.

You will recall that we said that the initial data points were used to set the initial control limits. Once the process is actually running with the feedback benefits of control charts, the control limits should be reviewed. Often they can be tightened because the process is running so much better. This will give operators an earlier warning when the process is beginning to drift. In rare situations, however, the control limits must be loosened because the process is always "in yellow" (in this graph, however, in light gray).

An operator using this kind of control chart will quickly learn that he or she can see trends in either the average or the variation and use that information to help debug the process. The information is intuitive and requires little training. This is especially critical where personnel changes are frequent. This is a key advantage of the simplified control chart over the traditional control chart, which is far less intuitive.

When we set up the control limits, we assumed that the process specification was greater than the $\overline{X} \pm 3S$ we calculated from the in-control process. If the specification had *not* been greater, the control chart could still have been used, but we would have had to adjust everything for a reduced quality level. For example, if the fit had only allowed 2.8 sigma between the $\overline{X}$ and the nearest tolerance limit, the upper control limit could have been set midway between the upper spec and ($\overline{X} + 2.5S$). The lower control limit would have been midway between the lower spec and ($\overline{X} - 2.5S$). Also, the vertical display bars that were calculated based on the last 11 readings would have been calculated at ± 2.5 sigma. However, 3-sigma limits are the norm and that should be your target.

CASE STUDY: SIMPLIFIED CONTROL CHART'S PERCEIVED SIX SIGMA

A customer was unhappy with a supplier's product and deemed it only a 2.5-sigma process (99% within tolerance). In response to the customer's complaints, the supplier's quality manager began measuring product and identified time periods when the process was running well and seemingly in control.

When the quality manager taking these measurements suggested implementing simplified control charts, the response from the engineers, operators, and plant manager was that the plant could not use control charts without some specific process directions. They wanted the quality manager to give them specific process directions before implementing what they thought would be a failure. However, the quality manager was insistent and they all finally agreed to try simplified control charts.

The feedback system and control chart display screen were designed and the quality manager met with the operators to get them "on board." (This product was run 24 hours a day, seven days a week, so four operators were involved.) The operators were largely noncommittal in these meetings.

During the first trial, only one of the operators ran within the control limits. The quality manager then met with each operator individually, explaining that one operator had been able to use the simplified control charts successfully. He told them he wanted to do another trial and asked for their cooperation in trying to use the simplified control charts. On the next trial, two operators ran in control. By the third trial, all four operators were running in control. The system was then made permanent.

After six months, the results were analyzed. First, to the surprise of all, yields had actually improved with the simplified control charts. This was apparently because the tweaks the operators now did to the process were less disruptive than the major changes the operators had been making. Also, their customer now deemed them a 6-sigma supplier (three defects per million product). This really surprised the supplier, because the in-house quality checks indicated that they were supplying a 3.5-sigma product (465 defects per million). Apparently the specification was tighter than what the customer required, so just eliminating the out-of-control defect spikes satisfied the customer.

Use Simplified Control Charts on Equipment or Process Output

Any piece of equipment or process that makes product that is generally acceptable to the customer, with the exception of defect excursions, is a natural for simplified control charts.

TIP

Although the most common benefit derived from the simplified control charts is reduced defect excursions, its inherent feedback feature often helps drive process insights and breakthroughs. The case study below is the first time my team used the simplified control chart. This project shows that even operators who are assigned periodically to a line can easily understand the simplified control chart.

CASE STUDY: CONTROL CHART VANQUISHES LOSSES

A component manufacturing plant had an ongoing issue with a high-volume product. The problem was warping of a surface that was critical to the customer. The customer had rejected 1,000,000 of these products in the previous year due to this defect. The component manufacturing plant had not been successful in keeping the warp within specification, so they started a project to build an in-line inspection device to reject all products exceeding the warp specification.

Although the plant production people recognized the need for this inspection device, they were afraid it would reject more than 1,000,000 products per year because they had a strong suspicion that the customer was unknowingly using a lot of warped product that was out-of-specification. The plant would then be losing product in addition to what the customer was already rejecting.

To address this concern, the project to set up the automatic inspection included a plan to use the output data of the inspection device to give the operator feedback on warping. The plan was to display the warp severity on a computer monitor at the operator's station. This display was to be in the form of a simplified control chart, with the hope that this would help the operator reduce the degree of warp.

The simplified control chart proved to be more valuable than anyone predicted. Apparently one operator knew the process "secret" to reduce warp. He was not a regular operator on this line, so his success on minimizing warp was not noticed. Either no one had believed him or he hadn't gone out of his way to tell others. However, when he was operator on this line after the simplified control chart was in place, his success was obvious. Soon others began to learn and use his process "secret."

The on-line automatic inspection combined with the improved process drove returns from the customer to zero within a few months. Also, the simplified control charts combined with the new process knowledge caused the warp losses in the component plant to be very low.

CONTROL CHARTS FOR KPIVs

If the knowledge of a process is such that the key process input variables (KPIVs) are known, then simplified control charts can be used on the input variables rather than on the output. If the KPIVs are known, then the specification on each KPIV would be established and a simplified control chart would be implemented on each input variable just as shown above for the output. This is a preferred way to control a process, but such detailed knowledge of the KPIVs is rare.

If Uncomfortable, Go Traditional

Anyone uncomfortable with the simplified control chart because it's unconventional should use a traditional control chart. At the end of this chapter are two excellent references for traditional control charts. My experience is that the simplified version has many advantages, but *any* control chart will provide many of the benefits described in this chapter. It is one of the few tools that almost *always* generate improvement.

TIP

WHAT WE HAVE LEARNED IN CHAPTER 16

1. This chapter is used in the Improve and Control steps of the DMAIC process.
2. Traditional control charts that use both an average chart and a sigma chart are somewhat confusing to operators. Since a relatively few are in use, the full potential of control charts has not been realized.

3. Operators want to see specification limits on a control chart, which is not valid on a chart that reflects averages rather than individual readings.

4. The simplified control chart shown in this chapter is intuitive to an operator and satisfies the above two concerns.

5. Variables data and a computer system are needed for simplified control charts.

6. Control charts work best on processes that make products that are generally acceptable, other than for defect excursions. But the feedback feature of control charts also drives process insight on any process.

7. Process instructions on how to react to an out-of-control situation are not required to implement a simplified control chart.

8. Some computer skills are required to set up the simplified control chart screen, data feedback, etc.

RELATED READING

Statistical Methods for Quality Improvement, Hitoshi Kume (New York: Chapman & Hall, 1995).

SPC Simplified: Practical Steps to Quality, Robert T. Amsden, Howard E. Butler, Davida M. Amsden, 2nd edition (New York: Quality Resources, 1998).

PART VI

Statistical Tools for Design for Six Sigma

CHAPTER 17

What Tolerance Is Really Required?

What you will learn in this chapter is that most tolerances have *not* been determined by application needs. Tolerances often have little to do with what is really required. Therefore, tolerances can and should be questioned. You will also learn the RSS (root sum-of-squares) approach to calculating stacked tolerances. Tolerances apply to the Improve and Control steps in DMAIC. This chapter is primarily for those involved in design, manufacturing, or process work.

The initial tolerance on a part is often based on the machine that the designer believes will make the part. The tightest tolerance the machine can achieve is then used. Or, the designer just copies the tolerance from another similar part. An analysis of the real need is seldom done.

Sometime later, the customer may have some issue with the part and complain. Then the tolerance is tightened—whether or not the issue involved the tolerance. Because most tolerances have evolved in this manner, there is large savings potential in determining what is really required in a tolerance.

CASE STUDY: REQUIRED TOLERANCES ON MOLDS

Eight sets of interchangeable molds were used on several high-speed machines. These mold sets were very expensive ($100,000 per set), so they tended to be kept for many years. However, the customer complained that the "old" mold sets were making product with too much variation and wanted the old mold sets replaced.

When an attempt was made to correlate product variation with each mold set, however, it was shown that the age of a mold set had no correlation with product variation. Instead, it was concluded that several mold sets were made with excessive variation from the start. Confidence tests, as covered in Chapter 12, confirmed this.

The mold shape was very complex and the plant purchasing the molds was not capable of validating the mold dimensions. It had to use an outside firm with three-dimensional measuring capability to check the dimensions. When molds from each set were measured, it was found that *all* sets had some molds outside specifications. The problem mold sets just had more molds further out of tolerance than the other sets!

Over the years, in response to complaints, the mold tolerances had been continually tightened until the supplier was not capable of making molds within specifications. However, since the plant kept buying molds, the supplier kept selling them. The mold tolerances became meaningless.

Molds that were making acceptable product were studied and it was found that the supplier was capable of making molds that made acceptable product, even though many of these molds were outside the specified tolerances. The tolerances were then doubled to reflect the dimensions of the molds that made acceptable product, based on this real-need criterion.

Inspection procedures were put in place to verify that all future molds were within the new specifications. Molds beyond the revised tolerances were taken out of production and excess product variation was eliminated. With the more realistic mold specifications, the plant was able to find alternate suppliers and the mold costs were reduced 50%. Total savings were in excess of $100,000 per year.

TOLERANCE STACK-UP

When multiple parts are "stacked" and have cumulative tolerance buildup, the traditional way to handle the stack-up variation is to assume "worst case" on each component. (Allow for all parts being at the high end of the tolerance or all parts being at the low end of the tolerance.) "Stacked" parts are akin to having multiple blocks, placed one block on top of another.

Tolerance Stack-Up Analysis
This is the process of evaluating the effect that dimensions of all components can have on an assembly. There are various methods used, including worst case, RSS (root sum-of-squares), modified RSS, and Monte Carlo simulations.

Example, Part A

Assume there is a stack of 10 parts, each a nominal 1.000" thick, and the tolerance on each part is ±0.010" (the total tolerance on each part = 0.020"). Any traditional "worst case" design using this stack of parts would assume:

Maximum stack height = 1.010" * 10 = 10.100"
Minimum stack height = 0.990" * 10 = 9.900"

The total tolerance on the whole stack would then be ±0.100", for a total of 0.200".

The problem with this analysis is that the odds of *all* parts being at the maximum or *all* parts being at the minimum are extremely low.

RSS TOLERANCE CALCULATIONS

Now, let's use the RSS (root sum-of-squares) approach to calculating tolerances. What should be the tolerance on each part if we assume that ±3 sigma (99.73%) of the products are within tolerance?

Assume ±3 Sigma of Products Are Within Specification
Unless you have specific data showing otherwise, assume that ±3 sigma (99.73%) of the products are within tolerance. This is a general rule of thumb, since few products are made totally within specification.

Assume that in this example we want ±3 sigma of the total stack height to be within the 10" ± 0.100" tolerance specification, the same as assumed with the traditional approach to tolerances.

RSS: Calculating the Sigma S from Multiple Parts Stack-Up

$$S = \sqrt{(1.3s_1)^2 + (1.3s_2)^2 + (1.3s_3)^2 + \text{etc.}}$$

S = the resultant assembly stack-up sigma
s_1, s_2, s_3, etc. = the sigma of each individual part being stacked
Each sigma s is multiplied times 1.3 to allow for a long-term sigma drift.

If each of n stacked-up parts has the same sigma s, then:

$$S = \sqrt{n(1.3s)^2}$$

The 30% assumed long-term sigma drift (0.3s) included in the above equation is based on actual data analyzed many years ago. It puts a degree of conservatism into the RSS tolerance method.

In our example, we first solve for the total stack sigma S. Assume that the ±0.100" tolerance, or 0.200", represents 6 sigma (±3 sigma).

S = 0.200" / 6 = 0.0333"

This means that the sigma S on our total stack is 0.0333".

We then solve for the sigma s on each part, assuming we will have the same tolerance on each of the 10 parts. We can solve for s from the following:

$$S = \sqrt{n(1.3s)^2} = \sqrt{10(1.3s)^2} = \sqrt{16.9s^2}$$

$$s = \frac{S}{\sqrt{16.9}}$$

$$s = \frac{0.0333"}{4.111}$$

s = 0.0081"

The tolerance on each part can therefore be 6 * 0.0081" = 0.049", versus the 0.020" dictated by the worst-case tolerance method. This means we could more than double the individual parts tolerance, with resultant potential parts savings!

Example, Part B

Another way to look at the problem is to assume we keep the original 0.020" parts tolerance and see what kind of tolerance we can expect on the total stack assembly (again, assuming ±3 sigma parts within tolerance).

Solving for the parts sigma:
s = 0.020" / 6 = 0.00333"

We now calculate the stack sigma:

$$S = \sqrt{n(1.3s)^2}$$

$$S = \sqrt{10(1.3 * 0.00333")^2}$$

S = 0.0137"

So, we can analyze the total stack with a nominal height = 10" and a sigma = 0.0137". The six sigma tolerance is 6 * 0.0137" = 0.082", versus the 0.200" assumed in the worst-case analysis. This means anyone planning to use the stack can assume a more repetitive-sized stack with less than half the variation assumed with the worst-case analysis.

CASE STUDY: LOOSENING EXCESSIVELY TIGHT TOLERANCES

A machine had 160 multiple assemblies that opened and closed as the machine cycled. These individual assemblies had multiple cams, rollers, and other parts that contributed to a total variation in how much each assembly opened, which was critical. The tolerance of each of the parts that contributed to the assembly opening had been calculated using worst-case tolerance methods, since the stack-up of the tolerances was a concern. The resultant tolerances on some of these parts were 0.0003", causing the parts to be excessively expensive and almost impossible to manufacture.

When the parts tolerances were recalculated using RSS methods, the tolerances became 0.0008". Although these were still tight tolerances, the parts could then be made with standard machining methods at reasonable prices. Savings were over $70,000 per year.

Problem #1

A company was building an insulator stack that consisted of alternating fiber disks and glass wafers, with a quantity of 10 each. The nominal thickness of the disk was 0.100" and the thickness of the glass wafer was 0.500". Therefore, the total nominal height of the insulator stack was:

Nominal stack height = 10 ∗ 0.100" + 10 ∗ 0.500" = 6.000".

The company had determined that it required the total height of the insulator stack to be between 5.960" and 6.040", so the stack's tolerance was 0.080". The company designer calculated tolerances using worst-case design and divided the 0.080" tolerance equally among the 20 parts (0.004" each). Quotes were requested from various suppliers on the fiber disks and the glass wafers. The specification for the fiber disk was 0.098" to 0.102". The specification for the glass wafer was 0.498" to 0.502".

When the part quotes were received, the company was shocked to find that the glass wafers were going to cost five times what they had estimated. (The disk cost was about what was expected.) When they asked the suppliers why the glass wafer quote was so high, they were told that the 0.004" tolerance on the part required them to incorporate a grinding step after forming the glass. If they had a greater tolerance, they could eliminate the costly grinding step.

What would the tolerance be on the glass wafer and the fiber disk if the RSS method were used to calculate tolerances?

Assume that the tolerances on the wafer and disk are identical and that the total assembly is to be manufactured with ±3 sigma of the insulator stacks within tolerance. Since the customer had specified that the total assembly must be between 5.960" and 6.040", the total tolerance is 0.080" and will be equal to 6 sigma.

1 sigma S on the assembly = 0.080" / 6 = 0.0133"

$$S = \sqrt{n(1.3s)^2} = \sqrt{20(1.3s)^2} = \sqrt{33.8s^2}$$

$$s = \frac{S}{\sqrt{33.8}}$$

$$s = \frac{0.0133"}{\sqrt{33.8}}$$

s = 0.00229"

So, the part tolerance can be 6 * 0.00229" = 0.014", versus the 0.004" calculated by "worst case." This difference would enable eliminating the grinding step.

We have assumed in the above examples that the sigma is based on using ±3 sigma of the tolerance. If you have historical data on actual parts dimensions, you can get even more accurate estimates of the proper tolerance. There are even software packages that allow you to put in raw data on the components. The software then fits a curve for each component and you can do a Monte Carlo analysis, in which the software uses random numbers to generate data as if you were actually running thousands of parts. However, this is more sophisticated (and a lot more work) than generally required.

Add Only Stack-up Items on Axis
When using the RSS method of calculating tolerances, be careful to add only the parts' dimensions that are in the same axis as the stack-up dimension. If a part is at an angle relative to that axis, then you should include only the component in the axis direction.

TIP

> **Reviewing Tolerances on Real Parts and Processes**   **TIP**
> You are ready to review tolerances on real parts and processes.
> 1. On any part that is difficult or expensive to make because of tight tolerances, review the tolerances based on application requirements.
> 2. On any group of parts that are assembled such that their accumulated stack-up dimensions affect the total assembly's dimension, review the tolerances using the RSS tolerance method.

WHAT WE HAVE LEARNED IN CHAPTER 17

1. Tolerances apply to the Improve and Control steps in the DMAIC process.
2. Tolerances are seldom calculated based on requirements, so there are potential savings to be realized by reviewing tolerances that cause issues.
3. When there is a problem with a part, the reaction is often to tighten tolerances on that part, whether or not the tolerance is the issue.
4. If multiple parts are "stacked" in an assembly, the tolerances on those parts are likely to have been calculated using worst-case methods. Using the RSS method of calculating tolerances can open tolerances on those parts or show how the assembly has less variation than assumed.

RELATED READING AND SOFTWARE

Six Sigma Mechanical Design Tolerancing, Mikel J. Harry and Reigle Stewart, 2nd edition (Schaumburg, IL: Motorola University Press, 1988).

MINITAB 13, Minitab Inc., State College, PA, www.minitab.com.

Crystal Ball 2000, Decisioneering Inc., Denver, CO, www.decisioneering.com.

CHAPTER 18

Simplified Linear Transfer Functions

What you will learn in this chapter is to use simplified linear transfer functions to understand the effect of each component on the total variation of a part, an assembly, or a process. In this way you will know each component's contribution to the total variation and know where to focus your attention. Simplified linear transfer functions are used in the Analyze and Improve steps of the DMAIC process. This chapter is primarily for those involved in design, manufacturing, or process work.

Just as with DOEs, there will be some who think that this is too complex for this level of text. But, green belts *have* used this tool—and with great success.

The method used in simplified linear transfer functions is very similar to the RSS tolerance method we already covered. In fact, this type of transfer function is called the *root sum-of-squares (RSS)*, because it involves squaring and summing the contributing sigmas, as we did for tolerance in the previous chapter. We want to account for all the variation in an assembly or a process by identifying the contributing variation of each component.

RSS Linear Transfer Functions

$$S_t = \sqrt{s_1^2 + s_2^2 + s_3^2 + s_4^2} \text{ etc.}$$

S_t = the critical sigma of the total assembly or process

FORMULA

s_1, s_2, s_3, s_4, etc. are the sigmas of the variables linearly affecting the critical sigma of an assembly or process.

Each variable's influence must be stated in common units consistent with the part, assembly, or process. For example, if we are studying the thickness variation of an injected molded part and one of the contributing variables is the weight of the injected raw material, we need to state that variable's sigma in "thickness variation per sigma," rather than in "weight unit per sigma."

The best way to illustrate this is to tell about an actual project done in a manufacturing plant.

CASE STUDY: FINDING GRINDING ISSUE USING TRANSFER FUNCTION

A manufacturing plant was manufacturing an item that involved pressing a forming material into a defined cavity. Figure 18-1 is a simplified diagram of this process.

Figure 18-1. Diagram of forming process

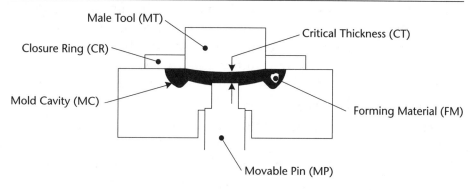

The critical thickness was varying too much and the plant wanted to run tests to see what was causing this excessive variation.

First, the team defined the things that could affect this critical thickness:

S_{CT}: total sigma on the critical thickness

1. S_{FM}: sigma of the forming material
2. S_{MT}: sigma of the shape of the male tool
3. S_{MC}: sigma of the shape of the mold cavity
4. S_{MP}: sigma of the moveable pin position
5. S_{AO}: sigma of all other unknown contributing variables

The formula of the total sigma S would therefore be:

$$S_{CT} = \sqrt{S_{FM}^2 + S_{MT}^2 + S_{MC}^2 + S_{MP}^2 + S_{AO}^2}$$

The team needed to run the tests such that they changed only one variable at a time. They could then see the effect of each contributing sigma without the effect of the other variables. The only variable they couldn't tightly control was the weight of the forming material, so it was decided to run that test first. Then, on tests for the other variables, they would analyze only product that had an average weight, eliminating weight as a variable on the remaining tests.

Test 1: find the sigma S_{FM} of the forming material weight.

Product was taken from one mold, where the pin was locked in position to eliminate any influence of the moveable pin. Only one male tool was used. The weight was allowed to vary over its normal range. The critical thickness on the resultant product was measured. From these data it was possible to calculate the effect of a weight change on the critical thickness, with no other variable changing.

There were historical data on weight variation, so the sigma in grams was already available. However, to get it into the common units needed, the team used the above data to convert the weight sigma to inches of critical thickness. This was a simple conversion, using the above data on thickness to determine what the equivalent thickness change was at the gram-weight value of the historical weight sigma. The team now had S_{FM} for the weight variation in critical thickness inches.

Test 2: find the sigma S_{MT} of the male tool.

Product was taken from one mold, where the pin was locked in position to eliminate any influence of the moveable pin. Multiple male tools were run. On products that had weights close to the historic average weight, the critical thickness was measured. In this way the team was able to find S_{MT} in terms of critical thickness inches.

Test 3: find the sigma S_{MC} of the mold cavity.

Product was taken from multiple molds, where the pins were locked in position to eliminate any influence of the moveable pin. One male tool was used. On products that had weights close to the historic average weight, the critical thickness was measured. In this way the team was able to find S_{MC} in terms of critical thickness inches.

Test 4: find the sigma S_{MP} of the moveable pin.

Product was taken from the same multiple molds used in the previous test, but the pins were no longer locked in position. One male tool was used. On products that had weights close to the historic average weight, the critical thickness was measured. The sigma was found for each individual mold. This gave a sigma for the moveable pin in that mold. Using the RSS method, the sigma from all the molds was then calculated. This gave the effect of many moveable pins. In this way the team was able to find S_{MP} in terms of critical thickness inches.

The total S_{CT} of the critical thickness was already available from historic data. The S_{AO} of the "all other unknown contributing variables" was the variable for which the plant then solved, since all the other variables were known and the S_{CT} equation had only one unknown. If the S_{AO} of the "all other unknown contributing variables" had not been small compared with the other identified contributors, the team would have known that they had missed some important variable(s) and would have had to go back and review their understanding of the process.

Here is the resultant RSS equation:

$$S_{CT} = \sqrt{S_{FM}^2 + S_{MT}^2 + S_{MC}^2 + S_{MP}^2 + S_{AO}^2}$$

$$0.0071" = \sqrt{0.0015"^2 + 0.0046"^2 + 0.0013"^2 + 0.0049"^2 + 0.0011"^2}$$

When the team analyzed the elements in the resultant RSS equation, they found that two variables were contributing most of the variation in the critical thickness. The highest, the moveable pin at 0.0049", was no surprise, and the plant already had projects underway to correct this.

The sigma on the male tool, which at 0.0046" was almost as large as the moveable pin, was a complete surprise. The male tool, whose surface was periodically reground in the plant, was varying far more than anyone had thought. It was discovered that the check procedures that were supposed to be used to verify that the male tool grinding wheel shape was correct were no longer being followed. This was quickly corrected and almost a third of the problem of critical thickness variation was eliminated within a day, at almost no cost.

In solving this problem, the team took care to make sure that each sigma contribution related directly to the change in the critical thickness, with the units being consistent with the product effect being measured. In this way comparing the sigmas to see which variable was more critical was valid.

No attempt was made to detail the transfer function to the point that the formula for the "shape" of the male tool was included in the formula. In an ideal world, it would be nice to have the transfer function defined by the geometry and position of parts in space. It just is not normally required or practical!

> **Non-Linear Transfer Functions**   TIP
> There are some processes that are non-linear and have complex interactions among variables such that they can't be represented with a simple linear transfer function. Chemical processes are often that way. The resultant transfer function is non-linear and requires partial derivatives.
>
> Tests to identify the components of non-linear transfer functions are extensive, with a large number of test iterations required. This is beyond the scope of this book. Also, processes requiring non-linear transfer functions are seldom defined completely.

WHAT WE HAVE LEARNED IN CHAPTER 18

1. Simplified linear transfer functions are used in the Analyze and Improve steps of the DMAIC process.
2. Use simplified linear transfer functions to understand the effect of each component on the total variation of an assembly or process.
3. The sum-of-the-squares of the contributing variables' sigmas must equal the square of the sigma of the total assembly or process. If the sum is too little, one or more variables are missing.
4. Each sigma contribution must have units consistent with the product effect being measured. In this way it is valid to compare the sigmas to see which variable is more critical.
5. Non-linear transfer functions, which require partial derivatives, are beyond the scope of this book (and most Six Sigma work).

RELATED SOFTWARE

Crystal Ball 2000, Decisioneering Inc., Denver, CO, www.decisioneering.com.

PART VII

**Six Sigma Data and
Quality Management Data**

CHAPTER 19

Comparing Six Sigma Data with Quality Department Data

This chapter applies to someone interfacing Six Sigma data with quality department data. Quality department data are often based on averages rather than individual data points.

This chapter does not include a Six Sigma tool, but it *does* show how someone can use data collected by quality departments to compare with samples collected doing Six Sigma work. This chapter is primarily for those involved in manufacturing or process work. What you will learn here is that quality department systems often use child distributions based on sample averages and the sigma of multiple sample averages, rather than using the individual data points.

To do statistical analysis, we use data in various ways. The previous problems in this book used the average and sigma of individual data points. This is called a *parent population*. Many quality departments deal primarily with sample averages and the sigma of multiple sample averages. This is a *child distribution*. Quality departments often do not even retain the individual data measurements. One of the reasons this is done is to limit database memory requirements.

Parent Population and Child Distribution

A *parent population* refers to the individual data and their related statistical descriptions, like average and sigma. These are labeled $\bar{X}$ and S.

A *child distribution* refers to the sample averages and the sigma of multiple sample averages. These are labeled $\bar{x}$ and $s_{\bar{x}}$.

The average of the child distribution $\bar{x}$ will tend to match the average of the parent population $\bar{X}$.

The $s_{\bar{x}}$ calculated from multiple sample averages will be smaller than the population's sigma S. Note that the sigma $s_{\bar{x}}$ of multiple sample averages is *not* the same as the sigma s of individual data points.

The larger the individual sample size, the smaller the sigma $s_{\bar{x}}$ of the multiple means of the samples. You can't use the $s_{\bar{x}}$ of the multiple sample means as an indicator of the parent population sigma S without adjusting the $s_{\bar{x}}$ to account for the individual sample size. You can see in Figure 19-1 how the child distribution is "tighter" than the parent population.

Figure 19-1. Parent population distribution and child distribution

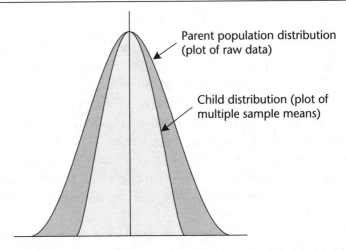

Parent population distribution (plot of raw data)

Child distribution (plot of multiple sample means)

To estimate the parent population sigma S from the $s_{\bar{x}}$ of a child distribution, multiply the child $s_{\bar{x}}$ by the square root of n, the individual sample size.

Estimating the Parent Population Sigma S from the $s_{\bar{x}}$ of a Child Distribution

$S = s_{\bar{x}} \sqrt{n}$

S = parent population sigma (sigma based on the raw data)
$s_{\bar{x}}$ = child distribution sigma (sigma of the multiple sample averages)
n = individual sample size (quantity in each raw data sample)

As noted, the $s_{\bar{x}}$ resulting from multiple sample averages will be smaller than the parent population's sigma S. This is illustrated below by showing the shaft data of 15 samples, with each sample having seven shafts (n = 7) from the parent population. The average of each sample of seven was calculated. Then the sigma $s_{\bar{x}}$ (one value) of these 15 sample averages was calculated. To estimate the population sigma S from the sigma $s_{\bar{x}}$ of these 15 sample averages, multiply the sample average sigma $s_{\bar{x}}$ by $\sqrt{7}$.

This is shown on the data below. All dimensions are in inches. The samples were drawn randomly from the parent population of shafts, which has an average of 1.0000" and an S = 0.0010".

Sample Diameters							
1	**2**	**3**	**4**	**5**	**6**	**7**	**Average**
1.0003	0.9994	0.9996	1.0012	1.0001	1.0004	0.9991	1.0000143
0.9982	1.0002	0.9989	0.9999	0.9996	0.9990	0.9980	0.9991143
0.9995	0.9999	1.0000	0.9976	0.9990	1.0005	1.0015	0.9997143
1.0022	0.9981	1.0003	0.9991	0.9994	1.0012	0.9987	0.9998571
1.0001	1.0008	0.9989	0.9994	0.9997	1.0018	0.9996	1.0000429
1.0014	0.9986	1.0009	1.0005	1.0010	0.9998	0.9977	0.9999857
1.0006	0.9996	0.9999	0.9995	0.9978	0.9990	1.0000	0.9994857
0.9995	1.0002	1.0015	0.9985	0.9998	1.0000	1.0007	1.0000286
1.0004	0.9992	1.0019	1.0009	0.9984	1.0010	0.9993	1.0001571
1.0016	0.9997	1.0007	0.9989	1.0003	1.0001	1.0011	1.0003429
1.0006	1.0020	1.0002	0.9994	0.9996	0.9986	1.0015	1.0002714
0.9991	1.0009	0.9992	1.0008	1.0006	1.0005	0.9996	1.0001000
1.0029	1.0001	0.9999	1.0012	1.0005	1.0007	1.0004	1.0008143
1.0023	0.9996	0.9997	1.0009	0.9990	0.9982	0.9996	0.9999000
1.0003	0.9991	0.9989	1.0008	0.9985	0.9998	1.0014	0.9998286
					Sample Average $\bar{x}$ =		0.9999771
					Child Sigma $s_{\bar{x}}$ =		0.0003850
Population Standard Deviation Estimate = .000385 x $\sqrt{7}$ = 0.001018614							

As you can see, the 0.999977" average $\bar{x}$ of these samples is close to the 1.0000" $\bar{X}$ of the population. The 0.000385" $s_{\bar{x}}$, however, is far smaller than the population S. As shown above, we can approximate the population S (which is 0.0010") by multiplying the sigma of the sample averages $s_{\bar{x}}$ by the square root of n, or $\sqrt{7}$ (which is 2.646). This gives us an estimated S = 0.001019", which is close to the population S of 0.0010".

Just for information, the actual average of the above 105 individual data readings is 0.999977" and the sigma of the 105 raw readings is 0.001075". But remember, quality departments often do not keep the individual raw readings, so this comparison would not be possible on those systems.

Problem #1

Our now-familiar lathe is machining shafts and, in this case, they are not averaging 1.0000" in diameter. We want to see if an improved setup for the cutting tool gives us shafts closer to our 1.0000" target diameter.

We first plot individual readings from the initial process. We then compare this plot with the plot of individual data points after the change. Assume that we see that the general shape of the distribution curve has remained the same.

Before the process change, the quality department had been taking samples of 20 measurements. They calculated the average on each sample of 20 measurements and then discarded the individual data values. They kept a running child sigma $s_{\bar{x}}$ and child average $\bar{x}$ based on the last 100 of these calculated averages.

After the process change, we check a sample of 60 shafts. Below are the results of the before and after process.

Before Data	After Data
child $\bar{x}$ = 1.0004"	sample $\bar{x}$ = 0.9999"
child $s_{\bar{x}}$ = 0.0003801"	sample s = 0.00173"
each child's n = 20	sample n = 60

What can we say about the average and sigma of the process "before" versus "after"?

The two sigmas can't be compared without some adjustment, because the "before" is a child sigma. However, we can estimate the population S from the $s_{\bar{x}}$.

$S = s_{\bar{x}}\sqrt{n}$

S = estimate of the parent population sigma of the "before" process

$s_{\bar{x}} = 0.0003801"$

$n = 20$

$S = 0.00170"$

Use the formula from Chapter 12 to see if the sigmas are significantly different.

Chi-squared test of a sample sigma s versus a population sigma S:

$$\text{Chi}_t^2 = \frac{(n-1)s^2}{S^2}$$

$n = 60$

$s = 0.00173"$

$S = 0.00170"$ (estimated from the child)

$$\text{Chi}_t^2 = \frac{(60-1)0.00173^2}{0.00170^2}$$

$\text{Chi}_t^2 = 61.1007$

We compare the calculated Chi_t^2 results with the values on the simplified chi-squared distribution table (Figure 12-1). If the Chi_t^2 test value we calculated is less than the table low value or greater than the table high value, we are 95% confident that the sample sigma s is different from the sigma S of the population. Since 61.1007 is between the table values of 39.662 and 82.117, we can't say with a 95% confidence that the sigmas are different.

We now test the averages. Since we are interested in which average is closer to the 1.0000" nominal, we will restate the averages versus the nominal as deltas: $|\bar{X} - 1.0000"|$ and $|\bar{x} - 1.0000"|$.

Before Delta

$\bar{X} = 0.0004"$

After Delta

$\bar{x} = 0.0001"$

$s = 0.00173"$

$n = 60$

t test of a population average $\bar{X}$ versus a sample average $\bar{x}$:

$$t_t = \frac{|\bar{x} - \bar{X}|}{\frac{s}{\sqrt{n}}}$$

$\bar{X} = 0.0004"$

$\bar{x} = 0.0001"$

$s = 0.00173"$

$n = 60$

$$t_t = \frac{|0.0001 - 0.0004|}{\frac{0.00173}{\sqrt{60}}}$$

$t_t = 1.343$

We then compare this calculated t-test (t_t) value with the value in the simplified t table (Figure 12-2). If our calculated t-test (t_t) value is greater than the value in the table, then we are 95% confident that the sample is significantly different from the population.

Since 1.343 is not greater than the table value of 2.001, we can't say with a 95% confidence that the changed tooling setup is different from the original process.

The Child Distribution Tends to Be Normal

TIP

When you plot the averages of multiple samples taken from a parent distribution of any shape, the distribution of the child population tends to be normal. This is especially true when individual sample sizes are 30 or more.
    This is known as the *central limit theory*.

When we looked at non-normal distributions, we gave the following examples:

Figure 19-2. Non-normal distributions

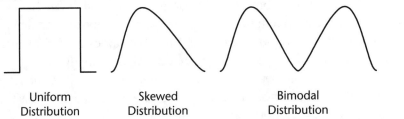

Uniform   Skewed   Bimodal
Distribution   Distribution   Distribution

If you took multiple samples of 30 from any of these populations and plotted the means of these multiple samples, the resultant child distribution (Figure 19-3) would be normal. In fact, from the shape of the child distribution, you could not guess the shape of the original parent population.

Be Careful Using Child Distribution

TIP

1. Since you can't tell the original parent population shape by looking at the child distribution (the plot of multiple sample means tends to be normal no matter what the parent distribution is), the parent distribution could change and you would not know it. You must periodically plot the raw data from the parent population to make sure the process has not changed.
2. Don't ever compare a child distribution sigma with a parent population sigma without first adjusting the child sigma by multiplying it by the square root of the individual child sample size.
3. Don't be misled into thinking a process is in control because the sigma of the child population is small. The *real* sigma of the parent population is always larger.

Figure 19-3. Plot of the means, samples of 30, from the above non-normal distributions

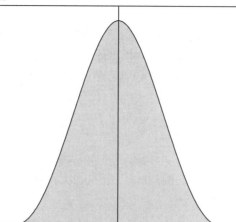

Be Careful Comparing Short-Term Data with Long-Term Data

TIP

When you are running tests, the data you collect are generally short-term (several days or less). Quality department data can contain both short-term and long-term data. Long-term data include some process drift, which will increase the sigma value. The rule of thumb is to assume a 1.5 sigma increase due to long-term process drift.

However, for your data comparisons, you are safer to use recent data with a time period equivalent to your test data, rather than assume a long-term drift value. This is because the actual long-term drift value can vary widely.

WHAT WE HAVE LEARNED IN CHAPTER 19

1. This chapter does not include a Six Sigma tool, but it *does* cover how someone can use data collected by many quality departments to compare with samples taken related to process trials or samples that are collected doing Six Sigma work.

2. Quality department systems often use child distributions, which are based on multiple sample averages, rather than the raw data itself. The raw data are often discarded after the average is calculated.

3. The sigma of the child distribution is always smaller than the sigma of the parent population, which is calculated using the raw data.

4. An estimate of the parent population sigma can be made by multiplying the child sigma by the square root of the individual child sample size.

5. The child distribution tends to be normal no matter what the shape of the parent distribution. This is especially true at individual sample sizes of 30 or over.

6. You have to be careful using a child distribution. It can hide a change in the shape in the parent population, therefore hiding a process change. Also, the child sigma can't be compared with a parent population sigma without first adjusting the child sigma with reference to its sample size.

RELATED READING

Basic Statistics: Tools for Continuous Improvement, Mark J. Kiemele, Stephen R. Schmidt, and Ronald J. Berdine, 4th edition (Colorado Springs, CO: Air Academy Press, 1997).

APPENDICES

The Six Sigma Statistical Tool Finder Matrix

Look in the Need and Detail columns in the matrix below to identify the appropriate Six Sigma Tool.

Need	Detail	Six Sigma Tool	Location
address customer needs by identifying and prioritizing actions	convert qualitative customer input to specific prioritized actions	simplified QFD	Chapter 3
minimize collateral damage due to a product or process change	convert qualitative input on concerns to specific prioritized actions	simplified FMEA	Chapter 4
identify key process input variables (KPIVs)	use expert input on a process	cause-and-effect fishbone	Chapter 5
	use historical data	correlation tests	Chapter 7
pinpoint possible problem areas of a process	use expert input	process flow diagram	Chapter 6
verify measurement accuracy	determine if a gauge is adequate for the task	simplified gauge verification	Chapter 9
calculate minimum sample size	variables (decimal) data	sample size—variables	Chapter 12
	proportional data	sample size—proportions	Chapter 13

Need	Detail	Six Sigma Tool	Location
determine if any statistically significant change on variables (decimal) data	compare a sample with historical (population) data	1. plot data	Chapter 11
		2. chi-squared test	Chapter 12
		3. t test	Chapter 12
	compare two samples to each other	1. plot data	Chapter 11
		2. F test	Chapter 12
		3. t test	Chapter 12
determine if any statistically significant change on proportional data	the mathematical probability of the population is known	Excel's BINOMDIST	Chapter 10
	compare a sample with a population where both proportions are calculated	sample/ population formula	Chapter 13
	compare two samples where both proportions are calculated	sample/sample formula	Chapter 13
minimize process defect excursions	applicable to variables (decimal) data	simplified control charts	Chapter 16
optimize key process input variable settings (KPIVs)	use on a current process	simplified DOE	Chapter 15
determine if tolerances are appropriate	how were tolerances determined?	need-based tolerances	Chapter 17
	are any stacked parts with tolerances at worst case?	RSS tolerances	Chapter 17
identify variation contributed by each component to the process or assembly variation	identifies problem components	simplified transfer function	Chapter 18

Six Sigma Tool Check-Off List

The example of the Six Sigma tool check-off list below can be used as a guideline for building a tool check-off list specific to your project. This example was used for a project to develop a laser and digital camera inspection device to measure the rim diameter of a product (case study in Chapter 2). Initial tests had shown that a series of lasers, if directed at the rim of the product, could project an image onto digital cameras, enabling a quick inspection of the rim diameter. The purpose of the project was to replace a slower gauge that used dial indicators. Although the dial indicator gauge gave satisfactory measurements, it was too slow to keep up with a planned increase in line speed.

Note that in this Six Sigma tool check-off list many of the tools are used in more than one part of the DMAIC process. For example, the simplified gauge verification is used in the Measure, Improve, and Control steps and the tests for significant change are used in the Analyze, Improve, and Control steps, sometimes comparing two samples and sometimes comparing the population to a sample. Where and how often each tool will be used is dictated by each project. Some tools, like the QFD and FMEA, should be used on *every* project, since input from people is always required.

This Six Sigma tool check-off list is sometimes modified during a program. Often as issues arise the proposed solutions include the use of additional Six Sigma tools. Each modification of this Six Sigma tool check-off list should be dated and prior lists should be kept for reference as part of the program file. The use of the Six Sigma tool check-off list should be in addition to whatever total program management tool is used. It is not a replacement for traditional program management techniques.

DMAIC	Tool	Use
Define	simplified QFD	Get input on detailed needs of project from inspectors, line maintenance, quality engineers, design engineers, production manager, and customers. Develop action list.
	simplified FMEA	Identify any other processes that may be negatively affected by implementing this project. (For example, the extra time required of line maintenance people may negatively affect the maintenance of other equipment.) Develop action list.
	fishbone diagram	Identify all the input variables causing the diameter to vary, to make sure we have samples of all types of diameter variations. This enables us to verify that all variations of diameters can be measured using the laser and digital camera device.
Measure	calculate minimum sample size, variables data	Determine the number of sample products required to run statistically valid tests on the new equipment.
	simplified gauge verification	Using product masters, verify that the *test setup* can sufficiently measure the product diameter.
Analyze	test for significant change, variables data (decimals) two-sample test	Run tests on the sample products using both the traditional manual dial indicator measurement method and the test setup. Verify that there is no significant difference between the two methods. If a difference is found, additional tests will be required to identify the reason(s).
Improve	simplified gauge verification	Using product masters, verify that the *production device* can sufficiently measure the product diameter.
	test for significant change, variables data (decimals) two-sample test	Run tests on the product samples using both the traditional manual measurement method and the *production device*. Verify that there is no significant difference between the two methods. If a difference is found, additional tests will be required to identify the reason(s).

DMAIC	Tool	Use
Improve	test for significant change, variables data (decimals) population/sample	Run tests on the production products using the new device. Verify that there is no significant difference between the new data and historical (population) data. If a difference is found, additional investigation will be required to determine why.
Control	test for significant change, variables data (decimals) population/sample	Using the output data, continuously calculate results on a running sample and compare the results with historical data. If the running sample results are statistically different from the historical population results, then the device may not be working properly. Line maintenance would then be alerted.
	simplified control charts	Using the measurement output of the new device, implement a simplified control chart to help the operator reduce diameter excursions.
	simplified gauge verification	Using product masters, verify that the production device can sufficiently measure the product diameter. Schedule this simplified gauge verification monthly.

APPENDIX C

Formulas Used in This Book

From Chapter 9

Simplified Gauge Verification, Variables Data

% gauge error = $\dfrac{5s + 2 * |\text{master} - \bar{x}|}{\text{tolerance}} * 100$ (ideally < 10%, maximum 30%)

$\bar{x}$ = average of *all* 21 readings of a master product

s = standard deviation of *all* 21 readings of the master product

master = standardized dimension of the master product

tolerance = allowable product tolerance (max − min)

$|\text{master} - \bar{x}|$ = difference between master and average $\bar{X}$, ignoring minus signs.

Use on Problem Type

You wish to verify that a gauge that measures variables data is not "using up" more than 30% of the tolerance. Have three inspectors read a pre-qualified master product seven times each, getting 21 total readings. The average and standard deviation are calculated on these data and entered into the above formula.

Both repeatability/reproducibility (ability to duplicate a reading) and accuracy (aim, or correctness of average reading) are included in the simplified gauge verification formula. The accuracy portion is

$2 * |\text{master} - \bar{x}|$

From Chapter 12

Estimating Population $\bar{X}$ and S from Multiple Samples of Similar-Size n, Variables Data

$$\bar{X} = \frac{\bar{x}_1 + \bar{x}_2}{2}$$

$\bar{X}$ is the population average
$\bar{x}_1$ is the average from the #1 sample
$\bar{x}_2$ is the average from the #2 sample

$$S = \sqrt{\frac{s_1^2 + s_2^2}{2}}$$

S is the population sigma
s_1 is the sigma of the #1 sample
s_2 is the sigma of the #2 sample

If you have three or more samples, modify the formulas accordingly, with more sample sigma or averages in the numerator and dividing by the total number of samples.

Use on Problem Type

You have multiple variables data samples with similar sample sizes, and you want to estimate the population's average and standard deviation.

From Chapter 12

Calculating Minimum Sample Size and Sensitivity, Variables Data

$n = \left(\dfrac{Z * S}{h}\right)^2$ to calculate minimum sample size on variables data

n = minimum sample size on variables data (Always round up.)
Z = confidence level (When in doubt use Z = 1.96.)
S = the population standard deviation
h = the smallest change we want to be able to sense
(When in doubt, use h = total tolerance / 10, or h = 0.6S.)

Note that the formula shown above can be rewritten as:

$h = \sqrt{\dfrac{Z^2 * S^2}{n}}$

This allows us to see what sensitivity h (change) we can expect to see with a given sample size and confidence level.

Use on Problem Type

Use to calculate the minimum variables data sample size you need to make estimates on a population. To use this formula, you have to define what change, or sensitivity h, you want to be able to sense. A rule of thumb is to use the total tolerance / 10.

By rewriting the formula, you can solve directly for the change, or sensitivity h. This provision is used when the sample size has already been determined and you want to see what change, or sensitivity h, you will be able to sense.

From Chapter 12

Chi-Squared Test Value of a Sample Sigma s Versus a Population Sigma S of Variables Data

$$Chi_t^2 = \frac{(n-1)s^2}{S^2}$$

n = sample size
s = sample sigma
S = population sigma

We compare the calculated Chi_t^2 results with the values in the following simplified chi-squared distribution table (Figure 12-1). If the Chi_t^2 test value we calculated is less than the table low value or greater than the table high value, we are 95% confident that the sample sigma s is different from the sigma S of the population.

Use on Problem Type

This is used on variables data when we want to test if a sample's sigma is significantly different from the population's sigma. We compare the calculated result from the above formula with the values in the simplified chi-squared distribution table (Figure 12-1) to determine if there is a statistically significant difference between the two.

This formula is normally used after we have already compared the plots of data from both the sample and the population and are satisfied that the shapes of the two distributions of data are not dramatically different.

From Chapter 12

t Test of a Population Average $\overline{X}$ Versus a Sample Average $\overline{x}$, Variables Data

$$t_t = \frac{\left| \overline{x} - \overline{X} \right|}{\dfrac{s}{\sqrt{n}}}$$

$\overline{X}$ = population average
$\overline{x}$ = sample average
s = sample sigma
n = sample size

$\left| \overline{x} - \overline{X} \right|$ is the absolute value of the difference of the averages, so ignore a minus sign in the difference.

We then compare this calculated t-test (t_t) value against the value in the simplified t distribution table (Figure 12-2). If our calculated t-test (t_t) value is greater than the value in the table, then we are 95% confident that the sample average is significantly different from the population average.

Use on Problem Type

Use this formula on variables data when you want to test if a sample's average is significantly different from a population's average. We compare the calculated result from the above formula with the values in the simplified t distribution table (Figure 12-2) to determine if there is a statistically significant difference between the two.

This formula is normally used after we have already compared the plots of data from both the sample and population and are satisfied that the shapes of the two distributions of data are not dramatically different and after the chi-squared test of sigma did not show a significant difference.

From Chapter 12

F Test Comparing Two Sample Sigma s, Variables Data

$F_t = \dfrac{s_1^2}{s_2^2}$ (put the larger s on top, as the numerator)

s_1 = sample with the larger sigma

s_2 = sample with the smaller sigma

    The sample sizes n should be within 20% of each other. There are tables and programs that allow for greater differences, but since you control sample sizes and get more reliable results with similar sample sizes, these other tables and programs are generally not needed.

    Compare this F_t with the value in the simplified F table (Figure 12-3). If the F_t value exceeds the table F value, then the sigmas are significantly different.

Use on Problem Type

This is used on variables data when we want to test if two samples' sigmas are significantly different. We compare the calculated result from the above formula with the values in the simplified F table (Figure 12-3) to determine if there is a statistically significant difference between the two.

    This formula is normally used after we have already compared the plots of data from both of the samples and are satisfied that the shapes of the two distributions of data are not dramatically different.

From Chapter 12

t Test of Two Sample Averages $\bar{x}_1$ and $\bar{x}_2$, Variables Data

$$t_t = \frac{|\bar{x}_1 - \bar{x}_2|}{\sqrt{\left(\dfrac{n_1 s_1^{2} + n_2 s_2^{2}}{n_1 + n_2}\right)\left(\dfrac{1}{n_1} + \dfrac{1}{n_2}\right)}}$$

$\bar{x}_1$ and $\bar{x}_2$ are two sample averages.
s_1 and s_2 are the sigmas on the two samples.
n_1 and n_2 are the two sample sizes.
$|\bar{x}_1 - \bar{x}_2|$ is the absolute difference between the averages, ignoring a minus sign in the difference.

We then compare this calculated t-test value against the value in the simplified t distribution table (Figure 12-2). If our calculated t-test number is greater than the value in the table, then we are 95% confident that the sample averages are significantly different.

Use on Problem Type

Use this formula on variables data when you want to test if two sample averages are significantly different. We compare the calculated result from the above formula with the values in the simplified t distribution table (Figure 12-2) to determine if there is a statistically significant difference between the two.

This formula is normally used after we have already compared the plots of data from both of the samples and are satisfied that the shapes of the two distributions of data are not dramatically different and after an F test of sigma did not show a significant difference.

From Chapter 13

Calculating Minimum Sample Size and Sensitivity, Proportional Data

$$n = \left(\frac{1.96\sqrt{(p)(1-p)}}{h} \right)^2$$

n = sample size of attribute data, like "good" or "bad" (95% confidence)
p = probability of an event (the proportion of defects in a sample, chance of getting elected, etc.)
(When in doubt use p = 0.5, the most conservative.)
h = sensitivity, or accuracy required
  (For example, for predicting elections it may be ±3%, or h = 0.03. Another guideline is to be able to sense 10% of the tolerance or difference between the proportions.)
  Note that the formula shown above can be rewritten as:

$$h = 1.96\sqrt{\frac{(p)(1-p)}{n}}$$

  This allows us to see what sensitivity h we will be able to sense at a given sample size and probability.

Use on Problem Type

Use to calculate the minimum proportional data sample size you need to make estimates on a population with a 95% confidence. To use this formula, you have to define what change, or sensitivity h, you want to be able to sense. A rule of thumb is to use the total tolerance / 10.

By rewriting the formula, you can solve directly for the change, or sensitivity h. This provision is used when the sample size has already been determined and you want to see what change, or sensitivity h, you will be able to sense.

From Chapter 13

Comparing a Proportional Sample with the Population (95% Confidence)

First, we must calculate a test value Z_t.

$$Z_t = \frac{|p - P|}{\sqrt{\dfrac{P(1-P)}{n}}}$$

P = proportion of defects (or whatever) in the population (historical)
p = proportion of defects (or same as above) in the sample
|p – P| = absolute proportion difference (no minus sign in difference)
n = sample size

If $Z_t > 1.96$, then we can say with a 95% confidence that the sample is different from the population.

Use on Problem Type

Use this formula on proportional data when you want to test if a sample is significantly different from a population.

From Chapter 13

Comparing Two Proportional Data Samples (95% Confidence)

We must calculate a test value Z_t.

$$Z_t = \frac{\left|\dfrac{x_1}{n_1} - \dfrac{x_2}{n_2}\right|}{\sqrt{\left(\dfrac{x_1+x_2}{n_1+n_2}\right)\left(1 - \dfrac{x_1+x_2}{n_1+n_2}\right)\left(\dfrac{1}{n_1} + \dfrac{1}{n_2}\right)}}$$

x_1 = number of defects (or whatever) in sample #1

x_2 = number of defects (or same as above) in sample #2

$\left|\dfrac{x_1}{n_1} - \dfrac{x_2}{n_2}\right|$ = absolute proportion difference (no minus sign in difference)

n_1 = size of sample #1

n_2 = size of sample #2

If $Z_t > 1.96$, then we can say with a 95% confidence that the two samples are significantly different.

Use on Problem Type

Use this formula on proportional data when you want to test if two samples are significantly different from each other.

From Chapter 17

RSS: Calculating the Sigma S from Multiple Parts Stack-Up

$$S = \sqrt{(1.3s_1)^2 + (1.3s_2)^2 + (1.3s_3)^2 + \text{etc.}}$$

S = the resultant assembly stack-up sigma

s_1, s_2, s_3, etc. = the sigma of each individual part being stacked

Each sigma s is multiplied times 1.3 to allow for a long-term sigma drift.

If each of n stacked-up parts has the same sigma s, then:

$$S = \sqrt{n(1.3s)^2}$$

Use on Problem Type

If multiple parts are "stacked" in an assembly, the tolerances on those parts are likely to have been calculated using worst-case methods. Using the RSS method of calculating tolerances can open tolerances on those parts or show how the assembly has less variation than assumed.

From Chapter 18

RSS Linear Transfer Functions

$$S_t = \sqrt{s_1^2 + s_2^2 + s_3^2 + s_4^2} \text{ etc.}$$

S_t = the critical sigma of the total assembly or process
s_1, s_2, s_3, s_4, etc. are the sigmas of the variables linearly affecting the critical sigma of an assembly or process.

Each variable's influence must be stated in common units consistent with the part, assembly, or process. For example, if we are studying the thickness variation of an injected molded part and one of the contributing variables is the weight of the injected raw material, we need to state that variable's sigma in "thickness variation per sigma," rather than in "weight unit per sigma."

Use on Problem Type

Use the simplified linear transfer function to understand the effect of each component on the total variation of a part, an assembly, or a process. The sum of the squares of the contributing variable's sigma must equal the square of the sigma of the total assembly or process. If the sum is too low, one or more variables are missing. Each sigma contribution must have units consistent with the product effect being measured. In this way, it is valid to compare the sigmas to see which variable is more critical.

This formula is not applicable to non-linear processes, like many chemical processes that have complex interactions among input variables and therefore require non-linear transfer functions. Non-linear transfer functions, which require partial derivatives, are beyond the scope of this book (and most Six Sigma work).

From Chapter 19

Estimating the Parent Population Sigma S from the $s_{\bar{x}}$ of a Child Distribution

$S = s_{\bar{x}}\sqrt{n}$

S = parent population sigma (sigma based on the raw data)

$s_{\bar{x}}$ = child distribution sigma (sigma of the multiple sample averages)

n = individual sample size (quantity in each raw data sample)

Use on Problem Type

This formula is needed in order to compare data collected by many quality departments with samples taken related to Six Sigma work. Quality department systems often use child distributions, which are based on multiple sample averages, rather than the raw data itself. The raw data are often discarded after the average is calculated.

APPENDIX D

Tables Used
in This Book

Abbreviated Binomial Table

Values within the table are the probability P getting exactly x successes on n trials.

n # of trials	x successes on n trials	p (each trial) =	0.125 (1/8)	0.167 (1/6)	0.250 (1/4)	0.500 (1/2)
2	0		0.7656	0.6944	0.5625	0.2500
2	1		0.2188	0.2778	0.3750	0.5000
2	2		0.0156	0.0278	0.0625	0.2500
		Sum of P:	1.0000	1.0000	1.0000	1.0000
3	0		0.6699	0.5787	0.4219	0.1250
3	1		0.2871	0.3472	0.4219	0.3750
3	2		0.0410	0.0694	0.1406	0.3750
3	3		0.0020	0.0046	0.0156	0.1250
		Sum of P:	1.0000	1.0000	1.0000	1.0000
4	0		0.5862	0.4823	0.3164	0.0625
4	1		0.3350	0.3858	0.4219	0.2500
4	2		0.0718	0.1157	0.2109	0.3750
4	3		0.0068	0.0154	0.0469	0.2500
4	4		0.0002	0.0008	0.0039	0.0625
		Sum of P:	1.0000	1.0000	1.0000	1.0000
5	0		0.5129	0.4019	0.2373	0.0313
5	1		0.3664	0.4019	0.3955	0.1563
5	2		0.1047	0.1608	0.2637	0.3125
5	3		0.0150	0.0322	0.0879	0.3125
5	4		0.0011	0.0032	0.0146	0.1563
5	5		0.0000	0.0001	0.0010	0.0313
		Sum of P:	1.0000	1.0000	1.0000	1.0000
10	0		0.2631	0.1615	0.0563	0.0010
10	1		0.3758	0.3230	0.1877	0.0098
10	2		0.2416	0.2907	0.2816	0.0439
10	3		0.0920	0.1550	0.2503	0.1172
10	4		0.0230	0.0543	0.1460	0.2051
10	5		0.0039	0.0130	0.0584	0.2461
10	6		0.0005	0.0022	0.0162	0.2051
10	7		0.0000	0.0002	0.0031	0.1172
10	8		0.0000	0.0000	0.0004	0.0439
10	9		0.0000	0.0000	0.0000	0.0098
10	10		0.0000	0.0000	0.0000	0.0010
		Sum of P:	1.0000	1.0000	1.0000	1.0000

Standardized Normal Distribution Table

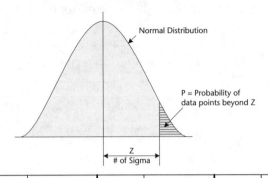

Z	P	Z	P	Z	P	Z	P
0.00	0.5000	0.05	0.4801	0.10	0.4602	0.15	0.4404
0.20	0.4207	0.25	0.4013	0.30	0.3821	0.35	0.3632
0.40	0.3446	0.45	0.3264	0.50	0.3085	0.55	0.2912
0.60	0.2743	0.65	0.2578	0.70	0.2420	0.75	0.2266
0.80	0.2119	0.85	0.1977	0.90	0.1841	0.95	0.1711
1.00	**0.1587**	1.05	0.1469	1.10	0.1357	1.15	0.1251
1.20	0.1151	1.25	0.1056	1.30	0.09680	1.35	0.08851
1.40	0.08076	1.45	0.07353	1.50	0.06681	1.55	0.06057
1.60	0.05480	1.65	0.04947	1.70	0.04457	1.75	0.04006
1.80	0.03593	1.85	0.03216	1.90	0.02872	1.95	0.02559
2.00	**0.02275**	2.05	0.02018	2.10	0.01786	2.15	0.01578
2.20	0.01390	2.25	0.01222	2.30	0.01072	2.35	0.009387
2.40	0.08198	2.45	0.007143	2.50	0.006210	2.55	0.005386
2.60	0.004661	2.65	0.004025	2.70	0.003467	2.75	0.002980
2.80	0.002555	2.85	0.002186	2.90	0.001866	2.95	0.001589
3.00	**0.001350**	3.05	0.001144	3.10	0.0009677	3.15	0.0008164
3.20	0.0006872	3.25	0.0005771	3.30	0.0004835	3.35	0.0004041
3.40	0.0003370	3.45	0.0002803	3.50	0.0002327	3.55	0.0001927
3.60	0.0001591	3.65	0.0001312	3.70	0.0001078	3.75	0.00008844
3.80	0.00007237	3.85	0.00005908	3.90	0.00004812	3.95	0.00003909
4.00	0.00003169	4.05	0.00002562	4.10	0.00002067	4.15	0.00001663
4.20	0.00001335	4.25	0.00001070	4.30	0.00000855	4.35	0.00000681
4.40	0.00000542	4.45	0.00000430	4.50	0.00000340	4.55	0.00000268
4.60	0.00000211	4.65	0.00000166	4.70	0.00000130	4.75	0.00000102
4.80	0.00000079	4.85	0.00000062	4.90	0.00000048	4.95	0.00000037

Simplified Chi-Squared Distribution Table

To test a sample sigma s (with sample size n) vs. a population of sigma S

	95% Confident They Are Different if Chi_t^2 Is				95% Confident They Are Different if Chi_t^2 Is		
	< Low	Or	> High		< Low	Or	> High
n	Low Test		High Test	n	Low Test		High Test
6	0.831209		12.83249	36	20.56938		53.20331
7	1.237342		14.44935	37	21.33587		54.43726
8	1.689864		16.01277	38	22.10562		55.66798
9	2.179725		17.53454	39	22.87849		56.89549
10	2.700389		19.02278	40	23.65430		58.12005
11	3.246963		20.48320	41	24.43306		59.34168
12	3.815742		21.92002	42	25.21452		60.56055
13	4.403778		23.33666	43	25.99866		61.77672
14	5.008738		24.73558	44	26.78537		62.99031
15	5.628724		26.11893	45	27.57454		64.20141
16	6.262123		27.48836	46	28.36618		65.41013
17	6.907664		28.84532	47	29.16002		66.61647
18	7.564179		30.19098	48	29.95616		67.82064
19	8.230737		31.52641	49	30.75450		69.02257
20	8.906514		32.85234	50	31.55493		70.22236
21	9.590772		34.16958	55	35.58633		76.19206
22	10.28291		35.47886				
23	10.98233		36.78068	60	39.66185		82.11737
24	11.68853		38.07561	65	43.77594		88.00398
25	12.40115		39.36406				
26	13.11971		40.64650	70	47.92412		93.85648
27	13.84388		41.92314	80	56.30887		105.4727
28	14.57337		43.19452				
29	15.30785		44.46079	90	64.79339		116.989
30	16.04705		45.72228	100	73.3611		128.4219
31	16.79076		46.97922				
32	17.53872		48.23192				
33	18.29079		49.48044				
34	19.04666		50.72510				
35	19.80624		51.96602				

Simplified t Distribution Table

To compare a sample average (size = n) with a population average or to compare two samples of size n_1 and n_2, using $n = n_1 + n_2 - 1$.

95% confidence (assumes two-tailed)—if the calculated t_t test value exceeds the table t value, then the two averages being compared are different.

n	t value	n	t value	n	t value
6	2.571	26	2.060	45	2.015
7	2.447	27	2.056		
8	2.365	28	2.052	50	2.010
9	2.306	29	2.048	60	2.001
10	2.262	30	2.045		
11	2.228	31	2.042	70	1.995
12	2.201	32	2.040	80	1.990
13	2.179	33	2.037		
14	2.160	34	2.035	90	1.987
15	2.145	35	2.032	100+	1.984
16	2.131	36	2.030		
17	2.120	37	2.028		
18	2.110	38	2.026		
19	2.101	39	2.024		
20	2.093	40	2.023		
21	2.086				
22	2.080				
23	2.074				
24	2.069				
25	2.064				

Simplified F Table (95% Confidence)

For comparing sigma from two samples (sizes = n_1 and n_2) (sample sizes equal within 20%).

$$n = \frac{n_1 + n_2}{2}$$

If calculated F_t value exceeds the table value, assume difference.

n	F	n	F	n	F
6	5.05	26	1.96	60	1.54
7	4.28	27	1.93	70	1.49
8	3.79	28	1.90	80	1.45
9	3.44	29	1.88	100	1.39
10	3.18	30	1.86	120	1.35
11	2.98	31	1.84	150	1.31
12	2.82	32	1.82	200	1.26
13	2.69	33	1.80	300	1.21
14	2.58	34	1.79	400	1.18
15	2.48	35	1.77	500	1.16
16	2.40	36	1.76	750	1.13
17	2.33	37	1.74	1000	1.11
18	2.27	38	1.73	2000	1.08
19	2.22	39	1.72		
20	2.17	40	1.70		
21	2.12	42	1.68		
22	2.08	44	1.66		
23	2.05	46	1.64		
24	2.01	48	1.62		
25	1.98	50	1.61		

Glossary of Terms

Accuracy Accuracy is a measurement concept involving the correctness of the average reading. It is the extent to which the average of the measurements taken agrees with a true value.

Analyze Analyze is the third step in the DMAIC problem-solving method. The measurements/data must be analyzed to see if they are consistent with the problem definition and also to identify a root cause. A problem solution is then identified. Sometimes, based on the analysis, it is necessary to go back and restate the problem definition and start the process over.

Attribute An attribute is a qualitative characteristic that can be counted.

Attribute Data Attribute data are data that are not continuous, that fit into categories that can be described in terms of words (attributes). Examples: "good" or "bad," "go" or "no-go," "pass" or "fail," and "yes" or "no."

Averages, Labeling *See* Labeling Averages and Standard Deviations.

Black Belt A Six Sigma black belt has Six Sigma skills sufficient to act as an instructor, mentor, and expert to green belts. A black belt is also competent in additional Six Sigma tool-specific software programs and statistics.

Chi-Squared Test This test is used on variables (decimal) data to see if there was a statistically significant change in the sigma between the population data and the current sample data. This test is done only after the data plots have indicated that there has been no radical change in the shape of the data plots.

Child Distributions   This term is used when interfacing with quality department data. A child distribution refers to the sample averages and the sigma of multiple sample averages. These are labeled $\bar{x}$ and $s_{\bar{x}}$.

Confidence Tests Between Groups of Data   These tests are used to determine if there is a statistically significant change between samples or between a sample and a population. These are normally done at a 95% confidence level.

Continuous Data (Variables Data)   Continuous data can have any value in a continuum. They are decimal data without "steps."

Control   Control is the final step in the DMAIC problem-solving method. A verification of control must be implemented. A robust solution (like a part change) will be easier to keep in control than a qualitative solution.

Control Chart   A control chart is a tool for monitoring variance in a process over time. A traditional control chart is a chart with upper and lower control limits on which are plotted values of some statistical measure for a series of samples or subgroups. A traditional control chart uses both an average chart and a sigma chart. *See* Simplified Control Chart.

Correlation Testing   This tool uses historical data to find what variables changed at the same time or position as the problem time or position. These variables are then subjected to further tests or study.

Cumulative   In probability problems, this is the sum of the probabilities of getting "the number of successes or fewer," like getting three *or fewer* heads on five flips of a coin. This option is used on "less-than" and "more-than" problems.

Define   This is the overall problem definition step in the DMAIC problem-solving method. This definition should be as specific as possible.

DMAIC Problem-Solving Method   DMAIC (Define, Measure, Analyze, Improve, Control) is the Six Sigma problem-solving approach used by green belts. This is the road map that is followed for all projects and process improvements, with the Six Sigma tools applied as needed.

Excel's BINOMDIST   Excel's BINOMDIST is not technically a Six Sigma Tool, but it is the tool recommended in this text for determining the probability of an observed proportional data result being due to purely random causes. This tool is used when we already know the mathematical probability of a population event.

F Test This test is used on variables (decimal) data to see if there was a statistically significant change in the sigma between two samples. This test is done only after the data plots have indicated that there has been no radical change in the shape of the data plots.

Fishbone Diagram This Six Sigma tool uses a representation of a fish skeleton to help trigger identification of all the variables that can be contributing to a problem. The problem is visually shown as the fish "head" and the variables are shown on the "bones." Once all the variables are identified, the key two or three are highlighted for further study.

Green Belt A Six Sigma green belt is the primary implementer of the Six Sigma methodology. He or she earns this title by taking classes in Six Sigma, demonstrating a competence on Six Sigma tests, and implementing projects using the Six Sigma tools.

Improve Improve is the fourth step in the DMAIC problem-solving method. Once a solution has been analyzed, the fix must be implemented. The expected results must be verified with independent data after solution implementation.

Labeling Averages and Standard Deviations We label the average of a population $\overline{X}$ and the sample averages $\overline{x}$. Similarly, the standard deviation (sigma) of the population is labeled S and the sample standard deviations (sigma) are labeled s.

Master Black Belt A Six Sigma master black belt generally has management responsibility for the Six Sigma organization. This could include setting up training, measuring its effectiveness, coordinating efforts with the rest of the organization, and managing the Six Sigma people (when Six Sigma is set up as a separate organization).

Measure Accurate and sufficient measurements/data are needed in this second step of the DMAIC problem-solving method.

Minimum Sample Size The number of data points needed to enable statistically valid comparisons or predictions.

n This is the sample size or, in probability problems, the number of independent trials, like the number of coin tosses, the number of parts measured, etc.

Need-Based Tolerances This Six Sigma tool emphasizes that often tolerances are not established based on the customer's real needs. A tolerance review offers opportunity for both the customer and the supplier to save money.

Normal Distributions A bell-shaped distribution of data that is indicative of the distribution of data from many things in nature. Information on this type of distribution is used to predict populations based on samples of data.

Number s (or x Successes) This is the total number of "successes" that you are looking for in a probability problem, like getting exactly three heads. This is used in Excel's BINOMDIST.

Parent Populations This term is used when interfacing with quality department data. A parent population refers to the individual data and their related statistical descriptions, like average and sigma. These are labeled $\bar{X}$ and S.

Plot Data Most processes with continuous data have data plot shapes that stay consistent unless a major change to the process has occurred. If the shapes of the data plots *have* changed dramatically, then the quantitative formulas can't be used to compare the processes.

Probability Determination This is the likelihood of an event happening by pure chance.

Probability p (or Probability s) Probability p or s is the probability of a "success" on *each individual trial*, like the likelihood of a head on one coin flip or a defect on one part. This is always a proportion and generally shown as a decimal, like 0.0156.

Probability P In Excel's BINOMDIST this is the probability of getting a given number of successes from *all the trials*, like the probability of three heads in five coin tosses or 14 defects in a shipment of parts. This is often the answer to the problem.

Process Flow Diagram The process flow diagram, and specifically the locations where data are collected, may help pinpoint possible areas contributing to a problem.

Process Sigma Level This is the formula for calculating process sigma level:

$$\text{Process Sigma Level} = \pm \frac{\text{Process Tolerance}}{2 * \text{Process Sigma Value}}$$

Proportional Data Proportional data are based on attribute inputs, such as "good" or "bad," "yes" or "no," etc. Examples are the proportion of defects in a process, the proportion of "yes" votes for a candidate, and the proportion of students failing a test.

Repeatability Repeatability is the consistency of measurements obtained when one person measures the same parts or items multiple times using the same instrument and techniques.

Reproducibility Reproducibility is the consistency of average measurements obtained when two or more people measure the same parts or items using the same measuring technique.

RSS Tolerances When establishing tolerances on stacked parts, the traditional method is to use "worst-case" fit, even though the probability of this fit may be extremely low. The RSS method (root sum-of-squares) of establishing tolerances takes this probability into consideration, resulting in generally looser tolerances with no measurable reduction in quality.

Sample Size, Proportional Data This tool calculates the minimum sample size needed to get representative attribute data on a process generating proportional data. Too small a sample may cause erroneous conclusions. Excessive samples are expensive.

Sample Size, Variables Data This tool calculates the minimum sample size needed to get representative data on a process with variables (decimal) data. Too small a sample may cause erroneous conclusions. Excessively large samples are often expensive.

Simplified Control Chart A control chart—traditional or simplified—is a tool for monitoring variance in a process over time. Traditional control charts have two graphs and are not intuitive. Simplified control charts have one graph, are intuitive, and are operator-friendly. *See* Control Chart.

Simplified DOE This Six Sigma tool enables tests on an existing process to establish optimum settings on the key process input variables.

Simplified FMEA This Six Sigma tool is used to convert qualitative concerns on collateral damage to a prioritized action plan. Unintentional collateral harm may occur to other processes due to a planned process or product change.

Simplified Gauge Verification This Six Sigma tool is used on variables data (decimals) to verify that the gauge is capable of giving the required accuracy of measurements compared to the allowable tolerance.

Simplified QFD This Six Sigma tool is used to convert qualitative customer input into specific prioritized action plans. The customer includes everyone who is affected by the product or process.

Simplified Transfer Function The simplified transfer function shows the variation contribution of each component to the total variation of an assembly or a process. This allows for component focus to effect total variation reduction.

Six Sigma Methodology The Six Sigma methodology uses a *specific problem-solving approach* and *Six Sigma tools* to improve processes and products. This methodology is data-driven, with a goal of reducing unacceptable products or events. The technical goal of the Six Sigma methodology is to reduce process variation such that the amount of unacceptable product is no more than three defects per million parts. The real-world Six Sigma goal is to reduce defects to the level at which the customer is happy with the product, supplier losses are low, and economics can't justify further improvement.

Standard Deviations, Labeling *See* Labeling Averages and Standard Deviations.

t Test This Six Sigma test is used to see if there was a statistically significant change in the average between population data and the current sample data, or between two samples. This test on variables data is done only after the data plots have indicated that there has been no radical change in the shapes of the data plots and the chi-squared test or F test shows no significant change in sigma.

Tolerance Stack-up Analysis This is the process of evaluating the effect that the dimensions of all components can have on an assembly. There are various methods used, including worst case, RSS (root sum-of-squares), modified RSS, and Monte Carlo simulations.

Variables Data Variables data (continuous data) are generally in decimal form. Theoretically you could look at enough decimal places to find that no two values are exactly the same.

INDEX

ABOUT THE AUTHOR

Warren Brussee spent 33 years at GE as an engineer, plant manager, and engineering manager. His responsibilities included manufacturing plants in the United States, Hungary, and China.

Brussee is a Six Sigma green belt and has taught Six Sigma classes to engineering and manufacturing teams. These teams excelled both on corporate tests on Six Sigma and in actual implementation of the Six Sigma tools.

Brussee has multiple patents, some of which were the outcome of his Six Sigma work. His teams generated several million dollars worth of annualized savings using the Six Sigma tools.

Statistics for Six Sigma Made Easy! was written to make the statistics involved with Six Sigma user-friendly and to introduce the Six Sigma methodology with a set of simplified tools. The intent of the simplifications is to get broader use of this powerful methodology. All the case studies portray real events, with some details changed to protect proprietary processes. The emphasis is on using the Six Sigma tools, not on the theory of Six Sigma.

Warren Brussee earned his engineering degree at Cleveland State University and attended Kent State University toward an EMBA.